INDIAN ACT

INDIAN ACT
Residential School Plays

edited by Donna-Michelle St. Bernard

PLAYWRIGHTS CANADA PRESS
Toronto

Salt Baby by Falen Johnson was originally published by Scirocco Drama, an imprint of J. Gordon Shillingford Publishing, in 2013, and is excerpted here with permission.

God and the Indian by Drew Hayden Taylor was originally published by Talonbooks in 2014, and is used here with permission.

Library and Archives Canada Cataloguing in Publication
Indian act (2018)
Indian act : residential school plays / edited by Donna-Michelle St. Bernard.
-- First edition.

Plays.
ISBN 978-1-77091-914-3 (softcover)

1. Native peoples--Canada--Drama. 2. Native peoples--Canada--Residential schools--Drama. 3. Canadian drama (English)--Native authors. 4. Canadian drama (English)--21st century. I. St. Bernard, Donna-Michelle, editor II. Title.

PS8309.I53I53 2018 C812'.6080352997071 C2018-902032-6

Playwrights Canada Press acknowledges that we operate on land, which, for thousands of years, has been the traditional territories of the Mississaugas of the New Credit, the Huron-Wendat, the Anishinaabe, Métis, and the Haudenosaunee peoples. Today, this meeting place is home to many Indigenous peoples from across Turtle Island and we are grateful to have the opportunity to work and play here.

We acknowledge the financial support of the Canada Council for the Arts—which last year invested $153 million to bring the arts to Canadians throughout the country—the Ontario Arts Council (OAC), the Ontario Media Development Corporation, and the Government of Canada for our publishing activities.

Canada Council for the Arts Conseil des arts du Canada

For those who do the work of facing truths and holding story. With respect to all the past stewards of Native Earth Performing Arts, with gratitude for the current leadership of Keith Barker and Isaac Thomas.

CONTENTS

MINNIE AFTER THE MUSH HOLE:
A Dialogue

"My mother lived at the Mohawk," my mother says.

"Lived." Is that the right word? If you consider that the Mohawk, less colloquially known as the Mohawk Institute, was the residential school on our reserve, Six Nations of the Grand River, known by the students as "the mush hole" for the unending porridge that got served up as daily bread. Consider that you know something of the darker truths of some of those schools, officially now, thanks to the efforts of the Truth and Reconciliation commissioners—does the word "lived" really fit?

I spent most of a year in that building, too, but I was working, my first job after school, and when I'd stayed the year I'd committed to, I left, got out of there and headed for Toronto. By my time the place had been transformed into the Woodland Indian Cultural Education Centre and I was the library researcher. Icy mornings that winter, I'd arrive early and the caretaker, who arrived before me, would unlock the front door to let me in, having already turned up the furnace and set the radiators ticking, sighing, the pipes shifting. I warmed up in the staff lounge, waited for my boss, and listened to the building, teasing myself with the possibility that those low-ceilinged abandoned dormitories on the third floor—I only knew the outlines of what such buildings represented in Canada's history then—were haunted.

"They taught her how to keep house," my mother says about my grandmother.

A limited sort of education, but one a woman might have been grateful for a century ago, and she learned those skills well. My mother provides details of cleaning, baking, and laundry, remembering my grandmother being out of their own Bleeker-near-Dundas-Street house in Toronto (a house that was in part during the '30s a boarding house for men come from our reserve seeking employment), working days all through my mother's younger years, like a reverse sort of immigrant, in the houses of Jewish families. She was so adept at the domestic arts she'd even spent one winter away in New York City, working for one of her families there.

Is that what they thought they were doing, I wonder, with the residential schools? Turning what they saw as "the Indian problem" into a class of servants? These people were always looking over their shoulders to their Mother- or Fatherlands, even though they wanted to call themselves Canadians. Don't they usually claim to have come here for something better?

My mother, having heard parts of the stories unearthed by the TRC, shakes her head when thinking about my grandmother. "She never badmouthed that place at all."

We know the men in power in government and the churches wanted to "kill the Indian in the child," so sure were they that Indians weren't quite up to the human measure, but what about those ordinary citizens who had these few dark-skinned creatures working for them behind the scenes? (My grandmother was one of the fair-skinned Tuscarora, so maybe I should go back to the haunting image?) Did those citizens not think about what was going on in the schools at all? Did they not imagine their leaders just wanting to get their hands on Indian lands?

I might have read some of *The Jesuit Relations* while looking for the answer to a question that came to me in the daily mail during that researcher job, or I might have read it earlier when working my undergrad summers at Indian Affairs in Ottawa, reviewing books for their education branch for an annotated bibliography of books by or about Indians, straightforwardly called "About Indians."

One thing I remembered the Jesuits found disturbing and deserving of correction about *les sauvages* was the way we treated our children. Our custom of not beating them to keep them in line, out of the way, quiet, just didn't jibe with their European wisdom, perhaps still presented most succinctly as "spare the rod, spoil the child." Despite their bravado about how civilized they were, if this was how they behaved back home, Europe must have been a less than pleasant place. No wonder they wanted to leave it. But then they brought that attitude here and intended to make our children its focus!

My grandmother and grandfather, by my time, had moved back to the reserve, having bought property and built a large log house there, to finish raising their half-dozen offspring. In addition to being a housewife, Grandma became a craftswoman (paper flowers, hooked and rag rugs, leather Indian-fringed coats and moccasins, beadwork, and cornhusk braided into dolls and rugs), and eventually a small business owner—I remember it as the community's first craft store—and one of the community's first elected women councillors.

None of her five girls had to go to the Mohawk. All went to public school, in the city or on the reserve. All of them came home for supper and slept under the same solidly supported roof. Not one of them did domestic work outside their own houses.

My grandmother lived after the Mohawk.

These plays show that other Indian girls and boys, and their spirits, survived and sometimes even thrived, too, despite the worst intentions of those men in government and in the church.

Maybe these plays can also help us understand a bit more about the immigrant mind and soul. Beside the political and sociological analysis, in addition to all the abstractions of crossed cultures and power, perhaps we'll figure out why they behaved so poorly.

They were welcomed here as guests in our many small nations; we performed ceremonies and observed protocols to make them our relations, but still they thought they should act as they did, as they would have over there, as if our attempts to make them family were foolish.

These plays help us make clear the human costs of their—at best—misguided project. These plays, to put it more humanely, show us how to heal.

Still, the bad results of the residential schools number as many as the Aboriginal children in foster care today.

When will we stop, these plays should help us wonder, beating the kids?

Maybe these plays can also remind those guests how they should behave if they really want to deserve to honestly use the word "Canada" when people ask where they come from.

They can ask themselves, "Am I from here yet?"

—Daniel David Moses, Six Nations/Toronto, ON, 27 July 2015

GROW UP ALREADY

So, I'm new here. By which I mean that I immigrated to Canada some three decades ago from a revolution-shaken Grenada and acquired citizenship by boning up on such vital cultural context as the difference between the Senate and the Legislative Assembly, the history of the United Empire Loyalists, and the process for extracting sap from a tree.

Okay, I'm lying. I never actually learned these things, being four years old at the time; they were learned by proxy, via my legal guardians. Nonetheless.

My formative years were driven by an anti-oppression impetus, inspired by the audacious injustices of the Jewish Holocaust, Rwandan genocide, the bombing of Hiroshima, and the global commercial terrorism of the Coca-Cola corporation. Despite being educated in the Canadian school system, which makes history a requirement at every level, I did not become acquainted with Canada's homegrown atrocities until well into adulthood. I first learned about residential schools when I was almost thirty years old. Shame.

As an adult Canadian theatre practitioner, I don't know what to make of the "legacy" handed to me upon arrival as a newcomer. I should have cut my political teeth on stories from my new home. I should have incorporated this sense of debt and displacement into my evolving immigrant identity. And consider that, since the age of four, I've read everything I could get my hands on: Farley Mowat, Edgar Allan Poe, Enid Blyton, and the immortal Bard. Where wasn't I looking? What wasn't I asking? I'm still not sure.

Lee Crowchild once said, "We are all stuck in a dogma given to us by government and religion," pointing out that the same distortions taught about Indigenous people were taught *to* Indigenous people, that we have all been similarly misinformed. So maybe we settlers and immigrants have been a nation of children, ceding to institutions authority over thought, judgment, and perception. Maybe we can all excuse ourselves for what we weren't told, as a child nation. Also, maybe it's time to grow up, to take responsibility, and to acknowledge that those schools, those institutions are made of people. Wrong, wrong people. And in many cases, mean, mean people.

Let us choose our teachers better.

In 2018 we are seeing Child and Family Services replicate Canada's paternalistic relationships with a number of nations still possessively referred to by well-meaning settlers as "our Native peoples." Indigenous children continue to be removed from their family homes "in the best interests of the child" just as once Indigenous women's wombs were removed "in the best interests of the women." The short life and tragic death of Tina Fontaine while in government care embodies the root and result of contemporary policy, which sees children warehoused in hotels and alienated from any sense of belonging. While the language of Indian Act policies have been revised and redacted, the institutional culture they represent is implicit, pervasive.

The residential school system is a dark spectre upon Canada's projected diplomacy, courtesy, fairness, social justice, and salt-of-the-earthedness. It encompasses a range of experiences and evokes complex traumas that are hard or impossible to articulate. Some of this trauma extends through generations, resurfacing as fear, anger, distrust, or damaged behaviour. Some surfaces as blunt humour, caregiving impulses, familial reconstruction, defiant pride, and deep empathy for others.

Verbally, we as a nation of many nations tend to be vague about this legacy, or graphic about its horrors in a general way.

Some of what we want to know would be unkind to ask. Some of those we want to hear speak have a right to their silence. The playwrights in this volume have started the work for us; they have generously opened very personal wounds, dug deep into research that they can't shake off. They outline a trajectory of impact that is not yet complete. They equip us to look at it from so many vantages that, cumulatively, we may have some hope of seeing the elephant.

These plays, each in their own unique way, take the theoretical space of "bad things that once happened" and populate it with people we know, behaviours we recognize, and patterns we can see being replicated. Michael Greyeyes's *Nôhkum* informs a more complex understanding of "the lesser of two evils." Tenderly wrung from shattered memory, Larry Guno's *Bunk #7* is an ode for boys far from home. Displaced from all that is familiar, the protagonists of Tara Beagan's *They Know Not What They Do* endeavour to resist redefinition. Drew Hayden Taylor troubles certainty when what has been suppressed resurfaces in *God and the Indian*. Extensive, lyric, and rife with ugliness, *A Very Polite Genocide or The Girl Who Fell to Earth* by Melanie J. Murray explores internal complicity in blood's erasure. Curtis Peeteetuce reveals the deep emotional underpinning of a practical decision in *kihēw*. And *Dear Mr. Buchwald* by Yvette Nolan evinces justifiable anger in a surprisingly generous piece of closure.

These works should be staged because they are good theatre. They are full of people driven but not always empowered to achieve their objectives, and confronted with barriers that test values. What happened here is part of our story, a part that is context to all other struggles in this place.

I owe this book to Larry Guno, to Helen Thundercloud, to John Sugar, to Ernie Crane Bear, to Tamara S., to Tina Fontaine, to the black-billed magpie, and to our community.

I'm sorry that it took so long.

—Donna-Michelle St. Bernard

"INDIAN"

The word "Indian," used throughout this volume by Indigenous authors in specific context and with purposeful intent, is not an invitation for settlers to casually adopt the word into their vocabularies. Falen Johnson addresses it better in her play *Salt Baby*, excerpted here:

Scene One

A café or a bar. It is late in the evening. A couple sits in first-date position, negotiating distance and affection.

ALLIGATOR: Really?

SALT BABY: Yep.

ALLIGATOR: Huh.

Beat.

Neat.

SALT BABY: Neat?

ALLIGATOR: Yeah, I don't know. Neat.

SALT BABY: What about you?

ALLIGATOR: Well my mom is Scottish and my dad is English and Irish. So I'm pretty white.

So what else are you? You're not full, right? How much Indian—shit . . . Sorry. Is that like totally offensive? Uh, Native or . . . Aboriginal or . . . any help here would be much appreciated . . .

SALT BABY: I say Indian but I don't like people to say that until we really know each other, you know? First Nations seems pretty safe to me, but everybody wants to be called something different these days.

ALLIGATOR: Okay so how "First Nations" are you? 'Cause you don't really, you know, you don't really look like one, a First Nations.

SALT BABY: Uh, I'm about three quarters.

ALLIGATOR: How does that work?

SALT BABY: Well my mom's half Mohawk. Her dad was a Mohawk chief, a hereditary chief. He was married to a white woman. And my dad's Tuscarora, full. So fractions, right? Three quarters. I guess. The government doesn't really agree with my math.

ALLIGATOR: What do you mean?

SALT BABY: In the opinion of the government, if you have one parent with any white blood it decreases the rest of your Indian blood. So by their standards I'm half, I think.

ALLIGATOR: You should find that out. I'd want to.

SALT BABY: I'm Indian enough to get the card, right?

ALLIGATOR: Aww! No way! Can I see it?

SALT BABY: All right but my head looks big.

ALLIGATOR: Even better.

SALT BABY: Screw you.

She hands him the card.

ALLIGATOR: Whoa! Your head is big.

SALT BABY: Told you.

ALLIGATOR: Wait, wait, wait . . . What's this? Expiry date?

SALT BABY: Yep. I expire. No longer Indian after 2012.

ALLIGATOR: What? That's insane. Hey can we use this here to pay for our food and stuff?

SALT BABY: Uh no. It doesn't work like that.

ALLIGATOR: No, eh? So can you say anything in Mohawk or Taah-ta—taahs *(he struggles)*—again a little help here . . .

SALT BABY: Tuscarora?

ALLIGATOR: Yeah. That one.

NÔHKOM

Michael Greyeyes

To my late father, George Greyeyes.

Acknowledgements

My thanks to Yvette Nolan, my dramaturg and director, as well as the Banff Centre and Brian Quirt for their role in developing this work in its current form.

Nôhkom was originally created in 2013 and directed by Michael Greyeyes for Intimate Portraits, a Signal Theatre / Banff Centre presentation in the Margaret Greenham Theatre, also featuring *Valley of Coal*, choreographed and created by Nancy Latoszewski (Greyeyes). *Nôhkom* was subsequently workshopped as part of the Banff Centre's 2015 Playwrights Lab and was performed most recently at the Woodland Cultural Centre near Six Nations territory in Brantford, Ontario.

Characters

Narrator
Maggie
Longneck

We hear the sound of wind, something that almost crackles. A howling. It could even be paper. A man enters the space regarding the audience. He is the NARRATOR. *A tripod holds a cast-iron pot upstage, with a few pieces of cut firewood. A long-handled axe lies on the ground, with a blanket folded neatly beside the tripod.*

NARRATOR: We come from the plains, west of here.

Just us. My older sister. My father. My mom.

Dad from Muskeg Lake. Mom from Sweetgrass.

The names of the communities around us formed the geography of my world. Muskeg. Marcelin. Beardy's. Mistawasis. Duck Lake. Okemasis. Carry the Kettle.

Saskatchewan.

Every kid who comes from Saskatchewan, by default, becomes a good speller.

Beat.

I remember the oddest things about growing up in Saskatoon. The longest summers in the history of mankind. *Spider-Man* (the television cartoon). Driving by car to North Battleford, to reserves off the main highways. Spying the strange aluminum bottles of Pepsi-Cola syrup, not yet mixed with carbonated water for the concession stands.

I remember my cousins. And my grandparents.

My mom's mom was Margaret. She was all shiny glasses and chubby cheeks. Long, beautiful braids. Linoleum floors and cool stuff everywhere. A rifle in the closet with the bolt removed! A bow. A blue fiberglass bow. Just sitting there! And on the wall of her basement, a drawing by my uncle of an Indian guy with big muscles and long braids. I think I stared at it for hours.

That was a happy home. Lots of laughter and food. And tears, of course. That was my mother's side.

There are two halves to every family. We all come from two strains of thought. Twinned strands of experience. But our visits to my dad's side of the family were more infrequent. This side of my world was distant from me, removed.

Nôhkom was very old. Her home was a shanty compared to the sturdy bungalow in Battleford. Dirty windows. The smell of smoke from a wood stove. She was very small. A handkerchief around her head. A patterned cotton dress, two sweaters. Brown nylons. And leggings underneath her skirt. She was layers upon layers of clothing. She only spoke Cree. My father was very caring toward her, deferential.

But I could only stare at her hands. Her skin was impossibly wrinkled. Her hands were soft and brown. Thin.

Like paper.

They were curled by arthritis. Her fingers twisted together like claws. It was a quiet visit. I wish I remembered more about it. Her eyes didn't see well at that point. Perhaps she couldn't really see me. Would I have disappointed her? Short and round, with a city kid's unmasked disdain for a poor house in the middle of nowhere.

I hope not. I think the sun was shining outside and that's where I wanted to be. It was the fall. The long light of summer beginning to fade. October.

This particular visit is still vivid to me. This is my clearest memory of nôhkom.

Everything else is from my father.

* * *

NARRATOR: My dad's name was George Greyeyes. George James Baptiste.

He is no longer with us now; he began his journey four years ago. But much of what I remember about him remains with me. When I see my sister, I see the outlines of his features. When I marvel at my own beautiful daughters, I feel him close.

Beat.

He is everywhere in *this* room.

I know that he grew up during the Great Depression, and that his mother raised him and his sister alone. His father wasn't there for him.

I know my dad went to residential school when he was five years old. I know he was a soldier. I know he was stationed overseas. These are all facts of his existence. But one part of his story has always gripped me, fascinated me beyond all else.

One winter he had to live in a tent with his mom and his baby sister.

I think about people who freeze to death in their cars, stranded by the side of the highway. Or hikers caught in a sudden storm. But my father, as a young boy, lived through an entire winter, a Saskatchewan winter.

I wonder, too, about how she, nôhkom, felt when November came, knowing what was coming. Freeze up.

In Cree, the months are named after their moons. November is the Freeze Up Moon.

Maggie

NARRATOR: My dad's mother was also Margaret, but they called her Maggie. She married my grandfather, William, whom they called Bill. She was from a neighbouring reserve, but Muskeg became her home.

I have no pictures of her. No physical descriptions—just a six-year-old boy's recollection of a tiny bird-like woman with claws for hands. I am filled with questions about her.

I asked my father about that winter. Where was grandpa? Why wasn't he there? How did you stay warm? What did you eat? How big was the tent? Were there no other relatives to take you in? His answers, like him, were straightforward. Unvarnished.

Music: "Gentle Paper (Longer)" fades in.

"It was a small tent. Just enough room for the bed and a stove. The stove was made from a washtub. We made stovepipe from it, so the tent wouldn't fill with smoke. The bed was on one side. It wasn't a regular bed. Just blankets laid on top of branches. To keep the frost off of us."

"Mum piled up snow outside our tent. Against the walls to keep the tent warmer."

"She was always chopping wood to feed the stove. Or melt snow. That's how we got our water. She melted the clean snow around the camp. And I remember we slept a lot. We laid there together, to keep warm."

Longneck

NARRATOR: There is a mystery surrounding my grandmother. I first heard of it through my sister, who spoke to me in low, conspiratorial tones. As if it was something secretive, shameful to my family. She said, "You know, there was a man. *Not* grandpa."

My grandmother had a lover.

LONGNECK enters, from stage left.

I don't know him. I don't know who he was.

But he visited her.

Softly.

At night.

In my grandfather's absence.

Beat.

It was only a few years ago that I learned his name.

Longneck.

This is what my father told me. I think he had trouble understanding it, even with age and experience. He told me that his mother had nothing. She had no money. They were hungry. And this man brought them food.

There was a kind of confusion that ran across my father's eyes when he spoke to me about this.

Dance: "Maggie's Courtship."

And we did not speak about it more than two, maybe three times in his entire life.

My father explained that when Longneck came into their tent, he and his little sister were there. Next to them. "Go to sleep," Nôhkom whispered.

Longneck, I was told, came from a strong family, but he was weak—perhaps it was physical. I don't know exactly, my father never explained. But he was clear about one thing: it was medicine that he used to charm her. That is how they explain it: my sister, my father. "It wasn't her choice," they said.

Maybe it was for money. To buy the food they needed.

Only whispers, my sister's whispered voice, giving me a sense of that history. Of that truth.

MAGGIE and LONGNECK dance as the NARRATOR stands facing away from them. MAGGIE and her lover intertwine, twisting themselves together. They finish their dance, breathing heavily, sitting, facing each other. LONGNECK stands and moves away as the NARRATOR walks to the other side of the stage.

Festival Moon

NARRATOR: December is called the Festival Season. Festival Moon.

My father would always remind me that New Year's Day is called "kissing day." He said people went all over the reserve to visit with each other. Share food. Kiss one another.

He told me about the Christmas they spent in the tent: "Dad came to visit us. He sat with us and brought gifts. For my little sister and me. They were wrapped in plain paper. He said, 'You open it.' So I unwrapped mine . . . *(blankly)* It was a toy airplane. *(almost shrugging)* We didn't know about Christmas. After an hour or so, he said, 'Maggie, I have to go.'

"That was all. Then he was gone again."

MAGGIE and LONGNECK dance. There is a new forcefulness to MAGGIE's movements, the choreography more visceral.

Music: "Cold White."

The dance ends and LONGNECK exits.

Whispers

NARRATOR: Now that George, my dad, is gone from here. I am alone with my questions.

Where was my grandfather? How could a man leave his wife and children—one barely more than an infant—to survive in a tent? In winter?

I know it was the Great Depression. I know there was barely enough to feed any of the children. And I know they experienced a poverty I can barely imagine. But I seethe when I think about a woman alone in a cloth tent, caring for two small children, while other families lived in their wooden houses, their doors firmly shut.

And the questions remain unanswered because the players in this are all gone now. My father was one of the very last to have died.

With his absence, all that I have left are whispers.

Half-acknowledged truths.

Insinuations and shards of a larger story.

MAGGIE and LONGNECK dance passionately. At times, we see her literally throwing her body against him, wrapping him in her limbs.

Grandpa was in the war. He wasn't the same when he came back. He couldn't be with them, Maggie and my father and his baby sister. He was dangerous to them.

And there were other women.

A white girl from a nearby farm. A pregnancy.

A painful whisper, "He was sent to jail for that."

A letter in the mail. Brothers and sisters that he didn't know about. Other families.

MAGGIE and LONGNECK dance, but in the end he, too, abandons her.

Music: "Inside Maggie's Head."

Her movements becoming more ragged, almost violent. Her body is angular, twisted. She falls continually, writhing.

She dances alone. Exhausted, she approaches the tripod, wood, and blankets. She lifts the pot off the tripod chain, tips it over. It is already empty. She then pushes over the tripod itself. It clangs to the floor. She takes the blanket and covers the items carefully. The materials under the blanket look like small bodies.

Silence, then the NARRATOR's voice is heard from the side of the space.

January. Moon of Exploding Trees.

The NARRATOR re-enters.

My father talked to me often about one night that winter.

It was in the dead of January, and I imagine that Nôhkom felt there was nowhere for her to turn. Her husband had abandoned her. His community had turned its back on her. How else to describe why a woman with two small children was left to live alone in a canvas tent?

She was outside the economy. My father remembers they had flour. Sometimes they had salt bacon. "I was hungry," my dad said.

Sound: the most brittle sound of cold imaginable, a screeching, grating sound against our ears.

"One night, she came to me. My sister was asleep beside me. Mom held my arms, looking into my eyes, she said, 'I just put some more wood in the stove. When it burns out, you're going to freeze . . . Do you understand? You're going to freeze tonight.' And then she kissed me and left the tent."

He said she walked away in the middle of the night.

MAGGIE leaves the tent.

A man came across her on the road into town.

The NARRATOR confronts MAGGIE as the man in the story.

Maggie, what are you doing? Where are your kids?

MAGGIE: Back in the tent. Sleeping.

NARRATOR: Go back home, Maggie. Do you have wood?

MAGGIE shakes her head, almost imperceptibly.

Go back to your kids. I'll bring you some.

MAGGIE turns slowly and walks back toward the blanket and her children. The NARRATOR takes the axe and looks for anything made of wood that he can chop. He grabs a wooden chair and smashes it to pieces. He takes the fragments of the splintered chair and lays them at her feet.

My father told this story to me again and again. Each time, it changed slightly. Sometimes there was no man. She just turned around of her own accord. Sometimes, Dad simply said, "You know, son? She couldn't do it. She didn't have the heart."

I imagine a four-year-old boy alone in a tent, with the fire dwindling. His two-year-old sister beside him. I imagine the terrible seeds of such a moment laid inside of him that night, growing outward.

* * *

NARRATOR: February is called the Great Moon. Hope of Spring.

Duck Lake

Sound: the cruelty of winter abates. We begin to faintly hear another sound: thawing. Water dripping, running.

NARRATOR: "After that winter, Mom sat me down one day and said, 'There's a school in Duck Lake. You're going to go there.'"

The NARRATOR shrugs as his father had done.

"So, I went."

The NARRATOR lifts his hand, five fingers outstretched, and in a hoarse, George-style whisper, says:

"Five. *(then more loudly)* I was only *five* years old.

"My father came in a car and took me to the school. She kept the girl. Jenny came a year or two later. We were together in the school, at least.

"St. Michael's, they called it. It had a big statue at the top of it."

Did you cry? I asked.

"Oh, I cried and cried. But I got used to it. There were a lot of little boys there and," he smiled, "we had good fun, sometimes. Laughed."

There is a lot of my family history at the Duck Lake school.

My great-grandmother, Sarah, was student number 001. The first student enrolled at St. Michael's when it opened in 1892. It closed in 1964.

When I asked my dad about the place, he always paused, and then usually said something that surprised me: "I remember it had steam heat and they had lots of food."

Residential school saved my father's life. They fed him, clothed him, kept him warm. They gave him English. My language.

Beat.

I *know* what I'm saying because he's told me the other stories. When we went back home, a year before he died, we visited Duck Lake. He wouldn't step out of the car.

The hardness and cruelty of it still shocks me. Knowing it informs my memories. Tip-toeing around him as a child. Stories of packed suitcases, waiting under the bed. His dangerous glares. My sister's fear and purposeful distance from that time. Seeing more than I.

But I also saw that anger burn out slowly through his long life. Time is an altar upon which even such damnable truth can wither and fade.

I am looking at the faded impressions of things that once were. Bits of paper. Echoes.

Music: MAGGIE's song begins very faintly.

"Maggie's Spring (Interlude)."

Nôhkom, my grandmother, is a fragment to me on a scrap of paper, held in someone else's hand for a long time before being put down or lost. Then someone tried to write her again, but only half of it was remembered, a shadow of a shadow.

We hear the sound of water, the snow and the ice beginning to thaw freely. The sounds of life—insects, maybe even birds—faintly, in the distance.

I've come to question much of the truth of my grandmother's story. As that time falls away into air and the land itself, as memories falter and the people who hold them leave us, it raises more questions than my dad had answers for.

Where is nôhkom's truth? When does she get to write over other men's voices? In the end, what do I really know?

My father told me she had a soft voice and that she loved to laugh.

She begins to dance. Choreographed by the performer, Nancy Greyeyes, this final dance contrasts starkly with the previous, often violent, choreography. MAGGIE *is light here—you can almost see her laughter in the movement.*

At the end of the dance, the NARRATOR *stands and brings a chair from the audience to his grandmother's side. He helps her sit, deferential toward her.*

He sits on the ground at her feet, looking up to her as if waiting for her to tell, nearly fifty years delayed, her story.

The light begins to fade.

We hear faintly a woman's voice in Cree, drifting like music over the entire audience. One word seems clear: "Naboose," the word MAGGIE *used to address my father.*

Darkness.

BUNK #7

Larry Guno

Bunk #7 is a dramatization drawn from Larry Guno's experiences at residential school. The plot centres on the influence a favourite supervisor has on improving the boys' lives, and what happens when that supervisor is suddenly fired.

The play began as a series of scattered writings as Larry chronicled his experiences at residential school as a Nisga'a youth. In 2000 he told his good friend in Terrace, BC, Marianne Brørup Weston, a director and actor in community theatre, the story of a riot in residential school in 1959. Marianne told Larry it would make a great play. "Funny you should say that . . . " was his response. They were both involved in Skeena River Players, a First Nations theatre company, at the time. Marianne suggested a dramaturg could help Larry shape the story into a play, and, to make a long story short, she found Yvette Nolan, a playwright working in Halifax at the time, and secured funding to bring Yvette to Terrace. Yvette took on the challenge. Shortly thereafter she was named Artistic Director of Native Earth Performing Arts and brought the play into her fold for development. Larry spent several years travelling back and forth to Toronto, working on numerous drafts. This work led to a staged reading at the Weesageechak Begins to Dance Festival in Toronto in 2003, which Marianne directed at Buddies in Bad Times Theatre. Larry continued to work with Marianne, Yvette, and a team of professional First Nations actors, criss-crossing the country, refining the dialogue and working on the story arc.

Bunk #7 was scheduled for its premiere Canadian production in Toronto in 2006. In June 2005 Larry went home to Terrace to finish the play, glossy flyer in hand announcing *Bunk #7* for Native Earth Performing Arts's upcoming season. Tragically, he very suddenly passed away that July. With the play unfinished and the playwright gone, the project was shelved, and many hearts were broken. Subsequently Yvette presented a staged reading and tribute to *Bunk #7* and Larry's legacy at Tarragon Theatre in Toronto, attended by the Guno family. Marianne vowed to make sure the play was finished and one day performed for Larry's people.

In 2008, Marianne, who now had stewardship of the play, granted by the Guno family on Larry's behalf, contacted playwright Michael Armstrong about the possibility of completing the play and bringing it to the stage. Michael flew to Terrace to work with Marianne to direct a series of readings of the play with at-risk Aboriginal youth and Indian residential school survivors in First Nations communities in northwest BC, including Larry's hometown of New Aiyansh. Subsequently Michael was awarded a Canada Council grant to work on refining the script. Using Larry's own extensive notes, several new drafts were completed. Larry himself became the narrator character in this version, which contains a series of monologues excerpted from Larry's notes, commenting on the past.

The play was dormant for several years. A northwest production to be directed by Marianne was in the works when Larry's younger brother Ray Guno unexpectedly passed away in November 2012; Ray, who also attended residential school in Edmonton, was to play Larry in the show.

In summer 2013 Yvette Nolan travelled to Terrace to meet with Marianne and for the first time witness Nisga'a Territory, the Nass Valley, and New Aiyansh. Yvette was doing research for her book, *Medicine Shows* which includes an excerpt from *Bunk #7*.

Cheryl Croucher of Porcupine Stone Productions discovered its existence while working on a history of the residential school. She has worked very hard in a very short period of time to create the opportunity to present *Bunk #7* concurrently with the Truth and Reconciliation Commission hearings in Edmonton in 2014, hosted by CKUA Radio and funded by Alberta Aboriginal Performing Arts. The Guno family attended the event and provided explicit feedback on new changes to the script that they were uncomfortable with, specifically the use of pig masks for the school staff, and the inclusion of Larry as the narrator.

Currently, Marianne is working with Eryn Griffith and the National Theatre School to pursue a production of *Bunk #7*.

Timeline

2001: Skeena River Players playwriting workshop with Yvette Nolan.

2003: Native Earth Performing Arts's Weesageechak Begins to Dance Festival staged play reading starring Lorne Cardinal as Gray and Michael Spencer-Davis as O'Keefe at Buddies in Bad Times Theatre.

2005: *Bunk #7* chosen for Native Earth's 2005/2006 season.

July 2005: Larry Guno passes away unexpectedly.

2006: Marianne Brørup Weston is given stewardship of *Bunk #7* by the Guno family at a feast.

Tribute to Larry Guno with a staged play reading starring Darrell Dennis as Gray at the Tarragon Theatre, Toronto.

2008: Northwest BC play-reading tour of *Bunk #7* sponsored by Kermode Friendship Society, bringing together at-risk youth and IRS survivors.

Michael Armstrong is contracted to take notes and assist with reworking *Bunk #7* to give the play a more active storyline.

2009: Workshop and staged play reading with at-risk youth, presenting the reworked script at Northwest Community College, Terrace Campus.

2012: Larry's brother Ray Guno passes away unexpectedly, halting plans to mount a full stage production of *Bunk #7* in northwest BC.

2014: *Bunk #7* staged play reading in Edmonton, directed by Michael Armstrong, at the CKUA Radio Hall, concurrently with the Truth and Reconciliation Commission hearings.

Characters

Gray
Gunay
Paul
Doug
Ernie
Head
O'Keefe

ACT ONE

Bunk Number 7

The setting is in an institution that is commonly called an Indian Residential School, sometime in the 1960s. Like all similar institutions, it is a brown, squat, three-storey building located in the Alberta prairies, near one of its major cities. A young Aboriginal, GRAY, *about eighteen, dressed in the style of the day and carrying two large bags, walks into a large dorm with a number of double bunks almost filling the room. There is the sound of a radio; a Sarah Vaughan tune is playing. He walks to a bunk where a teenage First Nations male, rather short but stocky, is lying on the top bunk.*

GRAY: Oh, excuse me. But is this bunk seven?

GUNAY: *(grunts)* Might be.

GRAY: It's the bunk that I'm supposed to be using.

Pause, looking around.

The principal said bunk number seven is where I sleep.

GUNAY reads a magazine without looking at GRAY.

GUNAY: Good for you!

GRAY puts his bag down.

GRAY: Look, I was told to go to the top dorm? . . . And that . . . my bunk is number seven. Is this it?

GUNAY: Hm hm.

GRAY: Pretty yappy guy, aren't you?

GUNAY sits up, swings his legs over the side of his bunk, and looks down at GRAY for a few seconds.

GUNAY: Where you from, Indian?

GRAY: From the coast, Indian! You?

GUNAY: The islands!

GRAY: The islands?

GUNAY: The Charlottes, where else? Jeez!

GRAY sighs.

GRAY: Just askin'.

GUNAY: Just get here, Indian?

GRAY: Look, what's all this Indian stuff . . . what are ya, a cumsewah?

GUNAY chuckles.

GUNAY: Hey, a little touchy—

GRAY: Fuck!

GUNAY: I was jus' . . .

GRAY: Being a jerk!

Pause.

Anyways, I jus' got here, okay?

GUNAY: How come you ya didn't come with us last week?

GRAY looks hard at GUNAY.

GRAY: You the principal around here? If ya gotta know, I was on the waiting list an' I didn't know until a couple of days ago that there was a spot . . .

GUNAY laughs.

GUNAY: You were on the waiting list?

He yells over to another teenager in the far corner of the dorm.

Hey, Paul, get a load of this new buck; he was on some kind a waiting list.

GUNAY laughs.

Waitin', to be in this dump?!

PAUL walks over.

PAUL: Hey, Gray, man it's good to see ya.

PAUL shakes GRAY's hand vigorously.

GRAY: Paul, ya little Dene, what a surprise. Whazzit about two years?

PAUL: Yeah left the ol' san, came straight here.

GUNAY: You were in the san, with this Indian?

PAUL: Two years ago.

GRAY: So ya haven't found home?

PAUL: Nope . . . allus I know is it's somewhere up north.

GRAY: And your folks? Find them?

PAUL: Nah, am still lookin', though. You? Ya get to see your family?

GRAY: Oh yeah, everyone's fine. Little brothers and sisters all growed up.

PAUL: Hey that's cool, man. So ya guys met each other? Gunay been givin' ya a hard time?

GRAY: Gunay?

PAUL motions to GUNAY.

PAUL: This rangy-tang is Harold Dick but we just call him Gunay. It means "dear boy" in Haida, you know. A term of affection, he says.

GRAY: Hello, dear boy! Or do you go by Harry, Harry Dick?

PAUL laughs.

PAUL: And Gunay, meet Edward Gray. In the san, we jus' called him Gray. He's Nisga'a.

GUNAY: Hello, Neesgaa, a grease-eater, huh?

GRAY: *(to PAUL)* What's bugging his ass?

PAUL laughs.

PAUL: Oh Gunay's jus' horsin' around. It's how those Haidas say hello. So ya gonna give school another go?

GRAY: Yep! Gonna giver this time.

PAUL: Hey, dat's cool, man, real cool!

GRAY: Well am two years behind now. Fucking guys at the school board won't accept that I finished grade twelve by correspondence while I was in the san. Gotta repeat it . . . I even got mostly As.

PAUL: Dat's stale . . . Still gonna be a lawyer?

GRAY: Betcha boots, buddy. Always wanted to be one, all I wanna do is finish this year and graduate.

GUNAY snorts derisively. GRAY looks at GUNAY.

Only reason why am here, even if I hafta put up with assholes.

PAUL: Oh it'll be all right. Better than the san.

GRAY looks around.

GRAY: Kinda crowded, ain't it?

GUNAY: Whadya expect? Private rooms?

GRAY: No, but I was hopin' there wouldn't be too many jerks.

PAUL: Well welcome to IRS.

GRAY: IRS are all the same. Been to one on the coast. Same smell, same crowded shit.

PAUL: Well, at least we get out of here during the week—bus leaves for school at eight.

PAUL walks over to the third locker by the right side, bangs it with his hand.

This is gonna be your locker.

GRAY: Shit, all my stuff ain't gonna fit into that little locker.

GUNAY: Hey, someone go get the bellboy for his majesty the Neesga.

PAUL looks around.

PAUL: Well ya hafta go an' see that creep Mister A. Boyce for the keys to the storage room where our bags are kept.

GRAY: *(tentatively)* Okay. Who is—

PAUL: And be sure to get a lock for your locker.

GRAY: Thanks!

GUNAY: Hey, Neesga, don't let me catch you getting into my locker—unless you want some serious beef.

PAUL laughs at GUNAY.

PAUL: Guys get real pissed off if they catch ya messing with their stuff—lots of fights happen that way.

GRAY glares at GUNAY.

GRAY: Yeah, some guys are already cruising for a bruising.

GUNAY jumps down from his top bunk and walks over to GRAY.

GUNAY: Stay out of my way, grease-eater, or—

GRAY moves forward so that he is almost nose to nose with GUNAY.

GRAY: Or you'll what?

PAUL and GUNAY start to laugh at GRAY's belligerence.

GUNAY grabs GRAY's hand and shakes it.

GUNAY: Gotcha goin' there, didn't I. Jus' don't take things too serious around here, except for Paul's farts, man. Small, but he carries killer gas.

They all laugh. Just then, a dark, scowling, heavy-set teen of about seventeen comes into the dorm, walks past the three without a word and into the small adjoining bathroom and shuts the door.

(in a near whisper) That's Doug the Slug—he's one mean Haida, boy! Just stay on his good side. Sorta runs the school, or thinks he does.

PAUL: Shsss, he might hear ya.

PAUL laughs nervously.

GRAY sits down on the bottom bunk.

GRAY: I been on the road for almost two friggin' days.

PAUL: Take the train?

GRAY: The bus. Oh man, it took that old bus a day and a half to get to here from ole Plince Luppet.

PAUL: Plince Luppet?

GRAY: Prince Rupert, it's on the north coast of BC.

GRAY looks around the dorm.

So where do ya go for a shower around here?

GUNAY laughs.

GUNAY: Lissen to him, Paul, he wants a shower—like now?

PAUL: I hear him . . . should we tell him?

GUNAY: Dunno, maybe wait till he finds out.

GRAY: What, what . . . I just want to shower. Where do I go?

PAUL: Down to the Pit, man.

GRAY: The Pit?

GUNAY: Yep, down the basement.

PAUL shivers exaggeratedly.

PAUL: Ooh, ooh!

GUNAY: Down a dark place they call a playroom—

GRAY: A playroom?

GUNAY: —right next to the shitters—a concrete pit with four shower heads, stink, dirty, and cold.

PAUL: Freeze ya balls off in the winter.

GUNAY: But there's hope, Gray, shower at the school. I do. Or be like Paul, he never showers.

PAUL gives him the raspberry.

GRAY: Take off, eh! Can't be that bad.

GUNAY: Worse! If you gotta shower here be early, gets kinda crowded.

PAUL: Yeah . . . lots a guys all wanting to wash off their dicks from wet dreams . . .

GRAY: Same ol' Paul.

GUNAY: He's what we call in Haida a "Gaay Kaaxiida," a horny old man.

PAUL: Up yours, Haida. Number one rule, if ya use the showers down there, doan be bending over, ole Dudley might come along.

GRAY: Dudley, who the fuck's Dudley?

PAUL stands up straight and strikes a pose of someone preaching in a high falsetto.

PAUL: I am the Reverend Asshole Dudley, I am the vice-principal, and you are my fuck . . . I mean my flock . . . If you follow God's rules, you will be saved, and if you follow mine, I will give you some candy—in my room, of course.

GRAY: Shit, Paul, ya think ya tellin' me something new? Jus' about every joint I been in there's someone like Dudley. I've learned to stay out of their way. Am not gonna hassle anyone and *no one* hassles me.

The door to the washroom opens and DOUG walks out, giving GRAY a quick appraisal as he exits to the left, muttering.

DOUG: Jus' stick to the goddam rules, grease-eater.

PAUL: Rules? Did he say rules?

GRAY: I know all about the rules, the rules are the same in every IRS.

GUNAY: Get use to them, grease-eater, 'cause there are lots of them. Rules rule this place. Some not bad, but most are aaghh. So stale.

PAUL: Jus' try and keep outta scraps an' keep your eyes open and your mouth shut, especially around staff.

GRAY: Which ones?

PAUL: Any one of them can get ya in real trouble, but if you get stuck ask Gunay, he's figgered out how to survive in this place, right, Gunay?

GUNAY: Some people around here don't know how to mind their own business. But we try look after each other.

He looks at PAUL.

Not always easy . . . It's jus' that there are some things you oughtta know.

PAUL: Rule number one: don't rat on anyone to the staff. You're in big trouble if ya do.

GRAY: So what else is new, Paul!

PAUL: Rule number two: thou shalt not know a girl.

GRAY: Know a girl?

PAUL sighs.

PAUL: You know how they say it in the Bible . . . in the Old Testament. That when David or Solomon knowed some woman—it meant he banged her?

GUNAY: What St. Paul here means is that we can't mix with the girls.

PAUL: Only time I get to see my woman is when we have church and . . .

GUNAY: Called the "non-fraternization rule." Get caught talking to a girl from the girl's side and you're in real shit, even if it's your own sister ya talkin' to.

PAUL: And watch out for the Bird Woman.

GRAY: Bird Woman?

PAUL: She's the senior girls' supervisor. Looks and acts like a bird.

He imitates a chicken fluttering and clucking.

Cluck cluck.

GUNAY: An' watches over them like a, a . . .

PAUL: Like a friggin' mother hen!

GUNAY: And she is Mr. Nelson's ah, ah . . . woman.

PAUL does an obscene gesture to demonstrate the Bird Woman's relationship to Mr. Nelson.

GRAY: Mr. Nelson?

GUNAY: The junior boys' supervisor. It's those little shits that do the supervisin'.

PAUL: He's from the States, Kansas. Says he's an ex-marine, but you'd never believe it, he's so skinny and nervous.

GUNAY: Shell-shocked.

PAUL: Sometimes the little guys make ole Nelson sing "Pumpkin Sue."

GRAY: Pumpkin Sue?

PAUL: Yahoo.

PAUL starts to jig and clap his hands rhythmically.

Gotta see it, Gray. Ole Nelson gets on that table in the playroom, not nervous anymore, gets kinda goofy, whips out his harmonica, plays a few bars, and then in that skinny voice starts to sing "Pumpkin Sue" . . . jus' a stompin'. All the little guys would clap and whoop it up.

GUNAY laughs.

GUNAY: Yeah, then at the end he bows around like he's Elvis. He's a'right.

PAUL: For a supervisor.

PAUL looks around.

It's Mr. A. Boyce ya gotta watch out for . . . dat man's mean, boy, especially early in the mornin'.

GRAY: Mornin', what?

PAUL: Usually around five-thirty he'll walk into the dorm without warnin', and if you're still in bed he'll give your bunk a real whack with that friggin' bat that he carries around all the time, and on his second round, if you're still in bed, he'll send ya flying, mattress and all. I think he jus' lives for those morning rounds. Jus' be up by five-thirty.

GRAY: Mr. Ayboys?

GUNAY: A. Boyce. A is for assface. A real mean shithead, ex-RCMP.

GUNAY laughs, poking PAUL.

This warrior allus buggers off whenever Boyce comes around.

PAUL: Bullshit, Gunay! Am not scared of ole Boyce.

GUNAY laughs.

GUNAY: Paul, you allus crap your pants when he comes around.

PAUL: He lies all the time, Gray. Rule number three: thou shalt remember your number.

GUNAY: Yeah, gonna lose your pants if ya forget.

PAUL: Hey, I gotta woman working in the laundry. She can get rid of all your skid marks. Cost ya ten ciggies.

GUNAY: That Paul's always talkin' about his women. Have yet to meet one of them.

PAUL: Fuck you, you goofy Haida. Anyways, Gray, forget your number jus' once, Doug'll brand it on your ass with a hot iron.

GRAY grows a little flustered.

GRAY: I'm not afraid of your jerk Doug.

PAUL: Oh ooh rule number four: thou shalt not call Doug a jerk. Not to his face, anyways. He'll have your balls for breakfast. He's beaten up a few guys for just lookin' at him the wrong way. Hey, Gunay, it's almost lunch, time to head down to the playroom for the lineup.

A bell rings and PAUL and GUNAY start to walk out the dorm.

GRAY: Hey wait a minute—you mean we still have to line up for meals? I thought . . . I mean, I was told . . . that there'd be no more lining up.

GUNAY: Yep, I doan like it either, lining up with the little guys. Like we're too stupid to know when to go to meals.

PAUL: Marchin' like prisoners into that stinkin' dining room next to the shitters, eatin' food that's not fit for dogs, havin' Doug as the table monitor.

GUNAY looks at the now despondent GRAY.

GUNAY: Hey, man, it ain't all that bad. Tomorrow morning, we're outta here . . . to school, broads, an' basketball.

GRAY: Good. Can't wait!

PAUL: C'mon, ya guys, we gotta get down there before Doug kicks our ass. Remember there ain't no Indian time here. Besides, I can't wait to see what's on the menu.

GRAY: Menu? You mean we get to choose?

The boys laugh.

PAUL: Gray, my son, we do get to choose. First there is spork, and if you doan wanna eat that, then there is spork, and if you wanna wait till supper there is always spork, and at supper the Spider Woman, the cook, might warm it up, but usually that's just for Sunday dinners.

GRAY: Aagh! I doan wanna line up for that kinda crap.

PAUL: Gray, get into the lineup or old Doug's gonna wreck ya.

GRAY: You guys are just shittin' me again, right?

GRAY laughs skeptically.

DOUG: *(voice from off-stage shouts)* A'right, you bunch of homos. Get into the fucking line.

Everyone hurriedly exits except for GRAY, who stands uncertainly and then grabs his bags and runs out after GUNAY and PAUL.

Dining Hall

The boys file in. GRAY *looks around for a place to sit, spots two younger boys, ages around ten or eleven. One is* HEAD, *and the other* ERNIE. GRAY *sits down to join them. They look at him in alarm.*

GRAY *is oblivious to their discomfiture.*

GRAY: Hi, fellows.

ERNIE: Hi

HEAD: Ooh.

He looks over in the direction where the supervisor on meal duty is standing.

Mr. Boyce is gonna see him.

He motions to GRAY.

You're gonna get us in trouble sittin' here . . . with us.

ERNIE: Haaah . . . you can't . . .

ERNIE *also looks fearfully in the direction of the supervisor.*

Please, you can't sit at this table, it's . . . not allowed . . . you'll get us in trouble.

GUNAY *comes hurrying over, flushed.*

GUNAY: Gray, are you crazy, you can't sit any ole place, man . . . ya sit in only one place and it's over that table where we are sitting—that's where all the senior boys sit. Not with these little twerps.

He pinches HEAD*'s arm.*

HEAD: Oww!

GRAY *gets up, smiling at the relieved boys.*

GRAY: Sorry, guys, gotta go sit with the big boys.

After GRAY *leaves,* ERNIE *watches* HEAD *playing with his food.*

ERNIE: So how ya doing, Head?

HEAD: I dunno—same ole stuff . . . hate goin' on the bus real early in the mornin'.

ERNIE: Why? It's fun . . . get to be away from here . . . for a little while.

HEAD: But it's so stale here, Ernie—and at school those white kids, making fun of my clothes an' the way I talk. Same ol' lunches . . . spork . . . no money for drinks.

ERNIE: Yeah . . .

HEAD: And every day I get picked on by that Cree guy . . . what's his name . . . Johnny High Feathers . . . and his white friends . . . thinks he's not Indian like us.

ERNIE: Come on, Head, you can take care of yourself.

HEAD: I can't. Too many big mean guys here.

ERNIE: Yes you can.

HEAD: I can't.

ERNIE: Chicken!

HEAD: Am not chicken.

ERNIE: Come on, Head, am just kiddin'—gonna eat your bread?

HEAD passes over his bread.

HEAD: I miss my mom real bad, Ernie.

ERNIE: What about your daddy, don't you miss him?

HEAD plays with his food with his fork.

HEAD: Doan have a dad.

ERNIE: Come on . . . we all have dads.

HEAD: There's jus' Mom and I.

Silence.

Ernie?

ERNIE: Yeah?

HEAD: Ya get lots a letters from your mommy?

ERNIE: Once a week.

HEAD: Me too. Used to. Now I never got one for a long time. Not like her. Last one there was a whole ten-dollar bill in it.

ERNIE: Head! You still got some of it?

HEAD: Oh yeah, hey next time we're allowed to go into town—we'll go to a movie, huh?

ERNIE: I hear there is a good Disney movie. *Tonka*? Sal Mineo plays this Indian kid who is in love with his horse.

HEAD: We'll go?

ERNIE: Yeah! Popcorn!

HEAD: And pop, a large one.

Silence.

Hey, Ernie.

ERNIE: What?

HEAD: Ya ever been to Bancouver?

ERNIE: Ya mean Vancouver? Yeah, once when I was little.

HEAD: Is it bigger than St. Albert?

ERNIE: Oh yeah, way much bigger. Why?

HEAD: In her last letter Mom said she was gonna go to Vancouver to look for a job. Maybe she got lost there.

ERNIE: Doan worry, Head, you'll get a letter from her soon. You'll see!

HEAD: I hope so, Ernie.

HEAD resumes eating as ERNIE looks on, silent, and then looks over to the table where the bigger boys are sitting.

GUNAY looks up at the approaching DOUG.

GUNAY: Oh hi, Doug.

DOUG ignores GUNAY and sits down across from PAUL and GRAY.

PAUL: Hi, Slug!

DOUG: Hello, Eskimo boy . . . and it's Doug, Eskimo!

PAUL: Am not Eskimo.

DOUG: Ya eat raw fish, don't ya?

GUNAY: Aw, leave him alone, Doug.

PAUL: *(defiantly to DOUG)* Am from the Northwest Territories but am not Eskimo, and anyways who the hell are you?

DOUG rises to his feet, pounding his chest.

DOUG: I am Doug and am a Haida!

PAUL: Well if I was as ugly as you, I'd hide away, too.

All the boys at the table laugh. DOUG jumps to his feet, and reaches across the table and grabs PAUL by the collar, trying to pull HIM forward. The smaller boy manages to twist away, causing DOUG to fall on his face on the table. He jumps to his feet again to get at PAUL.

DOUG: Why you little shit, am gonna tear you apart.

PAUL jumps around excitedly.

PAUL: Jus' you try . . . quick, someone hold me back or am gonna wreck him.

DOUG: *(spluttering)* You gonna wreck me? Let me at him.

GUNAY and GRAY jump up and restrain DOUG.

GUNAY: Shut up, Paul. Jeez, Doug, cool it, he was jus' horsin' around.

DOUG: Got my eye on you, Eskimo.

PAUL: It's Dene to you, you wagon-burning Haida.

GUNAY: Paul, shut the hell up!

The boys turn their attention to the food and soon the tension eases.

GUNAY stage whispers in a high falsetto.

Hey, Paul, hole me back, or am gonna wreck ole Boyce.

PAUL: Go jump in Sauce Lake.

General laughter. The boys banter as they eat: "Hole me baaack," "Gunay you're so stale," "Hey Paul, let's see that Cassius Clay move again." More laughter.

GUNAY: Hey, here come ole Nelson. Let's see if we can get him to sing his "Pumpkin Sue."

The boys, except DOUG, start to clap and sing "Pumpkin Sue." Suddenly everyone is quiet.

GRAY: What's goin' on, Gunay?

GUNAY: *(almost a whisper)* It's Boyce. He's comin' over this way.

Everyone furtively watches as Boyce's shadow goose-steps by their table.

GRAY speaks after Boyce seem to be out of earshot.

GRAY: So what's an ex-RCMP doing here?

PAUL: *(near whispering)* Be very careful what you say about him.

PAUL motions to the direction in which Boyce was heading.

Doan know how he does it, but he hears everything we say, seem like. Hey, you hear rumours that they are gonna be getting a new supervisor for the senior boys?

Laughs.

The last one, that Mr. McFartlane, the Mormon with the whistle? Remember him, Gunay?

GUNAY: It was McFarlay, dummy.

PAUL: Like McFartline betta.

Laughs.

He didn't stick around long after we went an' gave him the silent treatment. Shoulda seen him, Gray. Packed his bags and took off like a goose in the fall time.

GUNAY: Good riddance to him. To all of them pricks, most of these guys don't ever stay long—they jus' come and go. Except for that friggen' Dudley.

PAUL: Wonder where they come from, these white mans?

GUNAY: Who in hell knows . . . ya jus' gotta wonder if these cumsewah have a place of their own. They doan seem to have no families . . . belong to no tribe. Maybe they're just born to wander around the goddam country . . . just go from place to place and make life miserable for us Indians.

PAUL looks over his shoulder, leaning close to GRAY in a near whisper.

PAUL: They say that in another school . . .

GRAY: Can't hear ya.

PAUL leans closer.

PAUL: They say . . . in a school in BC, a kid went missing three years ago. They never found 'im, and they say that it was Boyce who was supervisin', and that he may have beaten him to death with a bat and throwed him in the ocean. I believe it. He's a real scary dog.

GRAY laughs.

What's so funny?

GRAY: You guys. Believe everything you hear.

GUNAY: You don't believe these things happen, Gray?

GRAY: Jus' about everywhere I've been I hear the same story, that some mean old white guy like Boyce has personally killed some kid with his bare hands. Some buried behind the cow barn or the utility building or even under the shit house. C'mon guys, give me a break!

PAUL: And you think that there aren't guys like assface around?

GRAY: All am sayin' is that ya can't take as gospel everything ya hear. Where's the friggin proof?

GUNAY: Oh ya gonna make a good lawyer someday, Gray.

GRAY: Well even if half of it is true what are we gonna do? What can we do?

PAUL: So we gonna jus' let guys like assface an Dudley get away with what they do?

GRAY: If you have any plans how ya gonna stop them, do it, Paul. Otherwise doan jus' talk about it. It just gets so stale.

GUNAY: Sometimes I get the feelin' that you're jus' chicken shit, Gray.

GRAY: Maybe I am, Gunay. You guys can fight your stupid wars, am not gonna get involved. I told ya: all I wanna do is jus' get through this year.

GUNAY and PAUL get up wordlessly, pick up their plates and utensils, and move offstage, leaving GRAY sitting alone.

Still Awake

Dorm. Lights out except for the light from the small toilet in the back—there is a low sound of music from someone's radio. Off in the distance is the whistle of a train rumbling by, the drone of the diesel—in the dark are the ghostly outlines of the double bunk beds.

GUNAY: Hey, Gray—are you still awake?

GRAY lightly kicking the bottom of the top bunk.

GRAY: Of course I am awake, you think this is all a dream—if it is, I am having one hell of a nightmare.

GUNAY chuckles, his head appearing from the side of the top bunk.

GUNAY: Homesick, huh?

GRAY: Nah.

He shifts his weight so that he is lying on his back.

Hear that train, Gunay?

They listen to the sound.

Kinda makes me wonder how the folks are back home.

GUNAY: They're so far away.

GUNAY sits up and swings his legs over the edge of the bed.

Some mornings . . . real early when you pricks are still snoring in both ends, I go to that window on the far side and watch the sunrise . . . and for a few moments . . . it's like looking out on the sea, watchin' the wind roll over those fields like waves out in Hecate Straits reflectin' the early morning light, an' I can almost hear the sea rollin' in like rumbling thunder that ends in a sigh. I swear I can even hear the screams of eagles echoing through the forest and, man, I can jus' about taste the salt in the air and in the distance those clump of little trees look like distant islands . . . in the mist.

GRAY laughs.

GRAY: Ya beginnin' to sound like ole Hank over there. He's allus goin' on about hearing stuff at nights. Bonkers!

GUNAY: Maybe! If things doan change around here we're all gonna be bonkers. An' seriously, Gray, we've been talkin' about getting' a student union goin' here.

GRAY groans audibly.

GRAY: Ohhh!

GUNAY: Anything would be better than this.

GRAY: It is the shits around here, especially for the smaller ones, but what can we do? A student union won't do dick all. Not one they'll allow.

GUNAY: But it will be *our* student union, Gray. That's how it works, working together . . . for changes to . . .

GRAY laughs.

GRAY: Oh yeah, I can jus' see the student union marchin' down to ole Stamp's office.

GUNAY: Here he goes again.

GRAY: *(in falsetto)* Gee, Mr. Reverend Sir, we's jus' poor little Indians an' all we's want is good grub.

GUNAY shakes his head.

GUNAY: Jeez, Gray, ya ever . . .

GRAY: *(continuing)* We want our own rooms, with TV . . .

GUNAY: You are bonkers, real savage.

GRAY: . . . more dances . . . with girls that is . . . more stuff to do, *and*!

GUNAY: *(startled)* And?

GRAY: And most of all, we wan' ya to kick ole Dudley and Boyce out. And ya wanna know what ole Stamp's gonna say, Gunay?

GUNAY: *(rolling his eyes)* What?

GRAY stands with a blanket wrapped around him like a clerical robe.

GRAY: He's gonna say, by Jesus, Mr. Gunay and all yous little red heathens, am gonna do jus' that.

GUNAY: You know, Gray, I can't figger out why ya wanna be a lawyer and be so scared to get into a scrap. I mean, I thought lawyers fight to make things right.

GRAY: Yeah, and make money at the same time.

GUNAY: Mostly make money, I hear. I think you're jus' all talk.

Pause.

GRAY: Maybe I am.

GUNAY: Jus' talk, talk, talk.

GRAY: Tell me, who's gonna back ya?

GUNAY: Well I've been talkin' to a few . . .

GRAY: How many, Gunay?

GUNAY: A few!

GRAY laughs.

GRAY: Tell ya something, Gunay. None of these guys are gonna stick their scrawny necks out. They'll all crap on it, and then when it does happen, if it happens, that is, every one of them will be fallin' all over themselves saying that they thought of it first.

GUNAY: Oh I dunno about that.

GRAY: And what about that creep Dudley. He's gonna fight this.

GUNAY: We can expose him.

GRAY laughs.

GRAY: He'll expose ya first, Gunay.

They fall silent and the music from one of the radios in the dorm becomes the hit of the day, "One little Indian, two little Indians . . . "

GUNAY: I think it's gonna work, Gray.

GRAY: What, exposing Dudley?

Both boys laugh.

DOUG: *(voice from the dark)* Hey, you pricks knock it off—for Chris'sakes, some of us are trying to get some sleep.

GUNAY: *(lowered voice)* Old Douglas, soundin' off again . . .

GRAY: Yeah! Wonder what's bugging his ass?

GUNAY: Oh he's all right, jus' likes to sound off. Anyways, as I was sayin' . . .

GRAY: So, Gunay—goin' out crab fishing this comin' summer?

GUNAY: Yeah, jus' can't wait—goin' out with my dad and Uncle Jim and two of my cousins.

GRAY: As the jo-boy, I betcha?

GUNAY: You're so stale, Gray. Ya know, Kellogg, this summer I get full share.

GRAY: Must be nice, sittin' on the deck drinkin' beer, chasing broads in every port. An' get paid for it.

GUNAY: Wish it was that easy. Can get kinda hairy out in the salt chuck.

GUNAY feigns puking.

But it's great . . . out there. Jus' hope it's gonna be a good season, sure can use the dough.

GRAY: Lots to learn to be on a crab boat? Think I can cut it?

GUNAY farts.

They listen to the music on the radio: "Hey Mister Custer I don't wanna go." The boys join in the chorus: "oompa, oompa, pah pah." The clock tolls.

Hear that clock, Gunay. Every goddam thing around here is by the goddam clock. Time is so big with them and it's like they fill our lives with it . . .

everything timed to the fuckin' minute. We get up to bells, we eat to bells, we line up to bells, we go to church to bells, and we go to our friggin' bunks to dem damn bells . . . bells, bells, bells.

Pause.

It's like they want us to die hearing them goddam bells.

DOUG'S voice comes from the dark, quiet but menacing.

DOUG: And if you don't shut yer yap you'll be hearing bells, sooner than you think.

Faint light starts to dim, and GRAY gets under the covers.

O'Keefe Arrives

Morning in the dorm. By the windows are two young boys, dressed in identical jeans and red/green plaid shirts. ERNIE is writing something on the window.

ERNIE: *(bubbling)* Ya hear that new supervisor, Mr. O'Keefe-guy is coming today.

HEAD: Is it true that he came all the ways from . . . England? That's what Mr. Nelson said.

ERNIE: I dunno . . . hey, maybe he might make things better, it's so stale here.

HEAD: What can he do, Ernie?

ERNIE: Jus' . . . more things to do . . . sports and stuff.

HEAD: Maybe teach us to play hockey?

ERNIE: Nah, those English don't ever play hockey—I don't think . . . boxer maybe. Who knows?

HEAD: Boxer? *(excitedly)* Maybe he might clean ole Dudley's clock, huh?

ERNIE: Jeez—I dunno.

Pause.

I just hope that he is not like dose other supervisors—like that scary Mr. A. Boyce—or Mr. Connelly—aagh he smells—like smoke and stinky beer.

They stand a little ways from the window for a quiet few moments—waiting, silently.

HEAD: *(tentatively)* Ernie . . .

ERNIE: Yeah?

ERNIE looks out the window intently.

HEAD: I . . . I . . .

HEAD is on the verge of tears. ERNIE turns from the window, almost impatiently.

ERNIE: What's a matter with you . . . Jeez!

HEAD starts to cry softly.

HEAD: I . . . I am scared . . . Ernie . . . am real scared.

ERNIE: Scared? Of what?

ERNIE looks around the empty dorm.

HEAD: *(blurts)* Of Dudley.

ERNIE takes HEAD by his shoulders.

ERNIE: He hasn't been—

HEAD: No, it's just that he's been really scary, and—

ERNIE: What . . . and what, Head?

HEAD: Jus' that, I jus' get scared the way he looks at me.

ERNIE: C'mon, Head.

HEAD: He gives me the willies, Ernie.

ERNIE: He gives everybody the willies.

HEAD: But his eyes—they're like . . . like . . .

ERNIE: Like what?

HEAD: I dunno, like snake eyes, small and . . . creepy. Jeez, I jus' wish my mommy didn't let me come here in the first place.

ERNIE laughs—grabs HEAD in a playful hammerlock.

ERNIE: Don't worry, Head, he ain't gonna touch ya . . . hear me?

HEAD: *(muffled)* Yeah, yeah. Lemme go.

ERNIE releases HEAD.

ERNIE: Anyways, ya ain't his type, Head . . . First of all . . . ya got a big head—an' you're too skinny, anyways.

HEAD: Anyways . . . anyways what, Ernie?

ERNIE: Well ya jus' gotta learn to pretend he can't see you.

HEAD: Huh?

ERNIE: Like get invisible . . .

HEAD: Oh yeah, get invisible . . . jus' like dat!

ERNIE: Ya can do it. Jus' be really still when he's around an' doan look at him. Make like he's not even there. My Chinee . . .

Just then, the sound of a vehicle coming up the school's driveway. The boys rush excitedly to the window—eager faces pressed against the glass.

HEAD: *(disappointed)* He looks kinda small and skinny, and look at those big glasses, like they are made of Coke bottles.

ERNIE: Yeah, and he's all sorta tweedy an' he's got his coat over his shoulders like some kinda gangster.

HEAD: And look, he's smokin' some skinny cigar, too!

ERNIE: That ain't no cigar. It looks like the stuff that you see in the movies. Like somethin' ya put cigarettes in. Boy, he sure looks kinda funny. Hey, Head, he's looking our way . . . and he's waving.

The two boys wave tentatively.

HEAD: Well if he's a boxer, he's gonna hafta be pretty good if he's gonna clean Mr. A. Boyce's clock.

O'Keefe Speaks

The scene is a small hall that on Sundays serves as a chapel. O'KEEFE *is standing by a small baby grand piano.*

O'KEEFE: I stand before you today as a humbled person. Humbled because I see in your shining faces hope. I see in each of you hope for a better future for your people. What others may dismiss as unteachable or hopeless, I see possibilities. For you represent the future. It is a future in which your people can take their rightful place in our society, as productive and useful citizens. What others may regard as backward and prone to drunkenness, I see potential. I see future doctors, lawyers, scientists, and leaders in this room. What others dismiss as a waste of time, I see great challenge. The challenge for each of you to be the best that you can be; to reach excellence in the fields of government, music, arts, culture, and in so many areas of Western life that have been deemed by others as out of reach for our red brothers and sisters.

It is my view that the government has not appreciated the full potential of this school. What is required, in my humble opinion, is that we—that is the staff and the students—work more diligently toward learning the arts, music, dance, and all other social skills that are the requirements of ladies and gentlemen.

The staff has done a superb job in maintaining a good learning environment here. But there is always room for improvement. I think that I have both the background and qualification to help you, and I look forward to working with both the staff and students to make this a better place to live, to study, and to learn new ways of relating to one another. I am sure that I can count on your cooperation.

In England there are schools like this, schools that have produced some of England's finest gentlemen.

I grew up in a school not unlike this one. Like some of you here, I was very small and scared. But I overcame my fears and doubts. Believe me, you have the capacity to do the same. One day you will look back to your experience here in this fine institution as the best of your lives.

Several of the boys laugh aloud.

HEAD: But sir, I jus' wanna go home and be with my mommy.

The boys shout their approval.

O'KEEFE: Well, young fellow, be patient. Things truly are going to change here. You will soon be so busy that you will forget about home. Most of you come from remote areas of Canada, and until now you have been exposed mostly to your old ways. I have done a good deal of reading about and studying the red Indians in Canada, which I found to be quite interesting. But the past is the past. It is gone. We must look to the future, to new ways, to attain an enlightened way of life. I promise that I will work very hard to introduce you to the finer things that a civilized life has to offer, such as classical music, modern dancing, good manners, civility, poetry, and athletics.

The students look on in silence.

I understand your plight, having come from very humble beginnings myself. In Great Britain, a fairly rigid class system exists, and it can be difficult to break through class barriers. I grew up in a working-class environment, but by working and studying hard I obtained good marks in the public school, and later I got a scholarship to attend a private school to study music. I was even selected to be one of the students to have the honour and privilege of playing the piano at a private recital for Her Majesty the Queen, a Royal Command Performance.

He pauses for dramatic effect. Then walks slowly to the piano, sits down solemnly, stretches his hands out to exercise his fingers, and proceeds to play some strains of Chopin before swinging into a rendition of Scott Joplin, then finishing off with some rock with a flourish. The student's cheer and clap.

You will find that I always try to be fair. I will go to bat for you in getting you special privileges, like going into the city, to visit the zoo, the art museum, and, for those of you who have demonstrated exceptional effort, to attend a musical concert. "Excellence through discipline," that is going to be our motto. It will guide all our efforts in the days to come.

After O'KEEFE's address, the boys are back in the dorm. GRAY is lying on his back on his bunk. GUNAY and PAUL are sitting on another bunk nearby.

GUNAY: Dat was one cool speech, man. I think O'Keefe's gonna be a'right. Whatya think, Gray?

GRAY: Heard it before.

PAUL: I think he's a cool cat.

GUNAY: Sure can play that piano.

PAUL: Good dresser too.

GUNAY: I liked what he had to say.

PAUL: He might be the guy to get stuff goin' around this stale place.

GUNAY: Maybe he can help us form that student council, huh, Gray?

GRAY: Give me a break, a student union?

PAUL: He can show me how to play the piano like Jerry Lee Lewis. Man, can you see all the girls?

GRAY: Ya guys are so stale. What's he gonna do? All I heard him say is that he's gonna kick our little red asses until we become big white asses.

GUNAY: Might help make some changes here.

GRAY: How?

GUNAY: I dunno, lots a things need to be done around here. Maybe us students can have more say.

GRAY laughs derisively.

GRAY: Forget it, they'll never allow it.

GUNAY: They might.

GRAY: Nope, never.

GUNAY: We'll see.

Pause.

I jus' doan get you, Gray?

GRAY: Gunay, I've told ya my only goal is to get through this year, graduate, and am outta here.

GUNAY: Doan ya care what's goin' . . .

GRAY: Nope, an' am not gonna get involved.

PAUL: Not even Linda Sue?

GRAY ignores PAUL.

GRAY: I doan care if we eat spork all the time.

PAUL: *(sings)* Spork in the morning, spork in evening.

GRAY: Doan care the staff are assholes.

PAUL starts to do the prairie dance.

PAUL: Heyaa.

GRAY: Doan care that there is nothing to do here after schools.

GUNAY: He's on a roll.

GRAY: Am jus' gonna work my butt off, see? I plan to go to university next fall. Understand? Am not on a mission to save my people.

PAUL: "Oh my people."

GRAY: I've heard speeches what's-his-name just gave before. They all sound the same.

GUNAY: More, more!

GRAY: As for that student union thing, Gunay, doan waste my time with that. It ain't gonna happen, not a real one, anyways. So my stale, little red brothers, beat it, this Indian jus' wanna get some rest.

GUNAY/PAUL: *(singing together)* One little Indian, two little Indians . . . oompa, oompa . . . "

DOUG, unseen in the background.

DOUG: SHADDUP!

Writing a Letter to Sue Ann

In the bathroom, GRAY is sitting on the toilet with a notepad on his lap, and GUNAY is sitting on the floor beside the toilet. The radio is playing some Perry Como ballad.

GUNAY: Jeez, am sure glad that you agreed to help me write this letter to Sue Ann.

GRAY: Fuck, Gunay, why can't you write this yourself? It's not that hard.

GUNAY: Well writin' is just not my thing. Especially to a girl like Sue Ann. I really want to impress her.

GRAY: Oh she'll be impressed all right . . . when she finds out someone else wrote . . .

GUNAY: Gray, ya gotta swear on a stack of bibles that you ain't gonna tell anyone.

GRAY: A stack a bibles, huh? You have my word, Gunay.

GRAY puts his hand on his heart.

On the honour of our horse named Billy, I swear that I will not tell Sue Ann that the words that she will read on the paper that Gunay has been fartin' on for a whole week are not his but come from the mind of—

GUNAY: Ssshh, keep it down. Come on, Gray, for Chris' sake, just do me this favour.

GRAY: Okay, but you gotta let me see her letter.

GUNAY: What, see her letter? No I can't let you see her letter.

GRAY: Well how else can I know how to reply unless I see what she wrote?

GUNAY: Well, I'll tell ya what she said, in general, like.

GRAY: Okay. Tell me in general, like!

GUNAY: Well I think that she really digs me and that she likes my . . . my body.

GRAY laughs.

GRAY: Likes your body?

GUNAY: Ssshh, keep it down. Just say that I really dig her too. And that I . . .

GRAY: Like her body too?

GUNAY: No, no, she might think that I am too fresh or somethin'.

GRAY: Okay, Gunay, how about this:

GRAY starts to write.

"Dear Sue Ann, you have no idea how my heart fluttered when I received your letter. I knew it was from you by the sweet smell comin' from said letter . . . "

GUNAY: "Said letter . . ." Doesn't it sound a little business-like?

GRAY: Well you said you didn't want to be fresh. Okay, how about, "when I got your letter, which I have been waiting for with so much longing."

GUNAY: Yeah, yeah, that sounds better.

GRAY sighs and rolls his eyes.

GRAY: "I long for your rounded body and your heaving breasts . . . "

GUNAY: Heaving breasts? Isn't that a little too fresh?

GRAY: Look, Gunay, this is not a business letter like ya said, and if you really want to impress her, you gotta take some risks.

GUNAY: Okay, okay. Heaving breasts it is.

GRAY: "I want you to know that I have eyes only for your . . . your . . . "

GRAY starts to laugh.

GUNAY: Come on, Gray, get serious.

GRAY: " . . . for your wonderful smile. It seems like eternity since . . . "

The music from one of the radios grows louder as GRAY continues to recite the words to the nodding GUNAY. The tune is "Since I Met You, Baby."

. . . And then say, "since I met you, my whole life has changed. Yours ever faithful, Gunay. PS. My friend Gray really digs you, too."

GUNAY: I don't think we need that last part.

GRAY: You mean the ever-faithful bit?

GUNAY: You know which part I mean. Well thanks, buddy. I owe ya.

GRAY: Ya owe me lots, man. Like that has to be the corniest letter that I have ever not written.

GUNAY: Well it may be pure corn, but it comes straight from my heart. Jeez, Gray, thanks. Where do you get this stuff, it's great.

GRAY: Jus' pure genius, I guess.

Pause.

Ya know, Gunay, as you were writin' your letter, I was thinkin' . . .

GUNAY: What?

GRAY: Well, am eighteen and I have never really been out on a real date except for the time that my ole friend Smitty and I got ditched by our dates after we paid their way into the dance. But we was only fifteen at the time.

GUNAY: Maybe next ya get luckier.

GRAY: Yeah, but by the time we get outta here, I'll be too old.

GUNAY: Oh you may never get too old. Some cowboy will probably shoot ya before ya hit twenty-one.

Pause.

Hey, Gray?

GRAY: What?

GUNAY: Ya write good, ya know?

GRAY: Yeah, I write okay.

GUNAY: Could be useful!

GRAY laughs.

GRAY: Like maybe I can use your letter to Sue Ann for my next English assignment.

GUNAY: Fuck that! I mean you could write that stuff . . . what you call it . . . for organizations?

GRAY: You mean the Constitution and bylaws?

GUNAY: Yeah, that's it, the constituuushun.

GRAY: This student union. Means that much to you, huh?

GUNAY: Yep. At least we get to have some say about things around here.

GRAY: God, Gunay, sometimes I envy you. Ya really believe this stuff.

GUNAY: Yes, and I think ya do too. You're allus goin' about the Negroes in the States an' how ya admire them for fighting for their freedom. Well it's same here.

GRAY: Hardly. They stick together, we don't. Anyways, I can't! Guess I've been on my own for so long, all I know is how to get by. To get through. To survive. That's all that matters to me.

GUNAY: Gotta do more than just survive, Gray.

GRAY: God, Gunay, they got us by the balls. I doan even wanna think about it. It jus' make me feel ashamed and pissed off. Okay?

GUNAY: So let's do like the Negroes and stick together.

GRAY groans.

GRAY: Oh, Gunay, leave me alone.

GRAY picks up a textbook.

I gotta get ready for my history exam, tomorrow morning.

GUNAY: You know what happened yesterday, Gray? Ole Hank came over to me and asked when are we gonna get goin' with this stupid students union thing.

GRAY laughs.

GRAY: He said that?

GUNAY: His very words.

GRAY: Holy!

GUNAY: Gray, lots a guys like Hank have been askin' about it. Gray?

GRAY: What, dear boy?

GUNAY: Promise me that you'll at least think about this student union thing.

GRAY sighs.

GRAY: Okay, Gunay, ya bug, but only after I've studied for the exams and written them, after I have taken Linda Sue to the movies, then I will think about it . . .

GUNAY: It can be done, Gray, especially if we can get the new guy, O'Keefe's, help. I know we can, but you gotta be there with us.

GRAY: What about sleeping beauty there?

GRAY motions to where PAUL is sleeping.

What does he think?

GUNAY: Paul? He's all for it.

GRAY: *(mutters)* Bunch of crazy Indians. So what ya gonna do, take over IRS?

GUNAY: If we hafta, yeah.

GRAY: Last thing I want is get kicked out with you renegade pricks.

GRAY starts muttering, almost to himself.

They think they can bring down a residential school.

Just then the door to the dorm opens and O'KEEFE walks in, beaming his flashlight at the boys.

O'KEEFE: Well, you boys mind telling me what is going on?

GUNAY: Well, sir, I . . . ahh . . . That is, we were . . .

O'KEEFE: You know the rules. After lights out, you should all be in your bunks, all radios should be out, and no conversation. Gray?

GRAY: Well, sir, we were just going to bed. I was just helping Harold write a letter to his aunt who is really sick at home.

O'KEEFE: Oh I am sorry to hear that, Harold. I hope that it isn't anything serious.

GUNAY: Oh no, not too serious. Jus' some woman thing.

O'KEEFE: I see. I am willing to overlook this. But next time you want to work on some correspondence like that, come to me and I shall see if something can be arranged. So that you can have some privacy. Anyways, we'll talk about it tomorrow. Good night.

GUNAY/GRAY: Good night, sir.

O'KEEFE exits as and the boys hurry to their respective bunks.

GRAY: *(whispering)* Hey, Gunay?

GUNAY: What?

GRAY: What's this about a woman thing?

GUNAY: Fuck, I doan know. I jus' said the first thing that came into my mind.

GRAY laughs.

GRAY: Ahh ya know, Gunay, this little limey may not be such a bad little shit after all.

GUNAY: I told ya!

GRAY: Good night, Dr. Gunay.

Dance Scene

GUNAY and GRAY are in the little hall/chapel.

GRAY: So what's happenin', why we all here?

GUNAY: I dunno . . . all I know is O'Keefe wanted—

PAUL walks into the room.

PAUL: What's up?

GRAY: Jus' tryin' to find out.

DOUG enters.

Hi, Douglas, howzit goin?

DOUG ignores GRAY's greeting.

DOUG: Who the hell called this meeting?

GUNAY: All I know is that O'Keefe wanted a bunch of us down here at seven p.m.

ERNIE and HEAD come in pushing each other.

HEAD: Quit that, Ernie.

ERNIE playfully twists HEAD's arm.

ERNIE: Grrrrrr . . .

DOUG: What are you little pricks doing here? Get back to your dorm.

Just then O'KEEFE *walks in wearing his tweed jacket and bright tie with a white carnation in his lapel.*

O'KEEFE: I invited them to be here, didn't I, Ernie.

He tussles ERNIE*'s hair.*

Okay, can you all gather around me?

The boys start to move toward him.

Now, you remember when I first met you, in my little talk, I told you that I was going to introduce you to the finer things in life. And that it would mean . . . some effort on your part. You see, in our world, one of the keys to success is that you take on the attributes of a gentleman—an educated, well-rounded gentleman.

At this the boys start to snicker. O'KEEFE *claps his hands impatiently.*

Okay, okay, I want your attention. We will start your education with learning some basic social skills such as ballroom dancing. I am going to teach each of you to dance with grace and dignity. Like a gentleman.

PAUL: *(incredulously)* Ya gonna teach us to dance?

GUNAY: Hey, I am a real good dancer already.

He starts to sing.

"Come on, baby, let's do the twist."

GUNAY *starts doing an energetic version of the twist.*

GRAY: Ballroom dancin', are you kidding? Only rock and roll here, man.

GRAY *starts to jive with an imaginary partner.*

HEAD and ERNIE start jiving, giggling.

O'KEEFE: Stop, stop.

He claps his hands.

Okay, boys, you've had your fun, now listen to me. That is all primitive stuff that is more appropriate for Negroes.

DOUG: For jungle bunnies.

ERNIE: Jungle bunnies—what does that mean?

DOUG: It means niggers, shithead.

O'KEEFE: All right, let's not be crude about it. What I mean is that there are other, more refined . . .

PAUL: More refined? What ya mean refined? Like sugar?

Laughter.

O'KEEFE: No! No! What I mean is that even in dancing you must learn some discipline.

GRAY: Discipline? God, we get enough of that around here.

O'KEEFE: You know what I mean, Gray, stop playing the fool. What I am saying is that the way to give a good impression of yourself, you need to show some self-restraint . . . not to jump around like some wild animal . . . Discipline, discipline is the mark of a proper gentleman. Watch me for a few moments.

O'KEEFE starts to demonstrate by gliding around the room with an imaginary partner, doing some fancy waltz, humming accompanying music.

The boys start to laugh as O'KEEFE glides around the room.

PAUL: He's dancin' like he's really with someone. Maybe he's thinkin' of Elizabeth Taylor.

GRAY: Or Rock Hudson, maybe?

ERNIE: Rock Hudson? But he's a guy!

GUNAY: I dunno, but he sure is dancing like . . . like he's somewhere else.

PAUL: He's a funny little guy, ain't he?

GRAY: Funny? He dances like he's got shit in his pants.

PAUL: Must be right about white guys!

GUNAY: What's that?

PAUL: That white guys don't have rhythm.

GRAY: Certainly not the limeys.

O'KEEFE stops dancing and walks back to where to boys are standing.

O'KEEFE: Now you get the idea?

The boys nod non-committingly.

Now we will begin with some simple steps. Paul, will you be my partner?

PAUL strikes a coquettish pose, batting his eyes.

PAUL: Why sure, big boy.

And sashays over to the waiting O'KEEFE.

GUNAY: Hey, wait a minute, hold the phone—where are the girls? How are gonna learn this stupid dance without girls?

O'KEEFE: We'll just have to improvise, Gunay. No girls today, I'm afraid.

He demonstrates the steps.

One, two forward, one back, one, two forward, one back, okay? Now let's give it a try. You will do the female part.

PAUL does an obscene bump and grind. The boys laugh, except for DOUG who is plainly uncomfortable.

Okay, let's be a little more serious about this. One day you will thank me for showing you how to dance properly. Now I want you to grab a partner.

The boys all exclaim dismay.

GUNAY: Am not going to dance with a guy. What do you think I am, some girley-boy? . . . I only dance with girls.

ERNIE: Oh jeez, what will my buddies say when they find out I am even doing this . . . ahhh.

GRAY: What the fuck is this all about . . .

O'KEEFE: Watch your language, Gray. Believe me, it will be all right. You may even enjoy it. Okay, Paul, you pair up with Ernie, Gunay with Gray, and Doug . . .

DOUG: No way, I am going.

DOUG starts for the exit.

O'KEEFE: *Douglas, you stop right there.*

O'KEEFE walks up to DOUG.

Did I say that you could go, Douglas? Did I?

DOUG just stands there, looking like he wants to throttle the smaller man.

You shall take part in this exercise because I say so, young man. Now your partner is Head. Okay, everyone, get in your positions.

DOUG scowls at HEAD.

DOUG: If you ever tell anyone that I danced with you, I'll break your skinny neck.

HEAD: *(quavering)* I won't, honest I won't.

PAUL: *(to ERNIE)* You woman, me man, okay?

GRAY: *(to GUNAY)* You will make a good wife some day, Haida.

GUNAY: Fuck you, and you're stepping all over my feet, you dumb Nisga'a.

O'KEEFE starts playing the piano.

O'KEEFE: One, two, three, one, two, three . . .

The boys start to dance, first awkwardly and then soon becoming more adept. O'KEEFE speeds up the tempo, and the boys are soon really flying—even DOUG seems to be enjoying it.

ALL THE BOYS: Wheee, yahoo!

Soon, though, they revert to rocking and rolling. O'KEEFE suddenly slams his hands on the keys. He raises the back of his left hand to his forehead and sighs.

O'KEEFE: Boys, boys, boys, what am I going to do with you?

PAUL: Mighta worked if you got the girls in the first place.

Dining Hall—A Hankering for Fish

In the dining room, the senior boys are having their dinner.

GRAY grimaces and looks at his plate.

GRAY: Aghh—the special of the day.

GUNAY: The special every day and that cook—the Spider Woman—she must be mad at us.

GRAY: She is plain mad—like the rest of the staff. Worst of all is that Dudley.

He eyes the patrolling staffer.

God—the meal is shitty enough without him watching us with those ice cube eyes.

DOUG eats with gusto.

DOUG: One of you girls pass the goddam ketchup?

Laughter from the table.

GUNAY: News for you, Doug: that ain't ketchup—but ya doan wanna know what it is.

GRAY: It's garbage like we get every day. Hey, Doug, trade you—

GRAY motions to his plate.

—for two cigarettes.

DOUG grunts an "okay." He quickly grabs the plate and sets it down beside his.

GRAY watches DOUG wolf down his food.

I dunno how you can eat this stuff—it's not what meals are like back home.

GUNAY: Yeah—fried baloney, right?

GRAY: Yeah. But not all the time—we only have that . . . on special occasions.

Pauses.

Sure miss it—the Indian food, especially salmon.

GRAY laughs.

My mom used to tell me I would miss it one day whenever I bitched.

DOUG: Ya allus bitchin'.

GRAY ignores DOUG.

GRAY: Now I really do—not just the food but all the stuff that went with it.

GUNAY: What stuff?

GRAY: Just stuff—you know—my brothers and sisters fighting, my dad yelling at us—

GUNAY: Yeah tell me about yelling and shouting!

GUNAY lowers his voice and leans over to GRAY, motioning his head toward the girls' side of the dining room.

I'll trade you my dessert for a dance with your old lady.

GRAY stands and swings playfully at GUNAY, knocking over the "red stuff" the Spider Woman passes off as ketchup, spilling it on DOUG's dessert.

DOUG jumps up menacingly.

DOUG: You pricks ever stop goofing around—jeez if you're not fucking around, you're griping about some damn thing.

GUNAY: Jeez, Doug—don't tell us you like this stuff.

DOUG: So what if I do? None of your friggin' business.

GUNAY: Ya doan ever get sick of it?

GUNAY drives his fork through the greyish piece of the processed meat and holds it aloft.

Spork this morning, spork in my sandwich, and now spork à la spork—

He begins to sing: "spork in the morning, spork in the afternoon, spork in the evening," and the rest of the boys at the table take up the chant.

DOUG: *Quiet*! What's the use of complaining—we're never gonna get what we want. Ya think I doan miss our food too? But I can't get it—I miss the herring eggs, the seaweed—I wish my Chinee can come though that door with a plate full of baked halibut stuffed with shrimps. And since Spider Woman never heard of a deer, am just not gonna get any of that stuff, so what? Why fucking beef about it all the time for Chris'sake.

PAUL speaks from the other end of the table.

PAUL: *(to GUNAY)* Hey, asshole. If you ain't eatin' that fish, pass it over—I'll eat it.

GUNAY looks down at his plate and then to PAUL, incredulously.

GUNAY: What fish—what—are you nuts? Here.

GUNAY passes his plate to PAUL, who solemnly places it in front of him.

PAUL points to the food with his fork.

PAUL: This—is a nice smoked spring salmon, just out of the smokehouse. Gunay—you wanna pass the oolichan grease.

PAUL motions to Spider Woman's brand of "ketchup" and begins to eat the "salmon" with relish. The others watch open-mouthed.

GRAY reaches over and grabs his plate back from DOUG.

GRAY: Sorry, Doug, I changed my mind because I want to have this, uum . . . fish.

The Deal

GRAY walks in a small room—O'KEEFE'S office—a little apprehensively. O'KEEFE is seated behind his desk with a cigarette dangling from his mouth.

GRAY: You wanted to see me, sir?

O'KEEFE: Oh hello, Gray. Please, have a seat.

GRAY slowly takes his seat.

GRAY: Look, if it's about my not being at the church service yesterday . . .

O'KEEFE: Oh, so you skipped another church service, Gray? My, my, what are we going to do about that?

GRAY: I was going, honest, but I just suddenly got sick. You can ask Gunay.

O'KEEFE laughs.

O'KEEFE: You can relax, Gray, this isn't about your impeccable record in church attendance.

GRAY: *(relieved)* Oh! What is it then that you . . .

O'KEEFE: Gray, I want to talk to you about a little project that I have been thinking about.

GRAY: Oh yeah?

O'KEEFE: I've been thinking how inspiring and creative it would be to have a choir comprised of the senior boys and girls.

GRAY laughs.

GRAY: A choir?

O'KEEFE: Why not, there are enough talented singers around here.

GRAY: Thanks but no thanks, sir. Am no singer. Can't carry a tune to save my life.

O'KEEFE: Gray, anyone can learn to sing. Natural as breathing.

GRAY: Nah, I'd rather not. No time, lots a studying to do.

O'KEEFE: It's not going to take much of your time, Gray. And your grades are fine. Besides, there is much to learn from music. I believe that it is one of the purest forms of the human endeavour. It involves harmony, balance, and a great deal of discipline, Gray. It was through music that I was able to fulfill my true potential.

GRAY: Sounds all right but . . . jus' doan have the time.

O'KEEFE: Forming this choir will lift the morale of the students, Gray.

GRAY: Why doan you ask Gunay or Paul. They're real good singers.

O'KEEFE: As a matter of fact, I did mention it to Gunay, and he said that if you join he would. The other students do look up to you, Gray.

GRAY: So?

O'KEEFE: So if you were to join this choir, the other students would follow your lead.

GRAY: Most of them would rather watch *Hockey Night in Canada* on the television. Including me.

O'KEEFE: You know, Gray, I know that the students have been discussing their desire to form a student union here, which if it happens would be a first. I think that I can be of assistance there, but I need to get that choir off the ground.

GRAY: Talk to Gunay, he's always going on about that stupid student union. For what I doan have any idea.

O'KEEFE: Hardly a stupid idea, Gray. There is so much that one can learn just in organizing such an endeavour, as an aspiring lawyer, taking part in its formation would greatly enhance your chances, Gray. Such a show of initiative can never hurt one's reputation. And it would be a first step for your people in becoming full participants in our society.

GRAY: Waste of time.

O'KEEFE: I don't understand what you mean by "waste of time."

GRAY: What is it gonna do other than plan a few dances. The school is never gonna allow it to have any more say than that.

O'KEEFE: I am sure that it can. I can help, Gray, but I want to work with you in getting it going.

GRAY: But it's Gunay's idea. Why doan you ask him?

O'KEEFE: Gray, I am firmly committed to turning this school around so that it will have a more effective learning environment. But there is still a lot of resistance. You saw how the ballroom dancing class degenerated into utter chaos, what with your pals jumping around like . . .

GRAY laughs.

GRAY: Like wild Indians?

O'KEEFE: That is not what I meant to say, Gray. Look, I don't think that you realize the opportunities that are there right before you. You are a leader, and this experience, if you choose to take it, will have immeasurable benefit for you when you graduate from this school. Maybe a scholarship. You will go on to university and become a lawyer. That will be no small achievement. There are not many Indian lawyers in this country. You will be a credit to your people. I have every confidence that you can fulfill your dream, Gray, but for now you have to become involved in working for change in this school. The boys will follow you.

GRAY: You know, I would be interested if I was sure that the student union could make a difference for the students here. But is Reverend Stamp gonna listen to us, even as a student union?

O'KEEFE: There is so much that it can do. But as they say, Gray, Rome was not built in a day. Small steps must be taken, to build confidence as you go. Getting this choir off the ground could be one of its first projects.

GRAY: Oh big deal!

O'KEEFE: Gray, it would impress Reverend Stamp immensely.

GRAY: Really?

O'KEEFE: I'll tell him that it would be a feather in his cap. This would surely be the first school to have a student union.

GRAY: And you, Mr. O'Keefe, what would you get?

O'KEEFE: If things go well, and the student union works out, which I believe it will, we all will have gained something. I hope that my approach in working with the students here will be recognized as a more effective one. It is so important that these students learn the tools to succeed in life on the outside. I think that we all want to be recognized for our work, Gray.

GRAY: If I do—an' am not saying yet—it's not gonna be a half-assed union. We need to have a way of being part of how things are done, like decent food, more activities. And most important, that we can be heard about . . .

O'KEEFE: Gray, you have my word. But you are going to have to show some good faith.

GRAY: Err, good faith?

O'KEEFE: By joining my choir, Gray. Deal?

GRAY: Am tellin' ya that you'll regret it. I can't sing a note.

O'KEEFE: Gray, you must stop selling yourself short. I am sure that in a very short time you will be singing along with the rest of us.

The Feast

The dorm, darkened. There are sounds of teens talking, laughing. Every once in a while DOUG'S voice is heard: "Keep it down, for fuck's sake." There is music—rock—and seated around their bunks are GUNAY, GRAY, PAUL, HEAD, and ERNIE. A small toaster has materialized and is sitting on the floor nearby. GUNAY takes some food out of a box and GRAY is plugging in an old kettle for tea.

GRAY: You little twerps, keep outta sight, okay.

GRAY motions his head in the general direction of DOUG'S bunk.

Don't allow junior kids up here after lights out.

ERNIE: Oh he won't say nothin'—he's my cousin, too. He's allus playing the tough guy, but he ain't bad.

GUNAY: Look, Douglas knows why we are having this get together and agrees to tell us if ole assface might show up suddenly.

GRAY: He'd do that for us?

GUNAY: Lots a things ya doan know about ole Slug. Okay you guys, let's try and keep this down. Doan want ole Boyce hearing what's goin' on.

ERNIE: Why we here, Gunay?

GUNAY stands up.

GUNAY: Okay, guys. We got it. The school is gonna allow us to have a student union.

HEAD: A student union?

GUNAY: Yeah, we can elect some students on it to speak for us, about gettin' some stuff like dances, sports, and better food.

HEAD: Will it let me go home to look for my mom?

GRAY: Prob'ly not, but we can help you write letters.

GUNAY: What we need to do tonight is to pick who we want to get voted on as president.

ERNIE: President? Is that like a chief?

PAUL: Better—girls can run to be president, right Gunay?

GUNAY: Yep, but we want to pick someone from amongst us. 'Cause whoever we pick, we have enough guys and girls who will support us to pick our first president, and . . .

GRAY: I nominate Gunay.

GUNAY: No way, Gray's the only guy that can do it. I nominate him.

The boys give a muted cheer.

GRAY: Hey, wait a minute, Gunay has been the one who has been pushing for this—I think that he should be the one to be our president.

PAUL: I second Gray's . . . ahh . . . whatya call it? Nomernation?

ERNIE: I third it!

HEAD laughs.

HEAD: I fourth it!

GUNAY cups his hand in the direction of DOUG's bunk.

GUNAY: Doug?

DOUG: Hate to admit it, but the grease-eater has my vote.

GUNAY: Okay, Gray. You's da man!

The boys do a quiet cheer: "Speech, speech, speech!"

GRAY: Jeez, guys, I doan know what to say. But thanks.

GUNAY: Gray, pass that box under your bunk

GUNAY takes the box from GRAY and begins to lay out the food, a big can of salmon, some dried herring eggs, and a plastic container of seaweed and white bread. GUNAY spreads out the food almost ceremoniously.

PAUL: Oh man, that smells some good.

He gets up hurriedly.

I am gonna see if I could trade with dem guys over there for some dried meat for this can of spork . . .

GUNAY and GRAY laugh.

GUNAY: You ain't gonna get dried shit for that—here.

GUNAY tosses a small can of salmon to PAUL.

You may have better luck with this canned salmon.

GRAY: You gotta be joking—canned salmon for dried meat . . .

GUNAY: It's chum salmon—we used to use it for trade with you Nisga'as all the time.

GRAY: *(slightly indignant)* That'll be the day when you Haidas can out-trade the Nisga'as. I'll have ya know that we used to feed chum guts to our Haida slaves.

PAUL: While you two re-fight your old wars, I, the great Inuit hunter, will get you some real good meat.

DOUG: *(from the back of the dorm)* You call blubber good meat, Eskimo.

PAUL: Same ole Doug. It beats that smelly, rotten fish eggs you people eat.

GRAY: Oh gwan, don't pay him no never mind. Hey, I got some dried fish we call kayuks and some grease that my mom sent me last week—no Nisga'a meal is complete without grease, especially Nisga'a grease.

PAUL gets up and goes to the back to trade.

GUNAY: Yeah, that's why we beat you guys in war alla time—we can smell you a mile away.

GRAY jumps on the laughing GUNAY, playfully pounding him with his fists.

GRAY: Actually our stories say that the Haidas never beat the Nisga'as. You tried to sneak on us, but our warriors were too good. Saw you pricks coming up the coast in those heavy canoes way before you got near us.

GUNAY laughs.

GUNAY: Yeah, gave ya guys enough time to hide with your women. Betsa we can beat you in basketball.

GRAY: I doubt it, eh? Never did hear of any Haidas at the Native tournament in Rupert.

GUNAY: Okay, tough guys, wanna try me out in an arm twist?

GRAY: Fuckin' right!

They sit opposite each other and begin to arm wrestle.

ERNIE: C'mon, Gunay, ya can beat him.

PAUL returns from his trading mission.

PAUL: If you two homos are done, let's get on with the feast. Here is some real good dried smoked meat that I got from Leroy Potsy, the Cree guy.

GRAY: Hey, cool idea, let's start the way they always do it at home.

PAUL: Yeah, like how?

GRAY: You know . . . with a prayer.

PAUL: Oh Jesus, we get prayers coming out of our ears around here.

GRAY: Yeah, but this will be to our own god.

GUNAY: Hey, that's a good idea. The old people at home always say their prayers in Haida before meals.

GRAY/PAUL: Be our guest!

GUNAY: Oh Jeez, I hardly know the language, how can I . . .

PAUL: Just make it up, for fuck's sake! Man, I'll starve to death before . . .

GUNAY: Hey, I just know some drinking songs but they're really dirty.

GRAY: Oh shit, Gunay, so what, God will understand.

ERNIE: Yeah, cousin, Grandmother allus tell us to thank the creator for the food.

GUNAY: Join hands and form a circle.

The boys join hands in a small circle in the darkened dorm. Several radios play softly in the background. They stand there silently for a few moments.

Oh God, at this moment we are all thinking of home, of our families, of the places that we miss. We thank you for all the beautiful things, like the sea, the sound of the breakers rolling in, the call of the raven, the quiet murmur of the rivers, the sound of the voices of our forefathers from the forest, and most of all, God, the mountains and all our relations.

GUNAY softly begins a lament of loss. When he finishes, the boys quietly sit down.

GRAY: Jeez, Gunay, that was real good.

GUNAY: My ji taught me that. Funny, I thought I forgot it.

GRAY: Okay, guys, from what I remember, back home, at feast there is usually a speech of welcome before people eat.

PAUL: What? More stuff . . . am hungry, and all this food . . .

GRAY: Well, if we are gonna have a feast, Indian style, Paul, then we have to do it like back home. Feasting is not just about eating, you know.

PAUL: Then get on with the other stuff—back home we eat then we make speeches.

GUNAY: Fuck, Paul, how'd you know, you said you left when you were little.

PAUL: Well, I read about it in the *National Geographic.*

GRAY: Okay, okay, I think the head chief, what we call the Simoighet, who is putting up the feast, speaks and welcomes the people—so if you don't mind, I'll be the Simoighet . . .

GUNAY: Hey, I am putting up most of the food here—I should be the one . . .

ERNIE: Ah, just let him, Gunay. He is the oldest, and I remember my Chinee saying that we should always respect our elders. Some acknowledgement here of the fact that they just elected Gray chief?

GRAY looks at ERNIE dubiously.

GRAY: Thanks, Ernie.

He stands up, straightens himself, and in a sonorous voice begins to speak in halting Nisga'a.

Why Simgighets gans Simgitnaks . . .

PAUL: So what does that mean in English, Chief?

GRAY: I said, "I wish to thank you for honouring my feast with your presence. Eat carefully, so that you don't choke on your food, and that we doan wanna get the blame. Thank you." That's what I said in Nisga'a, I think.

GUNAY: That's pretty short—for a Nisga'a.

GRAY: Think this is too long—too expositional—something shorter? More clever?

PAUL: For Chris'sake, when do we start fuckin' eating?

The other boys laugh, and GUNAY *starts handing out food to them. They eat silently, with only the sound of other boys in the background partaking of their own food, in the darkened dorm, and the music from the radios in the background eerily starts to sound like First Nation music. Soon the boys start to talk, laugh, and the dorm seems to have transformed into a big feast.*

Lights fade slowly.

ACT TWO

Graveyard

It is outside the school building, in a small clearing—a small graveyard with little crosses. There are two boys: one is digging; the other is standing at the edge of the half-dug grave holding a lantern, looking around a little fearfully. It is a clear night, and a full moon weaves its way in and out of the high clouds. The wind is blowing softly through the small tree stands nearby. In the distance, the howl of a coyote can just be made out. Quite clearly in the background, O'KEEFE's new school choir can be heard singing parts of Handel's Messiah.

PAUL: *(a little fearfully)* Gray . . .

GRAY continues to dig.

Gray, do you hear . . .

GRAY: *(grunting)* Dammit, Paul, keep still with that damn lantern, it's bloody dark down here.

There is a rustling nearby.

PAUL: *(yells)* Gray, there is something over there.

GRAY jumps out of the hole.

GRAY: What the fuck's the matter?

PAUL: I heard something move over there, growling.

GRAY looks in the direction that PAUL is pointing, then laughs.

GRAY: That's just some goof horsing around. Come on, let's get going—it's getting late, for Chris' sake.

He starts to climb back into the grave.

Hey it's your turn to go down there . . . I have been doing most of the goddam digging.

Just then, a coyote howls, but it sounds a little closer and louder.

PAUL: Maybe we should call it a night, huh, Gray?

GRAY: Your turn, buddy, dig.

PAUL: Hey, big shot, who the fuck appointed you boss, huh?

GRAY: Paul, ya little shit, it's your turn to dig! Gimme that friggin' lantern and get down there and start digging.

GRAY attempts to grab the lantern from PAUL. They struggle and then both tumble into the grave, putting out the lantern's light. There is the muffled sound of struggle and grunting. After a brief silence, the noises start sounding a little desperate.

Paul, get your fucking ass off my face . . . Paaaul!

PAUL is breathing hard.

PAUL: Not until you say uncle, assface?

GRAY: Paul, am gonna . . .

PAUL: You gonna what?

GRAY: Am gonna kill you, you little Eskimo.

PAUL: Little hard to do where you're at, grease-eater. And it's Dene to you, Jack.

GRAY: Okay, okay. Dene! Just get your skinny little Dene ass off my face.

GRAY starts to laugh. PAUL soon joins in, and they untangle themselves from the grave and each lean on the one side of the grave, looking at each other. The coyote howls again but they now ignore it.

GRAY re-lights the lantern.

It's bad luck, ya know, really bad luck.

PAUL: What is?

GRAY: Horsin' around like that.

PAUL: Shit, man, we're allus horsin' around.

GRAY: Not in a graveyard. Respect the dead our ol' people tell us.

PAUL: Yeah?

The choir singing is clearer in the background. The boys go back to work.

GRAY: Funny, the principal used to send guys out here to dig the graves for punishment.

PAUL: Now we get a whole three dollars and a quarter to dig a hole for some dead Indian from the san.

GRAY: Jus' be glad ya got a chance to make some money.

PAUL: Oh, Gray, what am I gonna do with all that money?

GRAY: You know our people doan jus' let anyone dig a grave, like we are doing for this poor soul from nowhere. Back home, from the time a Nisga'a is born, there is someone already picked to bury him when he dies.

PAUL: No shit! And who's gonna bury you? Soon I hope!

GRAY laughs.

GRAY: I dunno. But if I die here in this damned place, I guess you will, Paul.

PAUL: They gonna have to pay me big bucks. More than three bucks and a lousy quarter.

PAUL grabs the shovel and goes in and begins shovelling. He stops.

I wonder who it is?

GRAY: I dunno.

Pause.

A person dies back home, everything comes to a stop. Everything. Here, all it means is pocket change, never thinkin' whose grave we are diggin'.

PAUL: I do!

GRAY: What?

PAUL: Wonder whose grave we're diggin'?

GRAY: What's it to you?

PAUL: Might be a relative.

GRAY: Oh yeah.

He looks around at the small, unmarked crosses.

I hear that the people that are buried here are from way up north.

PAUL: Wonder if any student is buried here. You know, from the olden days.

GRAY: I dunno. Hear stories. Never paid much attention to them.

There is silence as GRAY moves to the other side of the grave. The moon is now obscured by cloud. The choir is singing the sombre part of the Messiah.

PAUL: Or maybe someone I know could be here. Remember Sam, at the TB san?

GRAY: Uh huh?

PAUL: Well he died shortly after you left the place. Boy, he was there a long time. Tol' me a little about where I come from 'cause he's from there too. He might jus' be buried here for all we know. Doan think even his relations know he died.

GRAY: A shame . . .

PAUL: I sorta took ol' Sam as my uncle.

PAUL resumes digging with vigour, and then stops.

He was kinda strange, ol' Sam. Sometimes he'd go into some kinda trance and just sit there for a long time as if he was seeing something.

GRAY: Oh, like what?

PAUL: I dunno, just something that only he could see. Other times, he would look at me like he could see right through me and know what I'm thinkin'. He was kinda spooky, but I was never scared or anything.

GRAY: Maybe he was a medicine man or somethin'.

PAUL: He was allus talking about gettin' some Indian medicine from home that could cure better than white man's medicine.

PAUL starts to dig again. The wind picks up, and the choir sings softly in the distance. He grunts.

Anyways, it never came, that medicine, 'cause he died, it was sudden and during the night . . . man, I cried real hard. And then I got pissed off the way they treated him. Jus' wheeled his body out of the ward the next morning like he was jus' a load of dirty sheets . . . they just took his body away . . . an' the rest of the patients jus' looked the other way as if nothin' was happenin'.

He looks around the graveyard, seemingly for the first time.

Lookit those numbers on the cross. That is all that is left of them. Numbers, that's all they give them even when they're dead—no name, no sign of where any one of them come from—whose family they belong—just bloody numbers.

He feels a chill.

It's getting cold.

GRAY: Yeah, buddy, almost time we went in.

Just then there is a rustle nearby, and both boys are momentarily frightened by it but laugh. The choir can be heard, now singing the "Hallelujah" chorus.

Listen to that music from the choir. Gotta admit that the little limey has done a great job. They sound real good.

PAUL: Can jus' see ole Gunay singing like some goddam angel.

GRAY: Better him than me.

PAUL: It's warmer in there.

GRAY: Rather freeze my balls off.

Both laugh. PAUL resumes digging.

Gunay was right.

PAUL: About what?

GRAY: The student union thing.

PAUL: Oh yeah, lots a the kids tell me they feel better 'cause of the student union now there.

GRAY: Jus' get worried.

PAUL: What?

GRAY: That they might expect more than we can give them.

The music from the choir is getting louder. PAUL stops digging and leans on the side of the open grave.

PAUL: Yeah, ole Sam deserved better than what they did to him. Too bad there was no student union then.

GRAY laughs.

GRAY: Yeah a patients' union.

PAUL: Man, am so excited about the student union I want to start by poppin' ole Boyce right on his red nose. Pow!

PAUL then looks around a little apprehensively.

GRAY: I think he'd like that.

PAUL: Who?

GRAY: Your Uncle Sam.

PAUL: Yeah, he allus was talkin' about the hunter-warriors back home, in the ole day.

GRAY: Okay, Einstein, get off your skinny ass and start digging—we have to finish this job by tomorrow.

PAUL resumes digging and grunting.

PAUL: From what I remember, it wasn't always bad there. Ya got to meet some pretty nurses, especially those young nurse's aides.

GRAY starts to laugh.

GRAY: Paul, did I ever tell ya about this ol' guy who once asked his wife who was visiting him, "Mabel, see that nurse over there, every mornin' she asks me if my balls moved durin' the night." The wife yells at him, "She means your bowels, stupid, not your nuts. She wants to know if ya shittin' properly."

The boys start to laugh uproariously against the sound of the choir, which is reaching the crescendo of the "Hallelujah Chorus."

Fade out.

Head's Dream

Outside the school—to the left, under a tree, which stands next to the graveyard—two boys sit.

ERNIE: What's a matter, Head? You haven't said a word for the last two days—you didn't even come down to the playroom to watch the big hockey game on TV last night.

HEAD: Ahh don't like watching TV no more.

ERNIE: Ya don't like watching TV?

HEAD: Well we never get to watch what we want; all those older boys boss the TV.

ERNIE: Yeah, but everyone likes hockey.

HEAD: I'd rather watch Ed Sullivan, used to watch it with my mom. It was our favourite.

ERNIE: Well we have to watch what we can, I guess.

HEAD: And I hate watching those commercials.

ERNIE laughs.

ERNIE: Jeez, Head . . .

HEAD: Can't stand seeing all them nice food on TV . . . jus' make me more hungry . . . at home, Mom would make popcorn when we used to watch TV.

ERNIE: Know whats a mean. I really get hungry when you see pies, ice cream, and all that neat stuff.

He pauses, looks over to his morose friend.

What's a matta, Head?

HEAD: I dunno, I jus' hate dis place more and more and more.

ERNIE: We all do, Head, but we are stuck here, can't run away.

HEAD: Why not? Hey maybe we can hop the train.

ERNIE: Are you crazy, we'll get killed or get arrested by the police.

HEAD: I doan care, I just wanna go home.

ERNIE: Why?

HEAD: 'Cause!

ERNIE: 'Cause why?

HEAD: Just because, that's why.

ERNIE: That's dumb—'cause why!

HEAD: I dunno, I just wish I can be home and be with my mom. I miss her real bad. I'm the only one who can make her smile.

HEAD gets up, picks up a pebble, and throws it at something on the tree branch above them—a bird, which flutters away. PAUL's voice is heard on the outside speaker—he is the DJ for the afternoon, playing the hits of the day over the PA system, chattering it up in comic imitation of the radio personalities of the day. In the background are the playful shrieks of younger kids.

Ernie?

ERNIE: Yeah?

HEAD: Do you get mail from your mommy?

ERNIE: Yeah sure, get 'em all the time, why?

PAUL's voice announces the tune of the day: "Blue Moon," by Elvis starts playing.

HEAD picks up a broken-off branch from the tree, swings it wildly.

HEAD: I dunno—what does she say?

ERNIE: Huh?

HEAD: In the letter—what does she write . . . I mean—

ERNIE: Oh stuff, ya know . . . like how she misses me and tells me how things are back there and even . . .

Pause.

HEAD: What?

ERNIE: Well . . . she says that sometimes she' sorry that she let me come to this place. And guess what, Head? Next week she said she's gonna send me a surprise.

HEAD: Wow! Can I have some, Ernie?

ERNIE: Sure, Head, if its somethin' ya can eat. It might be another sweater or somethin'.

HEAD: Yeah.

HEAD pauses, and then sits down beside ERNIE.

Ya know, Ernie.

ERNIE: What?

HEAD: It seems like it will be forever before we get to go home.

ERNIE: That's if ya get to go home.

HEAD: Whatya mean, sure am gonna go home . . . I mean my mom will want me home—she's gotta take me home—

HEAD starts to cry.

I hate this place . . . I hate it—

He jumps up and starts to bang the stick against the tree.

And I wish my mom could come and take me away right now.

ERNIE: You still haven't heard from her?

HEAD: Not for a long time . . . I am worried, Ernie.

ERNIE: Ah she'll write soon, you watch, Head.

HEAD: I had a dream, last night.

ERNIE: What dream?

ERNIE laughs.

A wet dream—

He jumps up and yells.

Hey guys, old Head had a wet dream last night.

HEAD: Sick!

ERNIE: So, Head, buddy, what was your dream about?

HEAD: Ahh it was nothin' . . . am just scared that somethin' mighta happened to my mom.

HEAD sits down and leans back on the base of the tree, aiming the stick like a gun at someone in the distance. Then he sits back and pokes at the ground with his stick.

It was good—that dream, at first, anyways—Mommy was all dressed up real nice, like she used to on Sundays, and sober too. Her hair was all shiny and so long and black, just like it was before.

Pauses.

Before—before bad things started happening back home. Her voice was so soft—she said that she was gonna take me away from here, too—and she said, "Mike, do you want to go to that café down the road and have some hambugga, with real thick gravy, mashed potatoes, and pie and ice cream." I was so excited, I said, "Yes, yes, Mommy." She bent down and kissed me, she smelled so good. I reached for her hand, and we started walking down the road toward town. I was not sure where we were but it looked like I knew the place. It seemed so nice and safe. And then we walked and walked and it got darker and darker and I was getting tired and I looked up and asked her, "When are we gonna get there?" She yanked me arm so hard. "Don't be so whiny," she said—I looked up again and it wasn't my mommy no more.

He pauses, blinking back his tears. The music in the background has now changed.

It was . . . that bird woman from the girls' side, and she was leading me down a long, dark hallway and—and there . . . at the end of the hall was Luddy, standing there with this funny smile, waiting for me. I started to scream and tried to get away from that awful bird woman. She jus' laughed and laughed, and then that's when I woke up . . .

ERNIE: Ah don't worry, like I said, you'll hear from her soon . . . Hey, wanna go play some touch football with the other guys?

HEAD: Yeah!

HEAD jumps up then and runs off, excitedly and awkwardly, with ERNIE.

Breaking the Deal

O'KEEFE and GRAY are sitting across from each other by a table in a room, most likely a small boardroom.

GRAY: Jeez, a meet and dance—here at the rez, two weeks from now.

O'KEEFE: And much still to do before then.

GRAY: We sure thank you, Mr. O'Keefe.

O'KEEFE: Don't thank me. It was your student union that came up with the idea to invite a group of white students from your high school for a friendly track and field meet here. A marvellous idea.

GRAY: Thank you.

O'KEEFE: I have talked to Reverend Stamp and everything seems to be okay.

GRAY: Oh, we got the ole Stamp of approval, huh?

O'KEEFE: Gray! He's actually looking forward to it. So we need to ensure that everything is in place. So what do we have?

GRAY: Well a group of senior girls are going to be in charge of decoratin' the chapel for the dance.

O'KEEFE: Fine! But who's in charge there?

GRAY: Well actually it's Linda Sue.

O'KEEFE: Of course!

GRAY: The girls picked her.

O'KEEFE laughs.

O'KEEFE: I know. How about the food?

GRAY: Well we hoped that you'd work with the Spider Woman. But we doan want any spork stuff, it would be embarrassing.

O'KEEFE: Gray, you know it's been a while since we stopped serving that kind of food. No, we plan to have hot dogs, hamburgers, potato salads. It'll be a tasty offering.

GRAY: And don't forget the soft drinks.

O'KEEFE: There will be plenty of soft drinks and juices. Now what about the track and field? Who is preparing the grounds for that?

GRAY: Well its jus' a soggy field out there, but Gunay and Paul are working to get it ready.

O'KEEFE: Gunay and Paul? Are you sure that those two are going to do a good job?

GRAY: There is no one else that can do a better job than those two. I trust them.

O'KEEFE: All right! Now for the officiating of the events. Have you lined up people to be the officials?

GRAY: Like who?

O'KEEFE: Well for one thing, we will need a starter for the races—you know, someone to fire the starting pistol to begin each race. How about Mr. Nelson for that role?

GRAY laughs.

GRAY: I don't think that Mr. Nelson should be the one to fire off a pistol.

O'KEEFE: Well you may have something there. How about Mr. Boyce?

GRAY: Another guy who shouldn't be near a gun.

O'KEEFE: Seriously, Gray, you need to have people in place to do those things.

GRAY: Don't worry, we have some students who have volunteered, and Mr. Holmes is coming here day before the events to train them to do those things.

O'KEEFE: Well, Gray, it looks like you have everything well in hand. What about the opening?

GRAY: The opening?

O'KEEFE: Yes, I think that it would be quite appropriate for someone from the school to welcome our guests.

GRAY: Well, we have . . .

O'KEEFE: In the ordinary course of events, it should be the principal, of course. Unfortunately, Reverend Stamp has advised me that he will be away until the afternoon of that day. So I think it is only proper that we should invite Reverend Dudley to . . .

GRAY: *No!*

O'KEEFE: No?

Pause.

Well, do you have any other suggestions?

GRAY: The student council have discussed this and they think you should do it.

O'KEEFE: Me? Why, Gray, that is such a grand thing for the students to do. I am deeply honoured. I am almost speechless.

GRAY: Well, gotta admit that you've done a lot since ya got here. You're not like those other guys.

O'KEEFE: Well we all have a job to do here at this school, but thank you, Gray.

O'KEEFE starts to gather his papers.

Well I think that we have accomplished a lot today. And I do have another meeting coming up.

GRAY: Errr . . . there is one other thing that I want to talk to you about.

O'KEEFE: Yes, what is it, Gray?

GRAY: It's about Dudley, sir. And Head.

O'KEEFE looks at GRAY for a long moment.

This is real hard, but I really want to talk to you about this.

O'KEEFE: Gray, I am not allowed nor am I inclined to talk about any member of the staff, and especially senior staff, with any student. I can't do that, Gray. I'm sorry!

GRAY: Oh it's okay to talk about Mr. Nelson and Boyce, but we can't talk about the Reverend Dudley.

O'KEEFE: Gray, I really have to be off for my next meeting.

GRAY: But this is important.

O'KEEFE: It may well be, but I'm not prepared to talk to you about those issues.

GRAY: Then ya know what I'm talking about.

O'KEEFE: I know nothing of the kind.

GRAY: Everybody seems to be so blind around here.

O'KEEFE: Gray, how can I say this. I am not prepared to talk about Reverend Dudley when he is not present.

GRAY: I think that you do know what is going on, but you're scared.

O'KEEFE: How dare you speak to me in that tone. I think that you have gone far enough, Gray. I am telling you to leave that issue alone. You are putting into jeopardy all that we have worked for.

GRAY: You told us from the beginning that we—that is, the student union would be listened to if . . .

O'KEEFE: But within reason, Gray, not to launch into some witch hunt?

GRAY: Witch hunt? I doan know what ya mean.

O'KEEFE: What I mean is . . .

He stops, now flustered.

Gray, we have enough on our plate for the next two weeks without getting into matters that will surely create more turmoil. I have worked very hard to get things to normal here, Gray, and I don't appreciate you trying to open up something that we have little if any control over.

GRAY: Not sayin' we doan appreciate them, but Dudley . . .

O'KEEFE: The Reverend Dudley, young man. Look, just consider what was there before. I mean, I have personally gone to bat for you on a number of things.

GRAY: And I've done my bit, too. And Gunay, Paul, and all those other guys and girls, too. All have chipped in, jus' to get stuff that other schools get all the time, anyways.

O'KEEFE: Gray. You have done such a great job that I am almost certain that the scholarship committee has your name on the short list. Things are going along so swimmingly.

GRAY: Swimmingly! So why is it that sometimes I feel like am gonna drown.

O'KEEFE: You have such a fine future, Gray, and the things that you have accomplished here in just a short time are all on record. Why would you want to put all that at risk???

GRAY: Because I . . . no I mean *we* take being on that student union seriously, Mr. O'Keefe. It's not jus' about putting up dances, planning for the track and field meets, which we appreciate, but we also want to make sure that the students, especially the younger ones, who are so far away from their parents, who miss them so much, are safe, sir. I . . .

O'KEEFE: Gray, it is . . .

GRAY: Jus' hear me out, please. Since my . . . well I heard that my little brother died two weeks ago back home.

O'KEEFE: Oh am so sorry, Gray, I didn't know . . .

GRAY: No, it's okay. I just couldn't get home to be at his funeral, but it opened my eyes about this friggin' place. How scary it really is. The younger ones have no one there to protect 'em except us, and that is what we are gonna do, Mr. O'Keefe.

O'KEEFE: But the protection of these children is our responsibility. They are our paramount concern.

GRAY: "Our paramount concern"?

O'KEEFE: Yes, the entire staff.

GRAY: Including the Reverend Dudley?

O'KEEFE stands up.

O'KEEFE: Look, Gray, I refuse to be interrogated by you any longer. This has gone far enough. Let's just concentrate on preparing for the big event you have been planning for the last month, shall we?

GRAY: Yeah, let's get on with the celebration, pretendin' nothing's happening.

O'KEEFE: Gray, just what is it that you want me to do here?

GRAY: We want you to go and talk to Stamp—I mean Reverend Stamp.

O'KEEFE: About what?

GRAY: About Dudley.

O'KEEFE: Just a minute, Gray, I don't think that we should be discussing anything concerning Reverend Dudley without him being present. He's just a few doors down, I can . . .

GRAY jumps to his feet.

GRAY: *No!* Jus' you and me.

O'KEEFE: Well?

GRAY: The other day little Ernie came to talk to me about Head, his friend. He's he . . . he's worried about his mother. But more than that, he says that Head is jus' frightened of Dudley.

O'KEEFE: Gray, I think that you are going to have to be careful here.

GRAY: Head's not the only one—lots of the smaller students are jus' plain scared of Dudley. But no one believes them.

O'KEEFE: But there is nothing to believe. Now I know that there are stories about Reverend Dudley, but they are just stories.

GRAY: They were hoping that you'd stick up for them. Head even thinks that you can clean old Dudley's clock. To them, you're their only hope. And I agree with them.

O'KEEFE: Well I know I have a certain rapport with the students, Gray. I like to think that it is because I am fair. But fairness goes both ways, does it not? I don't think that it would be fair to respond to every wild rumour about the staff in this school. There has to be proof.

GRAY: When a kid . . . a small kid like Head starts to throw up when he sees Dudley, isn't that some kind of proof?

O'KEEFE: Even if I were to go to the principal, what am I supposed to be telling him?

GRAY: Tell him that it is time somebody, from outside maybe, look into what is going on here.

O'KEEFE: What's going on here? What is that? *No!* I'm not going to the principal with a story about some kid's fantasy!

GRAY: It's you that's living in a fantasy if you think that these things are not gonna come out someday. Because all these things do. Then what is Mr. O'Keefe gonna say then?

O'KEEFE: *Gray, enough!* Whether you believe it or not, I do care for the students here. Remember I attended a school like this. There were stories that unsavoury things happened too. But when you come up with the reality—to shift through the myriad of the legalities—it just isn't that easy, Gray. Do you understand what I am saying?

GRAY: No I don't! I think that you're jus' yellow, Mr. O'Keefe, jus' worried about your fuckin' job!

O'KEEFE: That's it. Get out of my office, *now*!

GRAY: So you're not gonna do anything?

O'KEEFE: All am gonna do is call Mr. Boyce.

O'KEEFE starts for the door.

GRAY: Just a minute I'm not finished . . .

He grabs a hold of O'KEEFE's arm.

O'KEEFE: Get your filthy hands off me, you blubber-eating, dirty, stinking, wagon-burning savage, how dare you!

Both are now almost nose to nose.

GRAY: Savage!

GRAY laughs.

Savage?

O'KEEFE: And you should be so grateful that there are people like me who have enough interest in your welfare, to help elevate you to the status of the white people.

GRAY: So I see. It was never about us. You never really cared, in spite of your words about working with me, with the student union. I, we, we've been used by you.

O'KEEFE: Nonsense!

GRAY: It's all about you getting ahead in this place, isn't it? You want to show your bosses how well you have handled us savages, right, Mr. O'Keefe?

O'KEEFE: Gray, you have this singular penchant for being melodramatic.

GRAY: Bullshit, bullshit! You're no different than any of them. Worse, because you pretend to be our friend. At least ol' Boyce shows his colours about how he hates us.

O'KEEFE: No, it was I that was fooled. I thought that you had the maturity to be a leader and to help us create a better atmosphere for learning.

GRAY: Learning to be little white men.

O'KEEFE: Oh, Gray, you are getting so tiresome.

Pause.

There is another alternative for you, Gray. You are way past sixteen, so you are free to go home. We are not forcing you to be here. If you cannot abide by the rules, then maybe it is best that you go.

GRAY: Rules, but not for white man, hey O'Keefe? Well fuck you, Mr. O'Keefe—be glad to leave this place that stinks of lies.

O'KEEFE: Then go. Return to your reserve. You think this place stinks—what about where you come from? You think it will be any better there, Gray? But just remember, you will have spurned an opportunity to allow us to help you to be better prepared to live among the civilized people—to have some kind of future in our world—and that is the tragedy, Gray—you are one of the most intelligent ones here, and yet you seem bent on bucking the system all the way. So go, please.

Gray Not Leaving

In the dorm, GRAY *is by his bunk packing his bag, the ever-present rock hit of the day on the radio.* GUNAY *and* PAUL *walk in.*

PAUL: Hey, what's happening?

GUNAY: Goin' somewhere?

GRAY: Goin' home.

GUNAY: What happened?

GRAY: Jus' time to go home.

GUNAY: Whatya mean, what about the meet. Ya can't.

GRAY: I can leave any time I want to.

GUNAY: But goin' home? This is nuts, Gray. What brought this on?

GRAY: You guys have no idea how I've looked forward to leavin' this dump.

PAUL: But to go back to the reserve. What about your plans to be a lawyer?

GRAY: Right now am not sure where am goin'. Maybe Prince Rupert, look for work there.

GUNAY: Ya jus' gonna quit like this. I doan believe it.

PAUL: Oh leave him alone, he's going home. Wish I could . . .

GUNAY: No I wanna know, what changed your mind, Gray? I mean things couldn't be better around here. You're doing a great job as our president of the student union. Jeez, I thought you were jus' up in O'Keefe's office to talk about plans for the big meet comin' here in a couple of weeks.

GRAY: Well maybe all that stuff ain't what it's set up to be.

GUNAY: Well, Gray, you ain't makin' any sense. We've been talkin' and planning for that meet for weeks. Next to the graduation in little over a month from now, it's the biggest thing we're gonna have here. All the kids are lookin' forward to it.

PAUL: Ya got into a fight with O'Keefe over something, didn't ya?

GRAY: Let's jus' say that I doan feel like stayin' around here anymore. I'll finish the year out somehow but not here.

GUNAY: That's bullshit and ya know it, Gray! Whatever it is that you guys argued about, it can be worked out. O'Keefe's a pretty fair guy. He'll listen.

GRAY: Ya guys really have no idea what this guy is about.

PAUL: Whatever it is, ya guys have to work it out. Why, he'd never be able to do half of it without your help.

GRAY: Well maybe that's the trouble, Paul. Made his job too easy for him.

PAUL: What's he talkin' about, Gunay?

GUNAY: Look, man, you can't go jus' like that. Not now. We're jus' starting to get things going around here. Good things, too. And none of that woulda happened without you here. I mean that, Gray!

GRAY: Look guys, I really appreciate all ya say. And it's really hard to explain what happened and why . . .

ERNIE enters.

Hey, Ernie, you all right?

ERNIE: It's—it's Head, Gray, he's . . .

GRAY: What?

ERNIE: Taken off.

GUNAY: You mean run away?

ERNIE: He's gone.

PAUL: Maybe he's just buggered off somewhere outside.

ERNIE: He couldn't, doors were still locked.

GRAY: Wait a minute, Ernie, the supervisor, does he know?

ERNIE: Yeah, he went right out when he couldn't find him in the dorm. I . . . I . . .

PAUL: Jus' take it easy, kid.

ERNIE: He's run away, I know he did. He's all alone out there.

GRAY: I doan think he left the building. He's jus' a little guy.

ERNIE is half-crying.

ERNIE: Lately, he's been talking about running away. It's his mommy, Gray, he's gone to look for his mommy, he's so worried about her . . . Last night after lights out I heard him crying . . . whispering to himself, jus' saying Mommy, Mommy! I snuck over to his bunk, he jus' lay there under the blanket, but I could tell he was crying 'cause he was jus' shakin'.

GUNAY: Aw, poor kid.

PAUL, attracted by flashing lights below the dorm windows, runs over to look.

PAUL: Holy, there's a cop car down there.

GUNAY: The bulls are here? Son of a gun.

ERNIE: Oh . . . I jus' wish I'd gone with him . . . he's so scared of the dark . . . and that bull in the field. I jus' didn't think he was gonna do it, I thought he was jus' talkin.

GRAY: Ernie, don't blame yourself. He'll be okay. He can't have gone that far.

O'KEEFE enters quickly.

O'KEEFE: Ernie, there you are. The police want to talk to you about what you might know about Mike's whereabouts.

ERNIE: *No!*

O'KEEFE: Ernie, it will be all right. They just want to talk to all the younger boys from the dorm. You want to help us find Mike, don't you?

GRAY steps in front of O'KEEFE, they both look at each other.

GRAY: I'll go with him.

O'KEEFE brushes past GRAY with ERNIE in tow.

O'KEEFE: No, Gray, you have no more business in this school, remember. I will take care of this matter, thank you.

O'Keefe Fired

DOUG enters the dorm, where GRAY is sitting on his bunk facing the audience; the radio is playing a Mozart piano concerto.

DOUG: I hope you're happy, Gray.

GRAY: What the hell / are you talking about, Doug?

PAUL bursts into the room.

PAUL: Gray, ya hear O'Keefe's been fired? It's all over the school. He's gone! Just like that!

GRAY: What!?!

GUNAY walks in.

Gunay, What's goin' on. I mean . . .

GUNAY: Jus' heard!

PAUL: O'Keefe was waitin' for us out front when we were gettin' off the bus. He was almost cryin', man, sayin' he jus' got fired.

ERNIE climbs in through the window.

ERNIE: Guess what? Mr. O'Keefe jus' got fired. Boy, I bet it's because he went to Stamp about Dudley.

GUNAY: O'Keefe went to Stamp? Dudley?

ERNIE: Ask Gray, he went to O'Keefe about poor Head and O'Keefe went to the principal.

GUNAY: Ya went to see O'Keefe about Head?

GRAY: Well yeah, but what's it gotta do with O'Keefe gettin' canned?

DOUG: Ya dumb shit, I knew it was you. Got him fired. I oughtta kick the shit outta . . .

GUNAY: Hold on . . . we gotta figger this out. Gray?

GRAY: But I doan know what's goin' on, I mean . . .

DOUG: Best supervisor we ever had, gone.

GUNAY: But Gray, what's Ernie talking about?

DOUG: It's that fuckin' union thing. Everything was goin' fine until big shot here and his stupid union came on.

GRAY: But I didn't . . .

DOUG: At least before when I was in charge . . .

GRAY: In charge?

DOUG: That's right asshole, at least I took care of the little kids. I could protect them, Gray. I can't do that anymore.

GRAY starts to recover.

GRAY: Fat good you did for a kid like Head. Your buddy Dudley never had to worry about you.

DOUG: Am gonna rip your—

DOUG advances toward GRAY. ERNIE steps between them.

ERNIE: Doug, please. I am the one why O'Keefe got fired. I asked Gray to go and see him. He . . .

PAUL: About what?

ERNIE: Head was havin' nightmares, puking his little guts . . . he was gettin' more scared of Dudley.

PAUL: Holy.

ERNIE: And ole assface was gettin' meaner . . .

ERNIE starts to cry.

An' he never heard from his mommy for a long, long time.

GUNAY walks over to ERNIE and puts his arm around him.

GUNAY: It's okay, little cousin, it's okay.

GRAY: C'mon, ya guys, we don't really know what happened.

PAUL: Doug's right though. We never planned for the student union to get into this kinda shit. Man look at the other stuff we were gettin'.

GRAY: But Paul . . .

PAUL: Now that's gone, an' O'Keefe gone, too. Think you went too far, Gray.

GRAY: I went too far? I can't believe this, it was . . .

GUNAY: Ya shoulda talked to us first, Gray. No right to act on your own.

GRAY: Gunay, lemme remind you that you've been on my ass about gettin' this student union from day one.

GUNAY: But O'Keefe got fired. That wasn't supposed to happen.

GRAY: But we doan know why he got fired, for fuck's sake!

DOUG: He knows, he knows!

GRAY: Know what. Hey, Slug, you're their boy, how come you doan know? Huh?

DOUG: You call me that name once more I'll . . .

GRAY ignores DOUG.

GRAY: Anyways, I think it all has to do with what happened to poor little Head. I think ole Dudley is getting scared.

DOUG: What?

PAUL: You're nuts.

GUNAY: What are ya sayin'?

GRAY: Maybe O'Keefe is gettin' scared too, and maybe he did go to Reverend Stamp and Old Stamp fired him.

DOUG: So ya admit it was your fault.

GRAY: No. But what choice did I have. Ya guys elected me as president. I had to . . .

GUNAY: But that's not your job!

GRAY: Oh. Wasn't it you that kept tellin' me that we needed this student union so that we could also look out for the little guys.

GUNAY: It was *we*, Gray, *we* do that, not jus' you acting like the big shot.

GRAY: Big shot? Not fair, Gunay, not fair. I went to O'Keefe because Head was in real trouble. There's not always time to . . .

DOUG: Listen to him, tryin' to squirm. Like a friggin' worm.

PAUL: We shoulda jus' stuck to puttin' up dances and sports. Things were startin' to get better.

ERNIE: Not for everybody. Not Head.

GRAY: Am not a worm, Slug. Maybe ya should look . . .

DOUG advances menacingly toward GRAY.

DOUG: I told ya that next time ya call me that name am gonna . . .

ERNIE runs to the front and screams.

ERNIE: *Stop!* Please stop it?

GRAY: It's all right, Ernie, it's all right.

He turns to the other boys.

Ya know, am sorry to see O'Keefe go too. He was all right, most of the time anyways. And maybe he did go to Stamp and got himself fired. Good on him if he did. And yes, he did get a lot of things done around here that was all right. But he didn't do it alone. We did it.

He walks over to ERNIE and puts his hands on ERNIE's shoulder.

Ernie, your good spirits was always there, when things got real stale you were the one to cheer us on.

He walks over to the uncharacteristically serious PAUL.

Paul, you may goof around a lot, but you can always be counted on to be there. You worked your ass off in gettin' things ready for the meet.

He walks over to GUNAY.

Gunay, you're the guy that makes people want to work for you, and you organized a lot a things that have gone on well.

He then approaches DOUG, *and stands almost nose to nose.*

And Doug, well, ya did your thing. But ya have so much to offer if ya jus' quit being pissed off all the time.

DOUG: Just a minute here . . .

GRAY *silences* DOUG *with a wave of his hand.*

GRAY: Not finished.

He puts his hands up and examines them.

See these hands?

He then taps his head exaggeratedly.

And this head? We all have them, jus' like them. To use!

Silence.

Without us, O'Keefe couldn't have done much here. So why are ya guys pissing and moaning that all these good things are gone jus' cause some little white man is no longer gonna be here to hold our hands. Jeez, is that being free if we have to always depend on one guy like that? *Huh*?

The boys stand silently before him. The music from the radio is sombre. GRAY *starts to walk out.*

He stops and turns to the boys again. Points to his heart.

And this, the heart, is what's missing with all them clowns, including O'Keefe. My Ye told me that it is what guides the hand and the head. That's what makes you different. You all have it!

GRAY turns and heads for the exit.

GUNAY: Hey, Gray, wait.

GRAY: Gunay, go fight your own battles.

The boys stand around uncertainly as GRAY exits.

Riot

GRAY enters and walks to his locker, fiddles with his combination lock and opens his locker. He takes out a book. The radio in the back is playing Johnny Cash's "Folsom Prison Blues." He then walks to his bunk and lies down. The music seems to get louder, and then suddenly the lights start to flicker and then go out, except for the dim emergency light by the fire escape. The music continues. GRAY starts to get up when PAUL runs in all excited.

PAUL: Holy smokes, holy shit, oh God, Gray, you gotta go down and see what's goin' on down there. Gunay and the rest of the guy's have—have—oh, Jesus.

GRAY: Hey, cool it, man! Is Gunay all right?

PAUL: Yeah, yeah, but—

He starts to giggle.

He's—they have got all the staff locked up in—

GRAY: Locked in, the staff? What the fuck is goin' on?

The music from the radio is now louder, "O Fortuna," the drums beating.

PAUL: Well, Gunay gets into this fight with ole Boyce . . .

GRAY: Fight? Gunay and Boyce.

PAUL: Yeah, yeah, and next thing ya know ole Boyce is running down the hall.

GRAY: Holy!

PAUL: An' yellin', "Help, help me," and then another kid pulls out the fire-hose from the firebox in the main hall?

GRAY: What?

PAUL: Then—you can't believe this, but they start to hosin' the goddam hall down—the staff starts screaming an' runnin' to their rooms and locking themselves in.

GRAY: Paul, am gonna bop ya if you're bullshittin' me.

PAUL: Gray, am not lying, come and see—and the girls from the girls' side? They've joined in, dancin' and yelling—really whoopin' it up.

GRAY: Holy.

PAUL: Next thing, Gunay has all the lights put out—

GRAY: Gunay did?

PAUL: —and little Ernie and the rest of the younger kids have headed down to the dining room to try and get into the staff dining room.

GRAY: Little Ernie's in it, too?

PAUL: Listen—can you hear them?—they're dancing. Down there. God, I feel happy and scared at the same time—what's gonna happen to us, Gray?

GRAY: Shit, I dunno. When I told that little Haida to go fight his own battle, I didn't think he was gonna . . .

GRAY laughs.

. . . start a war. C'mon!

Scene shifts to the front of the school, where in the light from the dining hall ERNIE and GUNAY are eating, sitting on boxes marked "spork." The shadows of the revelling students, boys and girls, dancing, splashing one another with fizzed pop, followed by rock and roll music and laughter. When ERNIE sees GRAY and PAUL approaching he jumps up and runs excitedly toward them.

ERNIE: Gray, Paul, you guys want some chicken? It's cold, but boy it's so good.

GRAY: Not right now, Ernie. Gunay, what the hell is goin' on?

GUNAY: We've taken over the school, that's what's happenin'.

GRAY: Dudley, Boyce . . . where are they now?

ERNIE: *(yelling)* They all got scared and locked themselves in their rooms, too . . . ain't that funny, Gray, them locked in instead a us?

GRAY: God almighty, Gunay, how did it happen?

ERNIE: Boyce called Gunay a bad name. Said he was a fu . . . a flippin' Arapaho.

GUNAY: Aw, ole Boyce was drunk again and mean, pushin' Ernie around, and I told him to pick on his own size. He got real pissed off, swung at me. I ducked, and sorta stuck my fist out, hit his face, he goes down like a bag of fish guts. And then everything sorta happened.

The music is getting more frenetic—the dancin' shadows are really rocking.

PAUL: Gunay, ya crazy Haida. Next time ya gonna start a war call me first.

He starts to dance like the Hollywood version of Indian war dancing: jumping around, doing war whoops.

GRAY walks up close to GUNAY.

GRAY: Hey, man, what have ya done?

GUNAY: Well like ya said, sometimes you jus' gotta do what you hafta.

GRAY: Yeah but ya know they're gonna come after you, after all this is over.

GUNAY: I doan care. Really don't. Tired of being bullied by guys like Boyce, listening to lies from Dudley. And you're right, Gray. We can't jus' go on as if nothing's happening, not after Head.

GRAY looks intently at GUNAY.

GRAY: You sure sound like that Chinee you're allus talkin' about, Gunay. Was he a warrior?

GUNAY: The best!

GRAY: What about O'Keefe, ya still sore at me for.

GUNAY: Forget what I said. O'Keefe prob'ly did what he had to, but mainly to save his little limey ass.

GRAY laughs.

GRAY: Well if we're gonna be in real shit.

GUNAY: Not if, Gray, am gonna be in deep shit.

GRAY: No, we are in this together, Gunay. So let's enjoy it while it lasts. *(yells)* Hey, Ernie, pass over the chicken.

ERNIE: There's lots a keen stuff, Gray. Those supervisors, they sure weren't eatin' spork. Ya should see the food they have in their pantry. Want me to get you some pie, some ice cream.

GRAY: Thanks, jus' the chicken will do for now, Ernie.

As ERNIE is walking away:

Hey, Ernie, you're a real warrior.

ERNIE: Thanks. But am doin' this for ole Head. I sure wish he were here to see this. He woulda really liked it. Prob'ly woulda ate all the ice cream, too. And he woulda thrown all that dumb spork into Sauce Lake. Hey, that's an idea.

He grabs the box of spork he was sitting on and takes it to the front stage.

Let's build a fort.

GUNAY: Great idea, come on, you guys, let's start movin' the boxes of spork.

The boys run toward the back of the building and return with boxes of spork until they have enough for a barricade. Meanwhile, the music from the dining room changes to a dance tempo, and the shadows are doing some kind of line dancing, but eerily taking on Indian traditional dancing quality. DOUG arrives on the scene.

GRAY: So how come ya not with the staff locked in?

DOUG: Fuck ya, Gray. Ya gonna need all the help ya can get. Ya think they gonna let this go.

GRAY: No, guess not.

DOUG: The bulls are probably on their way.

GUNAY: For sure! Prob'ly in the next half hour. Hell, let's enjoy.

PAUL: Ehh!

He throws away a piece of cheese and spits morsels out of his mouth.

This cheese is rotten.

GRAY: It blue cheese, you savage.

The boys gather around in a semicircle, partaking in the food ERNIE had brought out.

PAUL: Is someone gonna do grace?

The boys respond by doing the raspberry as the music inside becomes more festive. PAUL starts to do a jig, with the rest of the boys slapping their thighs in unison, yelling yahoos.

GRAY shouts over the din.

GRAY: Gunay, this chicken is good. Almost taste like grouse. Wonder who cooked it?

GUNAY laughs.

GUNAY: Maybe Linda Sue.

ERNIE runs to the barricade.

ERNIE: Look, look, flashing lights comin' down the road.

PAUL: Holy Jesus . . . here they come.

GRAY: *(barks)* Okay, guys, let's show 'em who we are . . . Gunay . . . Doug . . . c'mon, Ernie, let's link arms. No, *up there*!

GRAY points to the top of the barricade they just built.

The boys clamour on top of the barricade and link arms as the flashing lights reflect off their faces and bodies like war paint. The music is still going, but there is now loud whooping coming from the dining room.

DOUG: *(shouts) Okay, let the cowboys come!*

Farewell

In the dorm. GRAY, PAUL, DOUG, *and little* ERNIE *watch* GUNAY *pack. The radio is playing some quiet blues song.*

PAUL: Are ya gonna take your *Playboy* magazines . . . can I have a couple of them?

GUNAY: Take them all, Paul, you're always borrowing them.

GRAY: You ever watch how he takes the magazine to that little washroom, shuts the door real quiet—and how he walks like a priest goin' to a confession holdin' the *Playboy* under his robe?

GUNAY: An' it only takes him about two minutes.

GRAY: The quick draw Dene.

PAUL: Sick . . . so stale that ya doan know that there are real good articles.

GUNAY: A fast reader too.

They all laugh.

Well, Ernie, howsit goin'?

ERNIE: Oh okay. Just hate to see you go an I still miss ole Head.

GUNAY: Yeah, still can't believe what happened.

Pause.

Well, guys, it's almost two weeks since the riot and nobody got arrested.

ERNIE: I doan think it's fair that you get kicked out and not Dudley or Boyce.

GUNAY: Well, Ernie, I'll see you in a few months' time when you come home for the summer.

ERNIE: It seems like a long way away . . . ninety-six sleeps . . . 2,304 hours left to go.

GRAY: Okay, guys . . . jus' thought we'd get together an' wish Gunay farewell—hope that you have a good crab season . . .

PAUL: As if he ain't have enough crabs.

GRAY: Don't think we gonna miss ya . . .

PAUL: Not gonna miss the farts . . .

GRAY: Not that Haida accent . . .

GRAY imitates GUNAY.

"You guys are so stale, always horsing around."

ERNIE: Am gonna miss you, cousin Gunay.

DOUG: Gonna miss listening to all his lies about all the girls he's had.

GRAY: Am gonna miss helpin' you write those love letters . . . must be working. Judgin' from all those nice replies.

GUNAY: Jus' a minute . . . you been readin' my letters, you dog!

PAUL: Hey, we just got a glimpse of one that you left on your bunk . . . holy.

PAUL imitates GUNAY's female correspondent.

"Oh, Gunay, you say the sweetest things. I just can't wait to get your letters. They make me feel so special . . . you Haida hunk!

GUNAY laughs.

GUNAY: Fuck off, Paul.

GRAY: Ernie's right, Gunay. It's too bad ya had to take the rap for this. It wasn't your fault. All you were doin' was to stand up for the little guys. Jus' wish there is more that we could do.

PAUL: Maybe get some newspaper guy.

DOUG: Hear stories that there is gonna be some investigation.

GRAY: I hope so.

DOUG: And I think that Dudley and Boyce are gonna be gone. Soon. That riot really shook 'em up. The Church, that is.

PAUL: Shit, you deserve a medal for what you did to Boyce, Gunay. Oh boy, pow!

ERNIE: Oh I wish Head was there to see the scary look on Boyce's face after Gunay knocked him on his ass.

GUNAY: I never really meant to hit him. Not that hard, anyways.

GRAY: We really tried, Gunay, tried to tell 'em that you are the best student around here. All of us, Paul, Ernie, and Doug, we all went and lied for you.

The boys all laugh.

GUNAY: Makes me feel good ya guys did that.

Pause.

GRAY: Well, some nights I can't sleep thinkin' of Head. Wondering if we did go too far, or if I could have done things differently. I am the oldest and

I feel responsible. So yeah, am really thinkin' of going too. It's jus' not right that only you get sent home.

GUNAY: Forget it, Gray. We've been through this crap. You gave us your word, didn't he, Paul?

PAUL: Ya betcha boots he did.

GRAY: But . . .

GUNAY: If you leave, then what we did here two weeks ago will mean nothin'. We kicked their ass in that riot. I have no choice, I gotta go.

Pause.

And there is the meet in a couple a days. Everybody in this school voted ya back in when ol' O'Keefe tried to kick you out. They know it's gonna be like a celebration. That we won. You gotta be there.

GRAY: But Gunay . . .

GUNAY: Gray, can ya jus' shut up for one friggin' minute and quit arguing.

PAUL: He's gonna be a lawyer, whadya expect!

GUNAY: A lot a people with suits and briefcases are gonna be comin' around to find out what happened. The students will need someone to speak for them. That's gonna be you, Gray. You're gonna stay and look after Doug and them.

DOUG: No way some grease-eatin' Nisga'a is gonna look after this Haida. But if ya try to leave, Gray, I'll beat the crap outta ya.

All the boys shout their support—am gonna tie ya up if ya leave/we'll lock him up in O'KEEFE's old room, etc.

GRAY: Looks like am gonna have to stick it out for another few more weeks.

The boys laugh, cheer, and clap.

GUNAY: Gotta tell ya that am not too sad to leave this place, but am gonna miss you guys. It's funny that we live in this dump together for so long, but as tough as it gets, we all seem to enjoy being together—most of the time, anyways. I guess it's the best thing to the family we all left behind.

PAUL: Amen to that!

GRAY: Ya made it happen, bro. You made it happen.

All the boys cheer their affirmation.

So, Gunay, how do we say goodbye, say we're sorry to see ya sorry ass go.

PAUL: Let's give him the royal bumps.

ERNIE: Stale, that's for sissies. Dunk him in Sauce Lake.

PAUL: I know. Let's make him pray in Haida again.

PAUL laughs.

They allus sound like they're going up and down in a canoe out in the big waves.

GRAY: You know, back home goodbyes like this are treated real special. And to acknowledge him as a warrior.

DOUG: What are ya getting' at, grease-eater?

GRAY: Sing a song . . . an Indian song. Anyone know any?

The boys all murmur in the negative.

Well I sorta know one. Our people sing it when they celebrate.

ERNIE: Gee, let's hear it, Gray.

GRAY: Well it goes somethin' like this: "Gitchess Axe, Oh Gitchee Axe, am well lyin . . . ooh, ohh." What do the rest of you think?

DOUG shrugs.

DOUG: Sounds okay by me. How does it go, again?

ERNIE: What if ole Boyce hears us?

GRAY: Oh I hope he hears us. So ya haywire Indians sing so loud that even ole Stamp will hear us.

PAUL cups his hands and shouts.

PAUL: Hey, assface Boyce, we're gonna sing a song that says we ain't scared of you no more.

PAUL giggles nervously, looking at GUNAY.

GUNAY: Hey, doan look at me, Paul. I give up fightin'. You gotta take him on now, Cassius.

Everyone laughs at PAUL's exaggerated shaking.

GRAY: Okay, you guys really listen because am jus' gonna sing it once more than we'll try it together.

He stops.

For Chris'sake, am beginning to sound like that little limey.

The boys laugh, and then GRAY starts to sing.

"Gitchee Axe oh Gitchee Axe, oh well lyin, ohh, ohh . . . " Ya got it? And Gunay, ya wagon-burning, assface kicking Haida, it's for you. To a warrior.

The boys all cheer.

ERNIE: And for Head, doan forget him.

GRAY: Yes for sure, for brave little Head.

PAUL: And for O'Keefe?

GRAY: Maybe jus' a little. Let's begin.

GRAY leads and the boys start a little tentatively, but soon gain confidence as if the song awakens in each of them their own song. PAUL grabs a bucket sitting by the washroom and starts to beat it like a drum. Then the boys get inspired by the ancient music and start to dance: first, mock ballroom dancing, then each doing his own dance to the singing, which now reaches a volume of twenty singers. They do the twist, the jig, and jiving. Then, as if called by the song, the boys start to dance some ancient steps. Then they line up, stamping to the music, starting with ERNIE, PAUL, DOUG, and GRAY. GUNAY dances to each of them and shakes their hands, giving a startled GRAY a hug, and then dances off the stage.

Curtain.

THEY KNOW NOT WHAT THEY DO

Tara Beagan

There are countless stories from people who survived residential school. There are many that will never be told, endured by those who did not survive to adulthood. This work is for those who did not escape, and for those who carry the memories of their stolen friends forward in every moment of their bravely lived lives.

Acknowledgements

Kind thanks to Frank Pio for asking this play of Native Earth, even though the Toronto Catholic District School Board could not bring it to fruition. Thanks to the artists who gathered to begin work on this, and thanks for their forgiveness when we did not go to full production. Thanks to Yvette Nolan for sharing stories of parents and Indian Residential Schools with me over the years at Native Earth. Thanks to DM for opening your Catholic heart to such articulate empathy. Thanks to Isaac Thomas for helping bring this script to realization and for helping put the production to a premature rest with such grace. Chi meegs to all staff of Native Earth past and present for fighting the good fight to offer a platform to the voices of our beautiful, brilliant peoples.

As ever, gookschem xhoo to my mom, Pauline Beagan, for braving a look into her own time at Residential School even when she didn't feel like doing so, for unpacking all of that hardship just because I asked her about school. I love you, Mom.

They Know Not What They Do was first produced for Native Earth Performing Arts's Made to Order program, as commissioned by Frank Pio of the Toronto Catholic District School Board. It featured the following cast and creative team:

Annie: Angela Analok
Donald and Elizabeth: Derek Garza
Brielle and Miss: Sarah Podemski

Director: Tara Beagan
Sound and Projection: Andy Moro
Stage Manager: Janet Antone
Fight Consultant: Aqua

Characters

Annie: Age five. Inuk, raised by her Grannie. First generation Anglican IRS student.

Donald: Ages seven and sixty+. First Nations, second generation United IRS student.

Elizabeth: Age eight, Brielle's best friend.

Brielle: Ages six then eight and sixty+. Métis, first generation Catholic IRS student.

Miss: A favourite teacher. White.

Three actors on stage, separate from one another. They stand, and each has a chair behind her/him.

Intro

ALL: My first day of school.

BRIELLE: I was six.

DONALD: Seven.

ANNIE: Five. My Grannie had me dressed in my best clothes. My hair all braided and smooth.

BRIELLE: My dad was getting ready to head out to the trapline, and my mom was hanging laundry. They were standing in the yard together, laughing and kidding around. We hadn't seen a motorized car come down that road before, so when me and Louie heard it coming we actually went down the lane toward it. Shiny and black.

DONALD: His parents had gone to their schools, and so they knew to retreat into the bush every August through to November, to hide my dad and his brothers. But my dad knew by then there was no point trying to disappear on them. They'd been circling like vultures, threatening, since June. A man like my father—a man who lived and learned in the open air his whole life—he wouldn't survive a week in any white man's jail. Our land had become too precious to them for us to keep getting in the way. Late August, my mom sat me down and explained this. Told me I was strong. Smart. I was the big brother! I could survive anything. So, Dad borrowed a wagon to bring me into town, to meet the truck.

BRIELLE: I had never seen two people all dressed in black like that before. They looked like shadows.

DONALD: A cattle truck.

ANNIE: I was pretty proud of how I looked.

BRIELLE: Tawnshi![1]

DONALD: Washed up and all, but still . . . the back end of a cattle truck. Not for some fun hayride, either.

ANNIE: My Grannie was proud, too. She smiled. But her eyes were sad.

DONALD: No . . . no fun, anymore. At all.

BRIELLE: I couldn't understand them, but they must have just said it, straight out.

ANNIE: And then the boat came. And she told me to hold her in my heart. Her voice sounded like it was already far away.

BRIELLE: That they were taking us—me and my brother—away. To school.

1 **tawn**-sheh = "hello." For audio sample, see http://www.learnmichif.com/language/greetings.

DONALD: I thought every school was like that.

ANNIE: I watched her become smaller and smaller as that boat pulled away.

BRIELLE: The woman—a sister—put her hands on our shoulders and led us away. Toward that car, which seemed to get shinier and blacker.

ANNIE: Takuniaqquguk![2]

BRIELLE: I thought my parents were coming with us. But when the doors slammed shut, they were still standing where we'd left them.

DONALD: This was no ordinary school.

BRIELLE: And then my mom started running toward us. But I couldn't shout out. And the lady shadow said something to us that sounded like someone saying sorry when they didn't really mean it. Because they still think they were right, even though someone got hurt.

ANNIE: *(as in prayer)* Grannie.

BRIELLE: And just that fast, we were gone. To school.

DONALD: I wouldn't be coming home after class.

BRIELLE: *(simultaneous)* . . . Mama.

ANNIE: *(simultaneous)* Grannie.

DONALD: I wouldn't be coming home on weekends.

BRIELLE: I didn't know I wouldn't be able to see him once we got there—my brother.

---

2 tah-koon-nee-ah-koo-gook = "see you in a bit." For audio sample, see http://www.tusaalanga.ca/glossary/inuktitut?pager=T , eighteenth word from the top of the list.

ANNIE: Grannie.

DONALD: Uncles.

ALL: This was no ordinary school.

DONALD: I could not see any of my family without a chaperone in the room.

BRIELLE: Without approval from the Mother Superior.

ANNIE: Without a "prearranged meeting."

DONALD: If they could afford to make the trip.

ANNIE: But my Grannie didn't have a phone. And could not write a letter in English. So, how . . . ?

BRIELLE: That motorized car had driven us through the night.

ANNIE: I didn't even know where they brought me.

DONALD: We didn't even have our own wagon, never mind a car.

BRIELLE: I didn't even know where I was.

ALL: "School," they said.

BRIELLE: For all the good that did.

ALL: I didn't even speak English.

All three brace themselves.

Scene 1

Projection: A nightmarish speech runs under a series of slides depicting clergical staff looming over students. Outdoor group scenes.

The actors stare up, uneasy, at the barking adult, who they cannot understand. Bewildered, they do a sort of inspection dance, in unison, as they are manhandled by an unseen staff member: turned to the side, mouths inspected, ears pulled, etc.

WOMAN'S VOICE: *(garbled speech)* Welcome, students. This is your new home. You will be brought to your dormitory after mass. Beforehand, you will be cleansed and groomed appropriately. You will be assigned a number. This number will appear in every item you will be issued today: clothing and bedding. You will be shown to your bed, which will coordinate with the number on your standard-issue items. Any student caught with an item that does not belong to him will be punished accordingly. Follow Sister Emma to service.

The students trudge around in a winding path. At one point DONALD *trips and gets yelled at.*

(garbled speech) Stand up, you imbecile. Stand up!

The others hold their breath as DONALD *stands back up.*

They wind along, finally landing back in front of the same chairs. They sit, at last.

Scene 2

They are at church.

Projection: Scary, bleeding icons and stained glass.

WOMAN'S VOICE: *(garbled speech)* Please stand for Father Campbell.

Pause.

Stand up for Father Campbell—mind your manners. Stand up. Stand up.

The voice pushes through the language barrier, and is finally decipherable.

Stand. Up!

All three stand.

Sound: music distorted and garbled, hymnal. Perhaps a church organ-styled "O Canada."

MALE VOICE: *(garbled, but less so)* Let us pray.

Slowly, each student kneels, perhaps emulating older kids around them. Silence.

All three students look around, wondering what the heck is going on.

Sound: MALE VOICE, garbled passages of scripture, incomprehensible.

They stand again. They sit again.

They kneel again. Silence.

BRIELLE steps out of the scene.

BRIELLE: Now, I don't know how it is for you, but when I'm starting to laugh when I know I'm not supposed to, it's way worse when I catch eyes with my brother, and see that he's about to laugh, too. They separated the boys from the girls as soon as we got to school, and it would stay like that until we finished school. But that day—the first time I was ever in a church—I was trying not to laugh at the strangeness of it all, and trying, also, to find Louie. I knew if he was smiling, that we were going to be okay. But I knew, too, that if we laughed in this place, it would be trouble. Still, I looked and looked. So many kids, all the smallest ones looking confused and scared— Louie!

BRIELLE steps back into the scene and gets the giggles.

She makes gestures toward her brother, making fun of the service—all of the standing and sitting and big gestures from the priest. This ends abruptly when—

Sound: a whip lashing skin. Focus zeroes in on BRIELLE as—

ANNIE and DONALD race to line their chairs up behind BRIELLE, and cower behind them, partly blocked by chair backs.

DONALD & ANNIE: SSHHHHHHH!

BRIELLE kneels beside her chair and sets her hands on the seat, face up.

Scene 3

BRIELLE: I learned English soon enough. You hear anything repeated often enough, you learn it. It gets into you and becomes the truth.

Sound: a door slams. Hard-soled women's shoes cross the floor and stop in front of BRIELLE.

WOMAN'S VOICE: You foul creature. You despicable, less-than-human thing. Laughing. As we think on our sins against our Lord and Saviour, Jesus Christ. What makes you exempt? What makes you immune to temptation? To sin? What? Answer me!

BRIELLE: I don't know, Sister.

WOMAN'S VOICE: Speak up.

BRIELLE: I don't know, Sister.

WOMAN'S VOICE: Oh, so you are exempt. Are you? You seem to believe so.

BRIELLE: No, Sister.

WOMAN'S VOICE: Absolution is not your right, little girl. He died for our sins that we may enter His kingdom after a life lived in His light. Do you think it funny that He died—crucified under the blazing sun—for your sins?

BRIELLE: No, Sister.

WOMAN'S VOICE: Say it.

BRIELLE: It isn't funny, Sister.

WOMAN'S VOICE: The suffering of our Lord, Jesus Christ, is not amusing.

Silence.

Say it.

BRIELLE: The suffering of our Lord Jesus Christ is not amusing.

Sound: lash on BRIELLE's hands.

WOMAN'S VOICE: Again.

BRIELLE: The suffering of our Lord Jesus Christ is not amusing.

Sound: lash on BRIELLE's hands.

WOMAN'S VOICE: I am unworthy of His love, and yet I strive for worthiness in every humble effort I may put forth.

BRIELLE only looks up.

Say it!

BRIELLE: I am unworthy . . . um. I am unworthy of . . .

Sound: lash. Lash. Lash.

WOMAN'S VOICE: I am unworthy of His love. And yet I strive for worthiness. In every humble effort I may put forth.

BRIELLE: I am unworthy of His love, and yet I strive for worthiness in every humble effort I may put forth.

Sound: lash.

WOMAN'S VOICE: You will never be worthy. You can't be. You were born rotten. Look at your eyes and your hair—the colour of dirt. At least your skin came out almost clean. I suppose you think you're a pretty thing. You mangy, halfbreed animal.

Lash.

Say it again.

BRIELLE: I am unworthy of His love, and yet I strive for worthiness in every humble effort I may put forth.

WOMAN'S VOICE: I didn't ask for this posting. In the middle of nowhere. If I were a Brother, I'd be choirmaster at St. Michael's in Toronto by now. Instead of herding halfbreed heifers around the prairie like a lunatic clergical cowboy.

Lash.

Again.

BRIELLE: I am unworthy of His love, and yet I strive for worthiness in every humble effort I may put forth.

WOMAN'S VOICE: I'll have to keep my eye on you. The others would be crying by now.

Lash.

BRIELLE: I am unworthy of His love, and yet I strive for worthiness in every humble effort I may put forth.

Silence.

I am unworthy of His love, and yet I strive for worthiness in every humble effort I may put forth.

Sound: hard-soled shoes walk toward the door. The door opens. Hard-soled shoes leave the room. The door slams. Hard-soled shoes walk far down the hallway until the sound of them disappears.

I am unworthy of His love, and yet I strive for worthiness in every humble effort I may put forth.

(whispering, now) "Halfbreed heifer. The Colour of dirt."

Beat. With conviction, now.

I am unworthy of His love, and yet I strive for worthiness in every humble effort I may put forth. I am unworthy of His love, and yet I strive for worthiness in every humble effort I may put forth.

The room darkens as night falls.

Each student crouches to the ground, shielded by their chair backs, all in a row.

Scene 4

A window shadow lights DONALD's face. The others can be seen a little less.

DONALD: Nighttime was the worst. I thought that first night would be the worst, but it got worse and worse. When they brought me here, I didn't know I had to stay. Boarding school, I guess you call it. United.

BRIELLE: Catholic.

ANNIE: Anglican.

DONALD: "Residential school." It was at night that I really missed home. In the day, we boys got to build things in the winter and help in the fields in fall and spring.

ANNIE: We worked in the laundry or sewing, making uniforms. Sometimes we had kitchen duty or we cleaned the school.

BRIELLE: But nighttime . . . nighttime it didn't matter that I ate more at that school than I ever did at home. Even if the carrots were soft or the porridge a little sour . . .

DONALD: A lot sour, in summer. Wiggling little worms.

ANNIE: And those teachers all had nice roasts and brand new potatoes and things.

BRIELLE: Still—we ate!

DONALD: But at night. At night . . .

Sound: hard-soled men's shoes walking slowly through a large room.

At night, we didn't even breathe.

BRIELLE: Didn't even dare sleep.

Sound: the shoes, still walking.

DONALD: Whenever he came into the dorm to pick someone. Whenever he stopped so close to me that I thought it was finally my turn . . .

ANNIE: I prayed that it wouldn't be me.

Sound: the shoes walk more slowly. They stop close by. Then they continue walking.

DONALD: And when it wasn't . . . I wondered what "God" would allow any kid to be chosen for that kind of horror. And if that God was the same God who spoke through that man who terrorized us at night—

BRIELLE: If that was the same God . . .

DONALD: —then who was it that I was praying to anyway?

Sound: the shoes come to a stop.

MAN'S VOICE: *(far off and whispering)* Wake up, son.

A BOY: *(moaning awake, and then)* I don't—

The boy's mouth is clamped over by the man's hand.

MAN'S VOICE: Shhhhh. Quiet, now. We all have to make sacrifices.

The sound of the boy's voice is jarring as he is picked up.

Shhhhhh . . .

The hard-soled men's shoes, heavier now, circle the room and leave.

DONALD: And in the morning, we could all tell who it was had been picked. And not one of us could look him in the eye.

ANNIE: Even those who'd been chosen, over and over.

BRIELLE: Families come together over hard times. But what that school did was destroy everything we ever knew good about families.

DONALD: The chosen boy was robbed of his childhood. And left alone in a school full of kids. For the rest of his life.

Scene 5

A school bell shrieks the room to brightness.

All three students jump out of "bed" and make their beds meticulously.

Sound: "God Save the Queen," in super fast tempo. Bedsheets snap.

Students brush off their legs, stomp into their shoes, lace them up swiftly, etc. At one point the actor playing BRIELLE *switches and becomes* MISS.

ANNIE: But there was this one teacher.

DONALD: She was pretty great.

BRIELLE: She made home feel like it wasn't so far away.

ANNIE: Especially when she told us—

MISS: *(a teacher)* Attention, students! Thank you for lining up so neatly to head to mass and mess.

Giggles from students.

I have a special announcement to make. In two weeks it will be the twentieth of December. On that day, you will travel home where you will remain for two whole weeks.

Cheers from the students.

Yes! Yes, rejoice and be glad in it. But keep it down. Father can hear you if he has the door open downstairs.

Quieter cheering.

Your family will come get you, or for some of you, travel will be arranged to take you to the nearest town to your community, and your family will fetch you there. Those students who have no family to return to, "yule" be in good company—that's a pun. Myself and Sister Margaret are in the same boat, and we will remain in the school to bring merry tidings into our halls, decked or not. You will not go without the Christmas spirit, here. So. Let us fall back in line and make our way down to morning service.

DONALD walks away quickly, trying to contain his joy. MISS holds ANNIE back.

Annie, can I speak with you a moment?

ANNIE: Miss?

MISS: A letter came for you, Annie.

ANNIE: But my Grannie can't write English. Can't write our words, either, I think.

MISS: It's not . . . from your Grannie.

MISS gives ANNIE the letter. Before she can open it, MISS speaks.

MISS: Annabeth. Your grandmother has passed on.

ANNIE: Passed . . . where?

MISS: She's passed away. On to a better place.

ANNIE: She died?

MISS: Peacefully, they say. It seems she was out walking, and her heart just . . . stopped. Out walking in that bitter cold. She must have been a hardy sort, your grandmother. It sounds as though she was several miles from the village.

ANNIE: Takuniaqquguk.[3]

MISS: I understand you have no other family.

ANNIE: I had a mom. My dad died before I got born.

MISS: Yes. Tuberculosis, I understand.

ANNIE: Huh?

MISS: It doesn't matter. You'll stay here with I and Sister Margaret over the holidays. Annie. You won't go without.

ANNIE: Who will lay her to rest, Miss? I'm her whole family.

MISS: Oh. Um. It's long over, Annie. You see, she died shortly after you left for school. It's just . . . it took some time for anyone to find her. And then . . . well, the letter only just arrived.

ANNIE: We used to go when it was our time.

MISS: Pardon?

ANNIE: I remember she told me. Our people. We used to go when we were no use to anyone anymore. The old ones. Or the ones who couldn't give. The ones who had no place. They would just . . . go. Maybe choose to be left behind. Or just walk away until they were let go from this world.

MISS: Well . . . that's not . . . Christian talk, now, is it?

A long pause.

ANNIE: No.

MISS: Why don't you rest, dear? I'll have the nurse write you a pass from morning service.

---

3 tah-koon-nee-ahk-koo-gook.

ANNIE: My Grannie isn't Christian, Miss.

MISS: Not everyone has had the benefit of an education, Annabeth. That is the sad truth.

ANNIE: My Grannie learned with her family. Not away. Stories and life and all kinds of laughing. At home. Before any white men came to the north.

MISS: The village sent you her things.

MISS fetches a tiny suitcase and brings it to ANNIE.

I'll see you in Home Economics this afternoon, Annie. Now, you're missing service, but . . . say your own prayers. You'll find comfort in them.

The teacher leaves swiftly.

DONALD and BRIELLE become ANNIE's idyllic imagining of her Grannie's family in the great pre-contact North. ANNIE becomes her own Grannie.

ANNIE: She says you could see nothing but clean, bright snow—no messy white man tracks in there—for miles and miles. Didn't even call them "miles." And her dad didn't have any TB. No way. He had dogs and a sky-wide smile. And he loved her pure and happy, with no devil in it. He could jump higher than anyone, higher, even, than the aqsarniq.[4] And her mom. Gave her hugs. And string to build her stories on. I don't have any string.

ANNIE sinks to the ground and sits, dazed and sad.

4 ak-sahr-nik = aurora borealis.

Scene 6

DONALD plays ELIZABETH in this scene.

BRIELLE: Elizabeth!

DONALD: *(as ELIZABETH)* Yeah?

BRIELLE: How come they're letting us go home this year?

ELIZABETH: Don't know.

BRIELLE: Grade One and Two, no luck. Then suddenly, we can go home.

ELIZABETH: Rules sometimes change, I guess.

BRIELLE: I didn't know rules about Indians ever changed.

ELIZABETH: Me neither.

BRIELLE: Do you think the rule about us coming to this school will ever change?

ELIZABETH: Jeez, Brielle, I don't know!

BRIELLE: Oh. Why do you think we suddenly got to come play outside?

ELIZABETH: Don't know. But I did hear Miss scream, before. When she went upstairs to the dorm. Maybe there's a mouse in there.

BRIELLE: Why would anyone scream about a mouse?

ELIZABETH: Well, I dunno. They really don't like it when we get to just talk to each other so much. What the heck is going on?

BRIELLE: Last time we suddenly got to play outside, they shut down the back stairwell for three days, and my brother said that one grade five boy, Maxime, they never saw him again. Got kicked down them stairs, they said.

ELIZABETH: Great. What if they shut down the dorm for three days? Where do we sleep?

BRIELLE: Ooo, maybe outside. Hey, I think we better make presents for our family, so when we get back maybe we can stay for good.

ELIZABETH: What are we supposed to do, make them uniforms? Even if we did, we wouldn't even be allowed to take them outta the school!

BRIELLE: Well, no! Not dumb uniforms. But we could make up songs or maybe find some really nice rocks out here in the yard.

ELIZABETH: You gonna give your mom a rock for Christmas?

BRIELLE: Hm. Well, I guess not.

ELIZABETH: And we'd get killed if anyone heard us singing songs they thought were Indian.

BRIELLE: Hm. Rats.

ELIZABETH: Could practice Christmas songs to sing for them, I guess.

BRIELLE: Ah! My brother Louie is a way better singer than me, so if maybe he has the same idea, then I could just sing real soft when he sings strong and we'd be pretty great, I guess.

ELIZABETH: Is Louie older than you?

BRIELLE: Only by forty minutes.

ELIZABETH: Huh?

BRIELLE: Yep. Twins. He came out first, and since he was a boy, my dad named him after Louis Riel, a great hero. Do you know Louis Riel?

ELIZABETH: Does he work at the school?

BRIELLE: No.

ELIZABETH: Oh. Then, no.

BRIELLE: Well, he got born and then my dad was so excited he had a boy that when I started to come out, he got even more excited because he thought "Here we go—two boys in one shot!" And I guess my mom kept saying "No, no, noooo!" which was maybe the first word I ever heard if I could remember when I was that little. So, my dad wanted to name me Gabriel after another great hero, Gabriel Dumont. Do you know him?

ELIZABETH: Um. I think so. I think he drives the bus into town when you have to go to the doctor, innit?

BRIELLE: *(doubtful)* Uh. Yeah, maybe. But anyways, I turned out to be a girl, so Gabriel was out of the question. Then my dad got a good idea, which was to name me Gabriella, but my mom said "No" again, or maybe she still was saying no from finding out there was two babies in one shot. So then my dad got an even better idea, which was to name me Brielle, which *is* a girl's name, too, and by then my mom was asleep. So now when he tells people our names, he gets to say "Louie, Brielle." Get it?

ELIZABETH: No.

BRIELLE: Oh.

ELIZABETH: Let's do the Satan one.

BRIELLE: Yes!

ELIZABETH & BRIELLE: God rest ye merry gentlemen,
Let nothing ye dismay,
For Jesus Christ our Saviour
Was born upon this day,
To save us all from Satan's power
When we have gone astray—

ELIZABETH: Ooo, hoo hooo! That part really scares me!

BRIELLE: Let's do it again.

ELIZABETH & BRIELLE: To save us all from Satan's power
When we have gone astraaaaay—

They laugh and spook, then carry on.

O, tidings of comfort and joy
Comfort and joy!
O, tidings of comfort and joy!

ELIZABETH: Again!

Scene 7

ELIZABETH and BRIELLE softly sing as ANNIE stands slowly.

She picks up the little suitcase that holds her grandmother's possessions. She looks up at the ceiling.

ANNIE: Higher, even, than the aqsarniq.

She walks upstage.

Before she leaves, she drops the suitcase. She disappears behind the screen.

Sound: a chair is dragged across a floor.

Wooden beams creak. A chair is kicked over.

Projection: close on feet swinging, cutting through daylight.

ELIZABETH and BRIELLE stop singing and look out to the auditorium. BRIELLE becomes a teacher again. She stands.

BRIELLE: Miss.

MISS: Annie? How are you, lamb? We missed you in Home Economics. Annie?

MISS runs behind the screen.

MISS shrieks.

Projection: the swinging feet fade to a whiteout until the screen is blank.

DONALD steps toward the small suitcase. He opens it toward the screen.

Projection: seemingly from the suitcase beams an unimaginable aurora borealis, dancing across the room.

Scene 8

DONALD steps away from the suitcase.

BRIELLE returns and sits again, in a chair. DONALD returns to his chair.

DONALD: Seems unfair to be sitting here telling my story when so many never will. But . . . hopefully our telling will honour them somehow. Huh . . . y'know? My first day of school? I didn't think I'd be staying overnight. And it turned into so many nights. But some kids never went back home, ever again. So many lost.

BRIELLE: When kids disappeared, you learned not to ask questions. I wondered, though, what their parents were told.

DONALD: When I did go back home for good, I realized I couldn't get used to being treated with kindness. Kept expecting the next fist to fall. Never did get good at sleeping, either. My dark thoughts. And fear. Seemed wrong in that warm little house.

BRIELLE: I couldn't even speak Michif anymore. The school had turned me into a stranger among family.

DONALD: Didn't know how to be a son, so I didn't ever bother becoming a dad. Hell, I can't even talk to a girl. How could I? I went twelve years only ever seeing them from far away.

BRIELLE: I was grown up before I understood it was the law. That parents had to send their kids to those schools. There were rumours among us kids at the school, but . . . it's hard to believe that kind of thing. Easier to believe—especially when the only adults around you were so insistent about your total lack of worth—it was easier to believe that you just weren't wanted at home.

DONALD: Didn't know how to fish or anything. Made me feel out of place at home. I knew how to rebuild an engine, though. But my folks still didn't have a car! Not one car on the whole reserve. So I moved to town.

BRIELLE: Our people have plenty of fight. I know now, if I had seen them fight for me, I would've fought all of those years at school. And might not have got out of there alive.

DONALD: And I never went back.

BRIELLE: Sometimes I wonder if I have. Gotten out of there alive.

DONALD: Those schools did what they were supposed to. Took us from home.

BRIELLE: That school. Took me away from myself.

DONALD: For good.

Beat.

Sorry.

Projection: Hammer home some archival images.

Sound: Harper's apology on a sardonic loop. "And we apologize for having done this. And we are sorry. And we apologize for having done this . . . " etc.

End of the play.

GOD AND THE INDIAN

Drew Hayden Taylor

To the lovely Janine, without whose patience and support I could not have written these words.

God and the Indian was first produced on April 7, 2013, at the Firehall Arts Centre in Vancouver, British Columbia, with the following cast and creative team:

Johnny: Tantoo Cardinal
George: Michael Kopsa

Director: Renae Morriseau
Set and Lighting Designer: Lauchlin Johnson
Costume Designer: Alex Danard
Stage Manager: Robin Richardson
Artistic Director: Donna Spencer

Characters

Johnny: Native woman, panhandler, residential school survivor, early fifties

George: Caucasian, assistant bishop in the Anglican Church, former teacher at an Anglican residential school, mid-sixties

Setting

The assistant bishop's office, located in an old mansion that has been converted to offices

Time

Early 2000s

ACT ONE

Lights up on a modest but well-appointed office in a heritage mansion that has been converted to offices. A large wooden desk sits in one corner. On the wall behind it hangs a painting of Christ with children gathered around him. An overstuffed chair, a mini-bar, a bookshelf, and a small couch and coffee table furnish the rest of the room.

It is Saturday morning. Scattered about the office is evidence of a small party from the night before: folding chairs leaning against one wall, wrapping paper from presents, trays of food in various states of consumption, and, directly in front of the door, a large cardboard box filled with empty wine bottles. There is silence. The door opens revealing Assistant Bishop GEORGE *Linus King. Looking content, he enters, sets his Tim Hortons coffee cup on the desk, and hangs up his coat. He is a well-dressed man of confidence and status, and it shows.*

GEORGE: *(addressing the painting)* Good morning, my Saviour. Another beautiful day you've given us.

He takes a sip of coffee.

As God is my witness, I do not understand the appeal of Tim Hortons. It's blander than a Catholic sermon. Still, it will keep me humble.

He begins making coffee in his own coffee maker.

Till I get to the good stuff.

GEORGE *looks around.*

My goodness, what a mess, but I'm not afraid to get my hands dirty. It's not exactly washing feet, but thy will be done . . .

He sniffs, noticing the smell from one of the trays.

Day-old sushi . . . and whole-wheat crackers . . . not quite five loaves of bread and two fishes . . .

Waiting for the coffee to brew, GEORGE *begins to clean up the office. He notices an overturned family photograph on the shelf. He picks it up and places it right side up on his desk. He smiles with satisfaction at this moment of domesticity and resumes tidying up. He places several bottles of expensive alcohol—gifts from the night before—on the desk. As he works, he begins to hum Anglican hymn 143, "Forgive them Father, for they know not what they do." He examines the bottles.*

Vermouth. Grand Marnier. Who gives these as presents to an Anglican minister? Is that your way of telling me I'm gonna really need this for my new position? I heard you work in mysterious ways, but that could have just been a rumour.

GEORGE *notices a wrapped box in the corner and picks it up. He tears away the wrapping paper to reveal a new espresso machine.*

An espresso machine! You do answer prayers.

GEORGE *continues cleaning up the room, humming to himself. Quietly, the door to his office opens. A Native woman enters. She is wearing many layers of old, torn clothing to keep out the cold, and her hair is dirty. She seems tired and worn out, and as though she's been left behind by both societies. Busy tidying,* GEORGE *doesn't notice her at first. Finally he turns and sees her in the doorway. He is startled.*

HOLY MARY MOTHER OF GOD!

GEORGE gathers himself together.

You scared me! I'm sorry, but this is a private office. You're not supposed to be in here.

The woman is silent for a moment, first taking in the room, then GEORGE, before responding.

JOHNNY: Nintoogeewaan. *(I want to go home.)*

GEORGE: I'm sorry. What did you say?

JOHNNY: Nintoogeewaan. *(I want to go home.)*

GEORGE: I'm sorry . . . I don't . . . It's okay. I think you've wandered into the wrong place. We can't help you here. But the shelter is just three blocks down. You can get warm there, and they have coffee. Food, too.

JOHNNY laughs.

What's so funny?

JOHNNY: "We can't help you here." Man, if you'd only known that forty years ago, you coulda saved us both a lot of trouble.

GEORGE: Ah, you speak English.

JOHNNY: Yep. You taught it to me. *A* is for "apple." *B* is for . . . "bullshit" or something.

GEORGE: *I* taught it to you?

JOHNNY: Yeah, you people. White people. Anglican people. White Anglican people. You almost taught me too good. What I just said is all I remember of how my parents talked. Their language. I remember it 'cause I used to say it to myself all the time. There at the school. So many times when I was lying in bed, or when I was locked in the closet. "I want to go home"—that's what it means. I could be dead a month and still be able to say it. Nintoogeewaan.

GEORGE: How did you get in here, anyway? The door should be—

JOHNNY: It is. But the thing about these old buildings is they often have old, very breakable glass somewhere around. You'll see that somebody broke into that room where the photocopier is, down there in the basement. You should be more careful; you never know who or what might crawl in here.

GEORGE: I see. And just why are you here?

JOHNNY: That's a very long story. But it's got a happy ending, 'cause I think I already found what I was lookin' for.

GEORGE: Perhaps I should call the police.

JOHNNY: You don't have to do that. I've already been punished.

JOHNNY holds up her hand, and it's bleeding.

GEORGE: Oh my God.

JOHNNY: That old glass is kinda thin and sharp.

She looks to her hand.

Sorta looks like one of those stig- . . . things . . . you know, bleeding like Jesus did that time on the Cross.

GEORGE: I think you mean stigmata.

JOHNNY: Yeah, that's it.

GEORGE: Well, I can assure you it's not. That's just Catholic superstition.

JOHNNY: Good. It would be very inconvenient to find out I was a Catholic saint.

GEORGE immediately becomes concerned with her wound. He looks around for something suitable to bandage her cut, but ends up using his scarf. JOHNNY flinches, seemingly afraid of GEORGE, but he continues to attend to her wound, being very careful not to come in contact with her blood.

GEORGE: Do you mind? I won't hurt you. Oh dear, that looks deep.

JOHNNY: Look at my blood. It seems so red, eh, and everything else so . . . colourless. The funny thing is, it don't really hurt. It should hurt. I used to hurt.

JOHNNY squeezes her fist so that blood oozes out.

Sometimes when I throw up, it's that colour. Funny, eh?

GEORGE cleans her cut very delicately, wary of getting any blood on himself. He grabs the nearest bottle of alcohol and prepares to pour some on the cut.

What a waste.

GEORGE: Those windows are filthy. You might need to get a tetanus shot. Now this is gonna sting a bit.

JOHNNY: Go ahead. Can't feel a thing.

He douses the cut.

GEORGE: Here, keep pressure on it. That looks nasty. I'm sorry, I didn't catch your name.

Pause.

You are . . .

Absent-mindedly, GEORGE *wipes some blood off the arm of the couch.*

JOHNNY: That's a good question.

Pause.

I don't know.

GEORGE: You don't know your name?

JOHNNY: I know who I used to be. I know who I was supposed to be. But that was a long time ago. Who I am today . . . like I said, that's one good question.

GEORGE: It's actually quite a simple question. You really should have somebody look at that. It's quite deep.

JOHNNY: I'll put it on my list of things to do.

GEORGE: Well, whoever you are, the hospital is two blocks away. They'll take care of you. I can find somebody to take you over there. I'd do it myself, but I have a lot of work to do.

JOHNNY: Like maybe . . . the work of God?

GEORGE: Well, we *are* the Anglican Church.

JOHNNY: Yeah, I saw the sign out front. I got a question for you. Me. You don't remember me, do you?

GEORGE: You? No. I can't say that I do. What's your name?

JOHNNY: What's my name?

GEORGE: Yes, what is your name?

JOHNNY: I would tell you, but I think maybe that's too easy. You see, sometimes I don't even know. Sometimes it becomes hazy. Sometimes I'm not sure I'm seeing what I'm seeing. It gets hard.

GEORGE: Listen, it's clear you have some issues, but I am not prepared to deal with them at the moment. I'm not without sympathy. Let me pay for a cab to—

JOHNNY: Like this morning. I was on my corner. It's not my usual corner. A couple of punks took it over a while ago. They don't let me sit there anymore. They have really bad attitudes. They don't love their neighbour. Me, I blame television. So I try this new place, just a couple of blocks down the street, in front of that Tim Hortons. I figure it's as good a place as any to make some money, and a lady's gotta do something with her life or she ain't a lady. Do you know what I'm saying, sir?

GEORGE: Look, I really . . .

JOHNNY: So, I'd been there about an hour, gotten a couple of bucks. Or maybe it was two hours . . . no more than three, I'm sure. Anyway, my fingers start to go numb from the cold, 'cause I'm out there so long. So, I'm sitting there, canvassing the citizens of this city for some *disposable income* . . . You know, I like talking like that sometimes. Makes me feel kinda smart. I learn more big words from them social workers than I did from you. Funny, eh?

> JOHNNY *appears weak at times. She is wracked by a seizure of pain. Her voice falters.*

GEORGE: What's wrong? Are you sick?

JOHNNY: Yeah, pretty sick. Both body and soul, as my noogoom would say . . .

GEORGE: We should get you to that hospital . . .

JOHNNY: Oh, been there lots already. So many people complain about hospital food, but hospital food is sure better than no food. Those hospital people can't do much for me, anyways.

GEORGE: Still . . .

JOHNNY: No, no, I'll be okay. It goes away after a while. Where was I . . . Oh yeah, I was sitting there at Timmy Hortons, watching people get their coffee this morning, when I saw you. You sure walk fast.

GEORGE: You followed me from . . . from the Tim Hortons?

JOHNNY: Yep. I recognized you.

GEORGE: Really, I don't think we've ever met. I'm new to the diocese.

JOHNNY: Oh, we met. Long time ago. Me, I've changed a bit since the last time you saw me. Put on about two feet and maybe forty or more pounds. All the doughnuts, I think.

JOHNNY starts to remove her outer layers of clothing.

GEORGE: Excuse me, please don't get comfortable. You can't stay here.

JOHNNY: Again, if you'd told me that forty years ago, it would have saved us both a lot of trouble. I get hot and cold flashes, which, depending where I am, don't help me a whole lot. If only I would get them hot flashes during the winter and the cold flashes during the summer, I think I'd be a much happier person. For sure. But like always, what I want makes no difference in this world.

Looks around.

This is a nice place, sir. I take it you're not a humble reverend anymore. I guess when you've taught at a residential school, there's no place to move but up.

GEORGE: How . . . how did you know I used to teach at—

JOHNNY: Ah, I think I got your attention now. St. David's. That's where I know you from. Did I mention you look a lot better now? Filled out a bit, and you sure dress better. You got a better job, too, I see. But yeah, it's still you. Someone can't change that much. You still stand the same and, after all these years, your hair is still the same. What's left of it. Yeah, I remember you, from St. David's, all that time ago. Some stuff in my head still works, but then again, you're a hard man to forget.

GEORGE: I think . . . that you need to leave.

JOHNNY: Boy, we've both come a long way, eh? Somehow, though, I think you did a little better in life than me. I guess it helps when you are the same race as God.

GEORGE is silent.

Like I said, you're a pretty fast walker. I mean, I'm younger than you, but, man, I had to race to keep up. Not bad for an old man. But then again, I ain't in the best shape myself. Still, I got hopes for the next Olympics. Thought maybe we could catch up on old times. See how the gang is all doing. That kind of thing. You see, I've been living on the street so long that I'm sure my invitation to the class reunion got lost in the mail. Remember them old days?

GEORGE: I taught there for only two years, before I was transferred.

JOHNNY: It's not how long you were somewhere; it's the memories you leave behind.

GEORGE: What did you say your name was?

JOHNNY: I didn't. That would be too easy. Remember how at school you always told us you couldn't give us the answers? That we had to find them ourselves? Now it's your turn.

GEORGE: Look, I don't know what you're up to but I don't have time for it.

JOHNNY: Really? I got nothing but time. To just remember the old days. In fact, that's my full-time job.

GEORGE: Remember the old days somewhere else!

JOHNNY is quiet, thinking.

Then tell me what your name is.

Pause.

Well?

JOHNNY: You can call me . . .

GEORGE: Yes?

JOHNNY: Johnny. Johnny Indian.

GEORGE: What is this, a joke? What kind of name is that?

JOHNNY: It's as good as any. Better than some. Johnny Indian. Me Johnny Indian. Like it?

GEORGE: Johnny is a man's name.

JOHNNY: It's also a white man's name. And as you can tell, I ain't neither. That much I'm sure of. That's all just part of the mystery of life I guess. Bummer, eh?

GEORGE: Fine. Johnny Indian. It's been a pleasure. Now please leave.

JOHNNY: You know, a long time ago, my people had long, beautiful Indian names that just rolled off the tongue. They sounded like the land we came from. Colourful names. Pretty names. Then you guys showed up and changed everything. You decided to give us names you thought were better. And easier. Smith. Williams. MacGregor. Scottish names, French names, English names, and a whole bunch of others. Names that weren't us. Names that were you.

GEORGE: You followed me here to give me a history lesson?

JOHNNY: I didn't like the name you guys gave me. It had too many bad memories. So I decided to get a new one. Now I am Johnny Indian. Ms. Johnny Indian. Kind of has a nice sound to it, don't it? I'd show you my ID if I had any. I'll answer to Johnny. Johnny Indian. Ms. Indian. Or just J.I.

GEORGE: Okay, Johnny, it's obvious you're ill, so I am going to call—

JOHNNY sees the family photograph on his desk.

JOHNNY: Hey, that your wife and kids? Good-looking family. Very white. You should be proud. I don't have a family myself anymore. At least I don't think so. Did I tell you things sometimes get a bit hazy? Sometimes I forget what I tell people. What are their names? Your family, I mean.

GEORGE: Their names are none of your business. Tell me, Johnny. Following strangers home from Tim Hortons . . . Isn't that kind of dangerous? Or is this some kind of shakedown.

JOHNNY: No. You're not a stranger, remember? We go way back.

GEORGE: Ah yes, you know me. From St. David's.

JOHNNY: Yeah, I know you. From St. David's. You could say we know each other in many ways. What's it called . . . in "the biblical sense." That's it, isn't it? Kinda a weird way to describe what you used to do.

That stops GEORGE in his tracks.

GEORGE: What?

JOHNNY: I used to have a picture of my family, a thousand years ago. Mom, Dad, my grandma, and my little brother. It was taken a month before we were sent to the school. They took my picture away from me, but I still have it up here.

JOHNNY indicates her head.

They can't take that away from me. God knows they tried. I can still see my family sometimes, when I close my eyes. My picture was in black and white, not colour like yours.

She notices the painting.

Wow! You know, because of you guys, I always imagined Jesus was white. That one painting in the rectory even had him with blond hair and blue eyes. Then I found out he was one of them Jews. Now I always picture him as that *Seinfeld* guy.

GEORGE: What did you say?

JOHNNY: *Seinfeld.* It's a show on television. Sometimes we watch it over at the shelter—

GEORGE: About us knowing each other. Did you just accuse me of something?

JOHNNY: I don't know. Did I?

GEORGE: All right, I'm calling the authorities. They'll know how to deal with you.

JOHNNY: Not very Christian, Reverend King.

GEORGE has the telephone in his hand, but stops when he hears his name.

GEORGE: You read my name on the door.

JOHNNY opens the door and looks at the nameplate.

JOHNNY: Hey, there it is. And you're an assistant bishop now, to boot. Good for you. You always knew how to go after what you wanted. The residential school couldn't hold you . . . unlike the rest of us. But who could forget the good Reverend George Linus King, the King of St. David's? A lot of the kids called you King David. But always remember, the higher up you are, the farther you have to fall. You taught us that. So, you just call the police. I'll wait over here. Rest my old bones.

JOHNNY picks up a bottle off the desk and squints at the label.

Grand Marn . . . iar! What the hell is that? Go ahead, call them police. We'll all have a drink and chat. I've got a few things to tell them, too. We'll talk all morning. You know I used to drink? A lot. I know I hide it well. Ooh, Scotch. Had a boyfriend who was Scottish, long time ago. Fresh off the boat. Man, he was a looker and, when he got drunk, his accent got thicker and thicker. When he was really blasted, it suddenly turned into a completely different language. I think he called it "garlic" or something. I knew a lot of old Indian drunks would do the same. Get drunker and drunker until they only spoke Indian. Mind if I take a sniff?

GEORGE doesn't say anything as he puts down the phone. JOHNNY removes the cap and inhales.

Wow, so that's what good Scotch smells like. Unfortunately, my street corner don't earn me enough money to buy this kind of stuff. My regular poison costs a little less. But a girl likes to dream. Boy, I bet this would taste great on ice cream.

GEORGE: Would you like a drink?

JOHNNY: Sir, I would really love one or two or maybe a few more. But I better not.

GEORGE: Afraid it will corrupt your palate?

JOHNNY: It's not even ten in the morning. You might want to see somebody about your wanting to drink this early.

GEORGE: I see. I figured someone in your position wouldn't be too particular about the time.

JOHNNY: Actually, a drop of the stuff would kill me, and it's a little early in the day for me to die. Still got a few things to do.

GEORGE: You're not going to die.

JOHNNY: I wish. I know you hated it when we didn't agree with you, but my liver's kinda shot. There's only sawdust left down there. The last time I was in the hospital, the doctor told me one more quickie love affair with the bottle, and I was history. My liver is looking for its own Wounded Knee. And the cavalry is usually 80 proof. So I must be . . . rude . . . and refuse your kind hospitality. I'm not ready yet to shuffle off this mortal coil. See, I still remember things from your class. And you said I'd never amount to much.

JOHNNY plops herself down on the couch. She and GEORGE stare at each other for a second or two.

GEORGE: I said that . . . about you, did I?

JOHNNY: Yep. You said I was kinda smart but didn't apply myself. Lo and behold, I guess you were psychic.

GEORGE: At St. David's?

JOHNNY: Yep. Back in the pre-Scotch days. Pre-wife and family. Your tastes seemed to have changed over the years.

GEORGE: I resent what you are implying.

JOHNNY: Me, I can't even spell "implying."

Beat.

GEORGE: So?

JOHNNY: So.

GEORGE: Why are you really here?

JOHNNY: Wow. That's a good question. I guess . . . why are any of us really here?

GEORGE: I'm here to work. To deliver the word of God. To make the world a better place.

JOHNNY: Me . . . I'm a memory. Whose memory, I'm not sure. I know that I am only half or a quarter of who I used to be. And somehow, I know that's not right. I was someone once. Or I was meant to be someone once.

GEORGE: What does that have to do with me?

JOHNNY: I think you know.

GEORGE: Let's pretend I don't.

JOHNNY: Okay, Reverend King—

GEORGE: Assistant Bishop King.

JOHNNY: Forgive me. *Assistant Bishop King.* See, there are parts of my life I don't remember. Or maybe I do. It gets hard to tell sometimes. I think I mentioned that. It's like I'm a ghost, floating through the city, just a shadow of questionable actions. Sort of like the ghost of abuse past. There are some things I remember but forget, and the other way around, too. But some memories are crystal clear and solid. Things that, as much as I try, as much as I drink, as much as I cry and bang my head against a brick wall, won't go away. They're like scars that sit on my mind, scars that can't be removed no matter what. And occasionally scars that walk out of Tim Hortons.

GEORGE: Are you trying to blackmail me? With these . . . these . . . lies? It won't work.

JOHNNY: No, sir. Not me. What's money to a dead Indian? And I'd be a little careful with that L-word. Keep in mind who's looking over your shoulder. I read somewhere your big guy don't like that.

JOHNNY points to the painting, squints at the image of Christ.

GEORGE: St. David's was a very long time ago.

JOHNNY: It was yesterday.

GEORGE: I think we're communicating on two different planes here. You've obviously had some problems. I understand. I've done some fieldwork with people who have suffered from substantial alcohol abuse. It does things to the mind. I know. You yourself have admitted your memory isn't what it used to be. That everything is hazy. I think possibly you're suffering from some sort of delusion. Let me help. I know a place that—

JOHNNY: No help. I've been helped before. By a lot of white do-gooders, and a few Indian ones. And trust me, there's nothing worse than a reformed alcoholic trying to dry you out. To me, that was even more of a reason to keep drinking. Those guys are good for a meal and an occasional warm bed. But have you ever seen those old-time photographs, where only the centre of the picture is clear and in focus and everything around it is fuzzy? That's what I remember. That is what I see in my mind.

GEORGE: That's the thing with delusions, sometimes they can appear so real—

JOHNNY: Sometimes them delusions *are* real.

GEORGE: And sometimes they're not. Sometimes the mind is your worst enemy. As I said, I've done some fieldwork and I know the reality of the streets. Yes, I was there at St. David's, but I don't remember you, Johnny Indian, or whatever your name is. And if you are implying what I think you are implying, your memory is worse than you say.

JOHNNY: Do you have any Aspirin?

GEORGE: Why?

JOHNNY: I hurt. Why else would somebody want Aspirin? So, do you?

GEORGE retrieves a bottle of Aspirin from a desk drawer and gives JOHNNY two tablets.

GEORGE: I really think you should go to the hospital—or let me call a doctor.

JOHNNY: You and your doctors and hospitals and clinics. They can't cure everything. Or is this just so you can get me out of here?

GEORGE: I want you to get the help that I can't provide.

Pause.

Where are you from, Johnny?

JOHNNY: Where am I from . . . That's a good question. Where *am* I from?

GEORGE: Do you have a good answer? I mean, St. David's served an area over three thousand square miles. About a dozen or more Native communities, if I remember correctly. Sometimes a few from even farther away. You said "noogoom" earlier. That's means grandmother, doesn't it . . . in Cree? So that tells me something.

JOHNNY: Ah, you know Cree . . .

GEORGE: A few words. I've worked with some Cree people over the years and picked up a little bit. It's a beautiful language.

JOHNNY: Sure, *now* it's a beautiful language. Not then. You got any water? These are a bitch to swallow dry.

GEORGE: There's a bottle in my jacket beside you.

JOHNNY pulls the bottle of water out of GEORGE's coat and notices something as she does so.

JOHNNY: Ooh, the fancy stuff. I'm used to water fountains. And can I have two more pills? Not everything makes it through my liver. I have to double up these days.

As GEORGE *dispenses two more pills,* JOHNNY *slips his cellphone out of the same pocket as the water and hides it under a cushion.* GEORGE *hands her the pills.*

You're a saint.

JOHNNY *swallows the Aspirin, drinks the rest of the water, then looks at the empty bottle.*

That's better. Water into wine. Remember that old trick, Assistant Bishop King? There have been a few times I wished I could do that. The best I could do was turn pocket change into cheap sherry.

GEORGE: You didn't answer my question. Where are you from?

JOHNNY: Far, far away. You can't get there from here. At least I can't.

GEORGE: Does this faraway place have a name?

JOHNNY: Home.

GEORGE: A more specific name.

JOHNNY: Again, that would be too easy. I need you to remember me, by yourself. I don't want to draw you a map. I want you to find your own way, like I did. But I will give you a hint. A small, round one.

Pause.

Oranges.

GEORGE: Oranges?! I don't understand. Are you talking about the oranges we gave you at Christmas?

JOHNNY: You do remember! Oh good. We never could figure out exactly what oranges had to do with Christ's birthday. We couldn't find anything in the Bible about oranges in the manger . . . but then, there was a lot we could never figure out about that place and that story.

GEORGE: I'm sorry. You've lost me. What does that have to do with you?

JOHNNY: Not with me. With you. There's so much more to those oranges than Christmas. Or don't you remember?

GEORGE: My memory is fine. I remember all the children being given fruit at Christmas. But that's all. That's all.

JOHNNY: Hmm, I was so sure you'd—

GEORGE tosses JOHNNY her tattered jacket.

GEORGE: Madam, I think it's time for you to go.

JOHNNY: And if I don't want to—

GEORGE: Let's not finish that sentence. Off you go. I've offered to help, but it's obvious—

JOHNNY doubles over in pain and falls to the floor.

JOHNNY: OH JESUS!

GEORGE: What's wrong?!

JOHNNY: I told you. I'm sick. Dying.

GEORGE: What? Here?

JOHNNY: Sometimes Aspirin just doesn't cut it.

GEORGE: I am definitely calling an ambulance.

GEORGE picks up the phone and begins to dial, but JOHNNY somehow manages to crawl over and rip the cord out of the jack.

Why the hell did you do that?

JOHNNY: I'm not done yet.

GEORGE: I was trying to help you! Look, I've humoured you as much as I can. I am obviously not who you think I am. I will not have you die in my office. I have a cellphone—

JOHNNY begins to hum a slow melody, "Yesterday" by the Beatles. GEORGE recognizes it and stops instantly.

JOHNNY: *(weakly)* Do you recognize that song, Assistant Bishop King?

GEORGE doesn't react.

I remember it so good. It's one of those real clear images that's at the centre of the fuzzy photographs in my mind. It wasn't until ten years after I left St. David's that I found out what it's called. "Yesterday" by the Beatles. I was in a shopping mall the first time I'd heard it since I'd left the school. I was sitting by the water fountain when it came over the loudspeakers. Almost immediately my whole body cramped. I was doubled over . . . started sweating and . . . my stomach was turning inside out. I couldn't breathe. I vomited. And vomited. It's not easy to vomit like that when you got nothing in your stomach. You used to sing us to bed with that song. That was your favourite song. It was the last sound we heard as we fell asleep . . . then later that night you would wake us up, for other reasons. I remember. My body remembers.

GEORGE: No, you don't. You just think you do.

JOHNNY: Then I got an awfully good imagination.

GEORGE: My child . . .

JOHNNY: My child . . .

GEORGE: It's obvious you've had a great deal of hardship in your life. I will say a prayer for you. But there's obviously something wrong here. I am not who you think I am. There is no possible way I could even contemplate doing what you are insinuating. It's impossible, I assure you. Now if—

JOHNNY: Do you know what's really sad? I actually like most of the Beatles's other stuff. Assistant Bishop King, isn't confession good for the soul?

GEORGE: You know very well it is. Do you have something you want to confess? Then confess directly to the Lord. He is ultimately the only one who can grant absolution.

JOHNNY: Do you think God has forgiven you for what you did?

GEORGE: I will not have this conversation with you. I've done nothing to be ashamed of. I'm not running. I'm not hiding. I am standing here looking you in the face, telling you the truth.

JOHNNY: Yeah, you know, almost like you've been expecting this to happen. What's it been, Assistant Bishop King, forty years, thereabouts? Waiting for that knock at the door. Wondering if somebody will show up and point their little copper finger at you? A lot of you churchmen aren't breathing too easy these days, are you, Assistant Bishop King? I hear about lots of court cases. Lots of apologies. Lots of . . . what are they called . . . accusations. A lot of money being given out. Ever get nervous?

GEORGE: No.

JOHNNY: Not even a little bit?

GEORGE: I have nothing to fear. I am innocent. I sleep well at night.

JOHNNY: Beside your beautiful family.

GEORGE: They and the Church are my life.

JOHNNY: Then I guess you're a lucky man. I had a family . . . once. I had to trade them in for your school. Do you think that was a fair trade, Assistant Bishop King? My old family loved me . . . I think. I don't know for sure. They, like a lot of things, were beaten out of me. My past is like a book with three out of every four pages ripped out. Hints of what my story was. At that place, I was told Jesus Christ and God were my new parents. Some parents.

Where were they when I needed them? I guess you could call them latchkey parents. I'd press charges, but I don't think either of them would show up in court. It's kind of hard to serve them papers. The Church, on the other hand, now that's different. They . . .

GEORGE goes over to the bookshelf and takes out a book, which he throws on the cushion beside JOHNNY.

GEORGE: Do you know what that is?

JOHNNY: I know I've been out of school a while, but . . . a book?

GEORGE: *A National Crime: The Canadian Government and the Residential School System, 1879–1986.* You should read it. It's all about what happened at the residential schools.

JOHNNY: When does the movie come out?

GEORGE: It deals with schools set up by the Catholic, United, and Anglican Churches.

JOHNNY: I knew about the Catholics, but the United, too? They always seem so nice.

GEORGE: I've read that book cover to cover. For years I sat on the committee set up by the Anglican Church to support healing in the communities. I do this because I know what went on.

JOHNNY: I bet you do.

GEORGE: Because I was there. Why do you think I was at St. David's for only two years? I hated it. It was a travesty of everything we were trying to do. I became a minister to make the world a better place. St. David's was nothing like they told us it would be. We weren't freeing minds or spreading the love of God. We were punishing children for the stupidest of reasons. Making them eat food we wouldn't give a dog. And then lying about what we were doing. St. David's was a four-storey lie shored up in red brick.

JOHNNY: Hey, brother, you're preaching to the converted.

GEORGE: So I left. I had myself transferred out. I had two eyes, two ears. I'm not stupid. The poor food, the substandard education, the hypocrisy, the abuse . . . Yes, there was abuse—and not just by the clergy, but by staff and other students. But not by me. I had trouble seeing the point of teaching there. It sickened me.

JOHNNY: So you ran away, while we had to stay behind. Cry me a river, white boy. If you were so innocent and clean, why didn't you tell anybody? Huh?

JOHNNY discovers the pile of food trays. She starts nibbling.

Mmm, food.

GEORGE: I was young. And naive.

JOHNNY: Naive . . . that's "native" without the *t*. I was younger than you. And I lost my . . . naiveness . . . and my nativeness.

JOHNNY is distracted for a moment by what she's eating.

Hey, vegetables, I gotta be careful; there might be a vitamin in here.

GEORGE: We did what we were told, but that doesn't absolve us. I've spent all these years with that sitting on my soul. I should have taken some responsibility and . . . and faced the evil . . . but I couldn't. I didn't know how. I was young. They were all my superiors. I was nobody. So I left. I ran away. And it's haunted me ever since.

JOHNNY: You were only following orders, eh? Hey, what kind of cheese is this?

GEORGE: Brie. But I'm not here to be judged by you.

JOHNNY: And yet, here I am.

GEORGE: How can you be so sure?

JOHNNY: That I'm here?

GEORGE: So sure that I did whatever you believe I did to you?

JOHNNY: Again, I was there.

GEORGE: So was I. And I remember it differently. How old were you when what you say . . . happened?

JOHNNY: You don't remember?

GEORGE: Answer my question. How old were you?

JOHNNY: I had just turned twelve. Somewhere around there.

GEORGE: That was so long ago. You were a kid, in a different environment. You were under such stress. I'm sure all the reverends looked alike. We dressed alike. Talked alike. You could be wrong about me. You *are* wrong. It wasn't me. Upon my faith in the Lord, I have many sins upon my soul, but I am not guilty of that.

JOHNNY: Sorry, but there are some things you just don't forget. Even if another forty years were to pass. Sounds to me like you're the one doing the forgetting. You don't even remember what's so special about the oranges. Maybe you got one of them old-men-losing-their-memory type diseases. Do you remember a little boy? His name was Sammy. Sammy . . . Indian?

GEORGE: Who was he?

JOHNNY: Another student. My best friend. My brother. My late brother.

GEORGE: If I don't remember you, how could I remember him?

JOHNNY: You couldn't. You see, he never existed. At least, that's what the records from St. David's say.

GEORGE: How can I know somebody who never existed?

JOHNNY: Now there's a deep question. 'Cause I remember him, so well. I remember playing with him in the woods. Swimming. I remember laughing with him at all his silly jokes. We used to fish and make forts in the fallen leaves. He was so trusting. I made him swallow a tadpole once.

GEORGE: I thought you said he didn't exist.

JOHNNY: He doesn't, anymore. We were there for nine months before he died, and I was only allowed to talk to him four times. Four times. You see, boys weren't allowed to play with the girls. I'd see him across the field sometimes. Sometimes he was so close, but I was always kept away from my sweet and precious little brother.

Pause.

Why? Which one of God's laws would be broken by letting a brother and sister play together?

GEORGE: I can't give you a logical answer. People there just thought boys and girls together might get into . . . mischief. I know it doesn't make any sense today. I never really understood it myself, but—

JOHNNY: It don't matter. He died of TB when he turned ten. He was just one of a bunch of kids who died that year at the school. But there's no record of him anywhere. Buried somewhere, forgotten. It's like God reached out and said, "Nope, nobody named Sammy Indian ever walked this earth that I made in six days." Him and hundreds of other kids over the years all gone, with families not ever knowing what happened to them. They didn't even let me say goodbye . . . How much mischief would that have caused?

GEORGE: You're right, you're right. I'm not sure—

JOHNNY: Tell me, Assistant Bishop King, what do you say to all those old Indian women with stretch marks that came from kids that were never born? When my parents came looking for Sammy later on, there was no record of him even being sent to the school, or having died at the school. Sammy ceased to exist. It's like he was a magician. *Poof*, and he was gone. One less Indian in the world. You guys tried to tell my mother and father that they had no second child there at the school. Oddly enough, they had trouble believing that.

GEORGE: I don't know any of that.

JOHNNY: But if he didn't exist, then where did my memories come from? Answer me that, Assistant Bishop King. The same place my memories of you came from?

GEORGE: I don't know anything about your brother. Or about you. That was more than forty years ago!

JOHNNY: Too bad. Maybe he died before you got to St. David's. You would have liked him. But maybe he was a little too young for you. And you liked little girls. Thank heavens for small mercies, eh?

GEORGE: Will you shut up! I am a man of God. A family man. A man of respect. I am not a monster.

JOHNNY: I wonder how many like you have said that over the years. Even the Jesuits thought they were doing something good, being productive. At least we got to martyr them, eh?

GEORGE pulls a photo album off the shelf and opens it, showing it to JOHNNY.

GEORGE: Look, here I am at the reading of the official apology, in 1993. That's me, in the back row, behind Archbishop Michael Peers. Would I be there if I was guilty?

JOHNNY: You've put on weight.

GEORGE: *(reading from the photo album)* "I accept and I confess before God and you, our failures in the residential schools.

"We failed you. We failed ourselves. We failed God.

"I am sorry, more than I can say, that we tried to remake you in our image, taking from you your language and the signs of your identity.

"I am sorry, more than I can say, that in our schools so many were abused physically, sexually, culturally, and emotionally.

"On behalf of the Anglican Church of Canada, I present our apology."

JOHNNY: Pretty words.

GEORGE: Heartfelt words.

JOHNNY: But just words. I could say I love you. I could say I can fly. I could say I'm the second coming of Christ, but we both know those would be just words.

GEORGE: They're not just words. We agonized over what to say. How to say it.

JOHNNY: It reads wonderfully for the news, but I was there. This is about me.

Pause.

I like this picture book of yours. It's like a time machine that shows you climbing your way up the Church's corporate ladder.

GEORGE: If that's how you want to describe it. One of my children put that together for me, two years ago. For my birthday.

JOHNNY: Your family must love you a lot. Do you love them?

GEORGE: What kind of question is that?

JOHNNY: A very important one, I think.

GEORGE: Of course I love them. They are my family.

JOHNNY: What's your wife's name?

GEORGE: I told you, that's not your concern.

JOHNNY picks up the family photograph, turns it over, and reads the back.

JOHNNY: Sarah. And your kids are Ruth, Daniel, and Mary. All good Christian names.

Still reading:

Mary's confirmation. Wow, people still wear white to those things.

GEORGE forcibly takes the picture from JOHNNY and puts it back down on the desk.

GEORGE: Leave them alone.

JOHNNY: Do you want to know why I'm really here?

GEORGE: You've made that painfully obvious, though you are profoundly misdirected.

JOHNNY: That depends on if you believe in God or not. God must have sent me.

GEORGE: God? Sent you? And just why would God have sent you here?

JOHNNY: It's amazingly obvious. He must have wanted me to come here. Why else would those punks have kicked me off my corner? Why would I have ended up at Tim Hortons? Why would you go to that same Tim Hortons? When I was there too? Don't you see . . . Tim Hortons must be part of his master plan!

GEORGE: We had a small party last night and I offered to clean up. I needed a coffee beforehand, so—

JOHNNY: What kind of party?

GEORGE: To celebrate my promotion to assistant bishop. Some of the staff thought—

JOHNNY: Well, congratulations, Assistant Bishop King! I didn't realize it happened so recently. So why would God arrange for you to be promoted at this very time? Holy mackerel, it must be some kind of miracle!

GEORGE: It is not a miracle. God has nothing to do with this. He doesn't send people to Tim Hortons out of some divine purpose.

JOHNNY: Pretty odd words for an assistant bishop. I thought God was in all things and all places?

GEORGE: Yes, but if you trip over a rock, I doubt if it's God's fault. It's your own clumsiness. This . . . so-called meeting has all been a coincidence, I'm sorry to say.

JOHNNY: Coincidence? I thought good Christians didn't believe in coincidence.

GEORGE: God works in mysterious ways. You may have heard me say that, too.

JOHNNY: He sure does. Like when he said, "Suffer the little children," did you guys have to take him so seriously?

GEORGE: Now you're being blasphemous. The passage reads, "And when Jesus saw it, he was much displeased, and said unto them, 'Suffer the little children to come unto me, and forbid them not: for of such is the kingdom of God.'" In that context, "suffer" means to permit. You're just trying to pervert his words.

JOHNNY: Monkey see, monkey do.

GEORGE: We can't change the past. We can only address it. That's why I want to help. You look so tired . . . exhausted.

JOHNNY: You're not going to start singing "Yesterday" to me, are you?

GEORGE: I was never fond of that song. Or the Beatles.

JOHNNY: You guys still upset over that "more popular than Jesus" thing? Lennon was probably right. More people know "Lady Madonna" than the Sermon on the Mount.

GEORGE: I think you're thinking of Reverend Anderson.

JOHNNY's face reveals her confusion.

He taught music, remember?

JOHNNY: Reverend . . .

GEORGE: . . . Anderson. Surely you remember him. Tall man. Bald. Always smelled of tobacco. Reverend Anderson. He used to hum that song all the time.

JOHNNY: No . . . no . . . it was you. I'm . . .

GEORGE: I was more into folk music.

JOHNNY: No . . . it was . . . you. You.

GEORGE: I'm sorry but, no, it wasn't. You look confused.

JOHNNY: It doesn't matter.

GEORGE: Yes, it does. If you were wrong about that, what else are you wrong about? I'm not angry, Johnny. Not at all. It's obvious what has happened to you over the years—how it's affected you—and it's not your fault.

JOHNNY: It couldn't have been him . . . *You* hummed it.

GEORGE: Don't you remember how he would sing that song at the Christmas concert? Usually off-key, but he would try.

JOHNNY: I'm not wrong.

GEORGE: You don't have to get upset. We all make mistakes.

JOHNNY: No, it's not a mistake. I have thought about this for forty years. It's always there. You're always there.

GEORGE: I hate to say the obvious, but look at how damaged you are. You can barely even sit up straight. So how can you trust anything? Could be delirium tremens or any of a host of other medical problems. You could be delusional, schizophrenic. All of what you remember about me you might have dreamed up during some drug or alcohol binge. It's certainly possible—in fact, it's more than likely. Your details about me are filtered through many years of abuse. Memories can lie.

JOHNNY: You're not a detail. You're a ghost, too.

GEORGE: I'm a ghost? How am I a ghost?

JOHNNY: You're a ghost. I'm a ghost. All these memories of what happened to me, to Sammy, to all of us. They're like ghosts seen out of the corner of the eye. No one wants to admit they're real. You can see through them. You can't prove them. Nobody believes. They don't exist. My childhood doesn't exist. It's dead. I'm a ghost.

GEORGE: You poor woman . . .

GEORGE moves in to comfort JOHNNY, who reacts violently.

JOHNNY: DON'T TOUCH ME!

GEORGE: It's okay. Everything's okay. Just relax. We're all fine here. Tell me some more, like why are you a ghost, Johnny.

JOHNNY: When my brother died, and my parents came to get us for the summer, they found out . . . and I died to them, too. I was supposed to look after him. But I couldn't do anything about him being sick. Nobody told me. I didn't know he'd died for a week, until one of you guys got around to telling me. Even though they kept Sammy and me apart, my parents blamed me for not looking after him. They didn't understand, so I became just as dead to them as he was. That's why I am a ghost. Those buildings created a lot of ghosts.

GEORGE: That's . . . that's horrible.

JOHNNY: Yeah, isn't it?

JOHNNY starts to breathe hard and fast. She slumps to the ground.

GEORGE: Here, let me help you.

JOHNNY: Okay. I would greatly appreciate it if you would confess. Pretty please?

GEORGE: You want me to confess? Fine, I will confess. I confess I spent two years at St. David's. I confess I heard about things that happened there, and other places. Horrible things. I confess I didn't do anything to stop it, as I should have. I confess I abandoned a sinking ship. I confess I should have done something. I confess. I confess I've had to live with that. I confess St. David's failed and I failed. But that's all I will confess to, because that's all there is to confess. The confessional is closed. Are you satisfied?

Neither of them says anything.

Let me get you up off the floor.

JOHNNY: No.

GEORGE: You're being silly.

JOHNNY: No, Sammy was the silly one. So silly . . .

GEORGE: I don't know anything about Sammy. I'm sorry.

JOHNNY: You don't seem to know much about anything, do you?

JOHNNY painfully rises to her feet.

An invisible brother. A ghost of a childhood. A song you didn't sing. Am I really here?

GEORGE: Yes, you are. So, do you believe me now?

JOHNNY: No. Maybe it was Reverend Anderson who sang "Yesterday" . . . I don't know anymore.

GEORGE: He's dead now. Though, I did hear rumours about him at St. David's. That's why I think . . .

JOHNNY: Maybe he did. Maybe he was one of the bad guys. But so were you.

GEORGE: Do you have proof? Other people accusing me? Otherwise, it's just my word against yours.

JOHNNY: No proof. No other witnesses. Just me.

GEORGE: Allegations like yours have to have some basis in truth—some evidence. We're not handing out blank cheques or apologies to whoever walks in the door.

JOHNNY: I told you. I don't want any money. Or an apology.

GEORGE: Then what?

JOHNNY: It's a big word, with a big meaning. Acknowledgement.

GEORGE: Of what? For something that may or may not have happened to you?

JOHNNY: No, I want acknowledgement . . . that I'm me. Me! I'm Sammy's sister. I am my parents' child. I don't want to be a ghost anymore. I want to exist. To be seen. To be noticed. To be acknowledged by you. And to have you admit what you've done.

GEORGE: I'm afraid I can't do that. And I think it's time to call the police.

JOHNNY: Oh, you can't do that.

GEORGE picks up the telephone.

It's broke, remember?

GEORGE: Damn it!

JOHNNY: Language, Assistant Bishop King.

GEORGE walks to the door.

GEORGE: Fine, I have a cellphone. I can—

GEORGE goes to his coat and searches inside the pockets, but can't find his phone.

My cell . . . it's gone.

JOHNNY: I guess God does indeed work in mysterious ways, eh?

GEORGE: Give me back my cellphone.

JOHNNY: That would make it a lot more difficult to finish our talk.

GEORGE: I've been very patient but there is a limit to all things.

JOHNNY: No more Mr. Nice Guy?

GEORGE: I'm afraid not.

JOHNNY: Okay. No more Ms. Nice Girl either.

JOHNNY pulls a pistol from deep inside a pocket of her discarded jacket. She points it at GEORGE, who freezes.

I didn't wanna do this.

GEORGE: Why are you pointing a gun at me?

JOHNNY: I want your attention.

GEORGE: Okay, you've got it.

JOHNNY: Those two years you taught at St. David's, when I was there, too, did you molest me? Did you touch me?

GEORGE: No.

JOHNNY: Did you stick your cock in my mouth? Did you fuck me? Yes or no?

Silence for a beat or two.

GEORGE: No!

JOHNNY: That's the wrong answer.

GEORGE: It's the only answer. You don't want to kill me, Johnny. It wouldn't solve anything. It would only make your life worse.

JOHNNY: I live on the streets, eat garbage, beg to survive, have nightmares—and I'm dying. How much worse could it possibly get?

GEORGE: Put the gun down.

JOHNNY: When I'm done with it.

GEORGE: I'm not afraid to die. Why do you want to do this?

JOHNNY: To end this. Make it stop.

GEORGE: Closure? You want closure? I'm sorry, but violence seldom brings closure. It frequently just complicates the situation even more.

JOHNNY: Assistant Bishop King.

GEORGE: We're adults now. You can call me George.

JOHNNY: No thanks.

GEORGE: Do you seriously want to pull that trigger and shoot me?

JOHNNY: No.

GEORGE: Then put the gun down. If you do, I will erase this whole thing from my memory and you can go on your way. No harm done.

JOHNNY: "No harm done." You have a bad habit of picking the wrong phrases. Actually you had a lot of bad habits. Oh, I know you tried to save the child by killing the Indian, but I think some of it managed to hide out somewhere, maybe behind my brown eyes, under my black hair, or beneath my thick skin. Killing an entire people can take a lot of time. I guess ten years wasn't long enough.

GEORGE: Think about this, Johnny.

JOHNNY: I have and I'm conflicted. Isn't that funny?

JOHNNY laughs a hearty laugh. GEORGE doesn't.

GEORGE: It isn't funny. Murder . . . revenge isn't funny.

JOHNNY: You sent a six-year-old to jail. For ten years of hard labour, and worse. Forty years of probation . . . I've had a long time to think about this moment . . . about you.

GEORGE: Johnny, please put down the gun.

JOHNNY holds the gun up to her head.

JOHNNY: I could just shoot myself . . . that would solve the problem just as easy. No more tears. No more anything.

GEORGE: Both would damn you.

JOHNNY: I don't think I'd notice the difference. What to do . . . What to do . . .

Lights go down.

End of Act One.

ACT TWO

GEORGE and JOHNNY are in the same positions as before; they hold them for a few moments.

GEORGE: Well?

JOHNNY: Well what?

GEORGE: For a moment I thought . . .

JOHNNY takes the gun away from her head.

JOHNNY: Just seeing if you were paying attention. God, sometimes you white people ain't got no sense of humour. Got any more of that brie?

GEORGE: Oh, Johnny, you play dangerous games.

JOHNNY: A girl's gotta have some fun, don't she?

JOHNNY walks over to the box of bottles, examines the Scotch. She sets the gun down on the coffee table. GEORGE watches her, still hopped up on adrenaline. He steps forward and JOHNNY immediately grabs the gun.

I hope you're not planning to go anywhere.

GEORGE: I go where I'm needed.

JOHNNY: You're needed here.

GEORGE: Just stretching my legs. I'm not a young man anymore. They do tend to get a bit stiff.

JOHNNY: I know stiff. We're good buddies. Assistant Bishop King, have you ever drank Lysol?

GEORGE: Can't say that I have.

JOHNNY: The first drink's the toughest. It burns. But after that, either the mind or the body blocks it out. Nice buzz though. And your breath smells pine fresh. We Native people like that; reminds us of the outdoors.

GEORGE: Am I supposed to laugh?

JOHNNY: You can do whatever you want. You always did.

JOHNNY holds up the Scotch, the gun in her other hand.

Bet this costs more than Lysol, don't it?

GEORGE: Substantially.

JOHNNY: Substantially . . . I gotta say, I am kinda curious 'bout what it tastes like.

GEORGE: Curiosity killed the cat.

JOHNNY: Not my clan. Are you really that concerned about my liver?

GEORGE: I am worried about every part of you.

JOHNNY: I bet you are. Why? Because it's your job?

GEORGE: Partially because of that. Partially because we may be to blame for what happened to you. Partially because I like to think it's the right thing to do and that I'm a nice guy.

JOHNNY: You are your brother's keeper.

GEORGE: Exactly.

JOHNNY: I tried doing that once. Like I said, it didn't turn out so well. Oh well, no use crying over buried brothers.

GEORGE: I can only imagine your grief. Let me help. Let us help. We have so many programs—

JOHNNY: *(raising her voice)* Oh God, if I go to one more life-skills class or one more AA meeting, I will shoot myself. If you're so eager to do something good, remember me. Remember Sammy. Remember everything. Take responsibility!

GEORGE: *(yelling)* But you're indicting me without any proof!

JOHNNY: But I remember you. I remember your smell. I remember your voice. I remember the pain. I remember it all. All the drinking in the world can't ever get rid of that. I remember.

GEORGE: You think you do!

Their shouting match halts for a moment as they regroup. JOHNNY's attention turns again to the photograph of GEORGE's family. She motions to it with the gun.

JOHNNY: Do *they* know what you did?

GEORGE: Johnny. I don't want to talk about my family. They're not a part of this.

JOHNNY: Okay, let's talk about mine. I almost had a family once. A brand new one. One of my own. About ten years or so after getting out of St. David's, I met a man. He was very nice, and I really liked him. We had a lot in common. He'd been to a residential school, too—a different one though. But he was just as fucked up as I was. Birds of a feather, you know.

GEORGE: Do you want me to call him?

JOHNNY: He was Cree, from way up north. A reserve with one of those long unpronounceable names. His name was Dick. We met in an upgrading class. I was thinking of going to college or something. I was trying to become smarter. God, was I stupid. You guys at St. David's did fuck all education-wise.

GEORGE: Where is Dick?

JOHNNY: I don't know. I lost him.

GEORGE: He died?

JOHNNY: No, I literally lost him. In a park. It was the weekend and we'd been on one hell of a bender. Came to early Monday morning, still time to get home and clean up before class, but no Dick. He was gone. I waited and waited, even called a few hospitals and jails, but nothing. He just disappeared. I guess he fucked off. That happens a lot in my life. Dick—

GEORGE: You said you had a family?

JOHNNY: You see, by then, I wasn't having my moon time . . . my period, as you white people call it.

GEORGE: You were pregnant?!

JOHNNY: Yeah, that happens with Dicks, I hear. But you don't wanna hear all this woman stuff. It'll just make you . . . sad.

GEORGE: It looks like it's making you sad.

JOHNNY: You know, I've never understood why the Church hates kids. I mean really hates them. No laughing, no playing, no talking, no love, no nothing. It was like we were being punished for being kids. Funny, eh?

GEORGE: You were mentioning something about you being pregnant . . . did you have a boy or a girl?

JOHNNY: *(working up strength)* A girl. Six pounds, nine ounces of the cutest little Cree girl you could imagine. Pure concentrated beauty. She looked so much like Sammy . . . so much. I thought I'd actually found something I could do pretty good. And I thought I could stop being a ghost, 'cause ghosts don't have kids, right? When I was pregnant, I stopped drinking . . . mostly, but—

She looks at GEORGE.

I think you know how this ends, don't you?

GEORGE: I have my fears.

JOHNNY: Seems I was wrong. I couldn't even do that right. The damage had been done. They called it fetal alcohol syndrome. I told you you didn't want to hear about this.

GEORGE: I'm so sorry.

JOHNNY: As you can tell, I'm not exactly great mother material. They took her away from me. Angela. My little angel. That's what I called her. I don't know what she's called today, but she was my little angel. At that moment, for the first time in a very long time, I actually believed in God, 'cause only God could make something so beautiful. Not somebody like me.

Silence.

GEORGE: It might be possible to find her. There are ways—

JOHNNY: And what possible good would that do? She was better off where she went. Couldn't have raised a kid on day-old doughnuts and handouts from the soup kitchen. Geez, she'd be . . . in her twenties by now. Wow. But ghosts can't have children.

She pauses, weary.

Like Sammy, it's like she never existed.

GEORGE: Johnny, I'm so sorry.

JOHNNY: So sorry. Afterwards, I was told, no more kids for me. Something got busted up in the process and they took some parts out. The moon never rose for me again. So, I started calling myself by a man's name. Might as well.

GEORGE: Johnny . . .

JOHNNY: That's me. I don't even have a picture of her . . . not like this one.

Pause.

What are their names?

GEORGE: You know their names. Can I ask you a question, Johnny?

JOHNNY: Sure.

GEORGE: Something you just said, do you believe in God?

JOHNNY: I think the more important question is, does he believe in me?

GEORGE: I think you know the answer to that. I mean, sitting here, listening to you, you sound so very lost.

JOHNNY: So very lost . . .

GEORGE: And while you have no reason to trust us, you should trust God. Men will lead you into the darkness, but his light shall lead you out.

JOHNNY: Hallelujah! I might have believed that once. You know, every once in a while I would go through moments of being sober. I would get a job, keep it for a couple months or even a few years. Then the nightmares would start . . . Anyways, during those times, I would try to lead a normal life. Hold down a job, pay taxes, ride the bus, ignore street people, feel guilty about my daughter—all the normal middle-class stuff. And it would work. Really. If you were to have seen me then, you wouldn't have recognized me. I had almost become what you and St. David's wanted me to be.

GEORGE: I guess the next thing to do is make those periods of stability last longer. Make your goals attainable.

JOHNNY: There are things I can remember, bits and pieces of stuff from the past forty years. I completely missed the disco years, but I managed to follow the rise of Shania Twain and the two middle years of *North of 60*.

GEORGE: Well, that's something, I suppose. Except for the gun, I'm finding you to be a lucid and intelligent—if misguided—woman. Johnny, you can have a future. It's not too late.

JOHNNY: You mean get a job? Settle down? Would you let a woman like me marry your son?

GEORGE: Johnny, Daniel is eighteen.

JOHNNY: Oh, how about your daughters?

GEORGE: Humour is an excellent sign of healing. So, Johnny, what . . .

JOHNNY: You had them kind of late in life, eh? Your kids. You must have been in your forties or something.

GEORGE: I didn't marry my wife till I was thirty-nine.

JOHNNY: Why?

GEORGE: I didn't meet her until I was thirty-five.

JOHNNY: I thought you religious people got married early in life. That "go forth and multiply" kind of thing.

GEORGE: Everybody is different.

JOHNNY: Was she older than I was when we met?

GEORGE: Of course. Substantially.

JOHNNY: There's that word again, "substantially." But good for you. You're adaptable. No more little Indian girls running around, so you had to make do with older white ones?

GEORGE: The filth that comes from your mouth.

JOHNNY: I only know what I see.

GEORGE: I am not a monster.

JOHNNY: So you keep saying.

GEORGE: I'm not. I can't even contemplate . . .

JOHNNY: Did your kids have nightmares, Assistant Bishop King, like me? Did you sing to them . . .

GEORGE lunges at JOHNNY, grabbing her arm forcefully.

GEORGE: You will not say such disgusting things about my children, you—

But JOHNNY still has the gun in her other hand and she waves it at GEORGE, who backs down.

JOHNNY: No, no, no, no. I have my get-out-of-jail-free card.

GEORGE: I told you. Leave my family out of this.

JOHNNY: I suppose you left your little girls alone. It's not often a bird will shit in its own nest. That's an old Indian saying or something.

GEORGE: I would have died before I let anything happen to my children.

JOHNNY: Children are so important. It's good you finally learned that. Better late than never, eh? "For I, the Lord, thy God, am a jealous god, visiting the iniquity of the fathers upon the children unto the third and fourth generations." That's your great-great-grandkids, Assistant Bishop King. That's a long time for your family to suffer because of your "iniquities." "Train up a child in the way he should go: and when he is old, he will not depart from it." Remember that? Basic residential school logic. The one who is hurt becomes the hurter. I'm glad my little Angela is with a good family far away from me, for that would be the last straw. I know the pain will end with me. Assistant Bishop King, I've got a question. Think you can answer it for me?

GEORGE: What?

JOHNNY: Catholic priests aren't allowed to marry or have sex. So, they got all these built-up, frustrated urges bouncing off the church walls. They got to do something with them, so they grab the nearest little girl, or boy, to get it out of their system. Maybe that's what's causing all their abuse problems, eh? I've heard people say that. But Anglican ministers, you guys can marry. You can fool around. You can even squeeze a boob without going to hell. And yet you still find the need to repeatedly diddle kids. Explain that to me?

GEORGE: I would if I could. I would if I were able. I would if I were responsible. But for the last time, you have the wrong man. At some point you're going to have to understand that and accept it.

JOHNNY: Turn the other cheek?

GEORGE: No. I agree that evil should be punished. Every man in this world has his own demons to fight. Some far worse than others. Why do people hurt children . . . I don't know. It's beyond me. Is it the Devil at work . . . I think people blame the Devil for too much and are afraid to take responsibility for their own actions.

JOHNNY: God made man in his own image. Does that make God a child diddler, then?

GEORGE: It's called free choice. Man makes his own choices. That was his greatest gift to us. And greatest curse.

JOHNNY: It depends on who has the free will. I certainly didn't. None of the kids at St. David's did. We couldn't do a damn thing. I don't think God likes Indians.

GEORGE: You are accusing God of being racist now.

JOHNNY: "In the beginning there was darkness, and God said, 'Let there be white.' And there was. And it was good."

GEORGE: He said, "Let there be *light*."

JOHNNY: Light. White. Right. Fright. Not much difference. And do you know what I find really funny? When good church people are faced with big, serious decisions in their lives, they say, "What would Jesus do?" I hope you weren't thinking that when you came for those evening visits all those years ago, Assistant Bishop King.

GEORGE: You will say anything, won't you? No matter how repulsive.

JOHNNY: Like I keep saying, I only know what I was told or shown. If you damn me, sir, you will damn me only for that. Then the fault is yours and St. David's.

GEORGE: You are blameless, then?

JOHNNY: No, sir. I am to blame for a lot of things. Too many things. Just ask whoever took care of Angela. I loved her with every part of me possible, and it wasn't enough. I had hurt her before I even knew she existed. And I go to bed knowing that every night. You see, I think hell is knowing everything you are responsible for. Blame . . . I have done a lot of things that I shouldn't have. I broke the law. Lied every which way possible. Sold myself. Stole. Hurt people. Practically everything the Ten Commandments told me not to do. It's not easy for a woman to stay alive on the streets. But us Native people, we have a really strong will to survive. You see, I think it comes down to the fact that the Church's will to destroy us was never as strong as our will to live.

Pause.

If you call this living.

GEORGE: Do you know they shut down St. David's? It's now just a ruin, a shell of a place. Maybe you should make a pilgrimage there. It might help you heal. Get rid of some of those—

JOHNNY: No. I don't think that would help.

GEORGE: You never know. It might.

JOHNNY: I think you've got the wrong idea. The school itself don't matter. It's just a brick building, a spiritless place that couldn't care less about Johnny Indian or Sammy Indian or anybody else. The Church don't have hands that touch you. It don't come to your room and hurt you. It don't lock doors. It don't sing songs. It don't make kids cry. But *people*—like you and other "servants of God"—are different. They have hands. They have tongues. They have cocks. They have needs. A building can't touch a kid. The people who work there can make kids cry. The Church was the gun, but you were the bullets.

They stare at each other as her words sink in.

GEORGE: I . . . I don't know how to respond to that . . .

Suddenly, JOHNNY once again seems wracked with pain. Moving away from GEORGE, she tries to make herself comfortable. GEORGE watches her closely.

JOHNNY: Shit, some of that free will sure comes back to haunt you.

GEORGE: You seem to be getting worse. Johnny, what are you going to do with me? At some point you are going to have to make a choice.

JOHNNY: What am I going to do with you? That is a good question. I don't know.

GEORGE: That's some master plan you have there.

JOHNNY: I got a short attention span. Every morning I wake up. That in itself is a good beginning. And then I'm just happy to make it through to nighttime. Usually that's a good day for me.

GEORGE: The gun. Where did you get the gun?

JOHNNY: I know. It's very American, isn't it? I found it. In the park. The same park where I lost Dick. Only I found this a lot more recently. The Lord did indeed provide, though I don't really think it's a fair trade.

GEORGE: That gun could have been used in a crime or something. You should turn it in to the police.

JOHNNY: One way or another, I'm sure it will find its way to the police. But I'm not done with it yet.

GEORGE: Do you even know how to use that thing?

JOHNNY: I remember my father going hunting. I'd watch him clean his gun after every trip. He let me shoot it once. Me, a five-year-old girl. Just about took my shoulder off. My mother chewed him out for that. Oh, was she angry. He just laughed.

GEORGE: Those were probably hunting rifles. That's a handgun. A very different weapon.

JOHNNY: I haven't remembered that in a long time. What do you know about guns?

GEORGE: Not much. But, like your father, I do know they need to be cleaned and oiled regularly. Especially if they've been left in parks. Dirt and dust can cause them to misfire. And somehow I don't think you have a gun-cleaning kit. You might end up doing yourself more damage than me if you decide to shoot that thing. Is that what you want? Give me the gun.

JOHNNY: I'll give you the bullet.

GEORGE: Very well.

Pause.

If you have a gun, why didn't you use it on those punks you said took your panhandling spot?

JOHNNY: I thought about it. Oh, that would have been so much fun, but there's only one bullet in this gun, and I wasn't going to waste it on them. I've been saving this bullet for a very long time.

GEORGE: I see.

Pause.

Well, I'm tired of all this. Do you mind if I pour myself a drink?

JOHNNY: If that's what you want.

GEORGE: What I want is to end this. But a drink will have to do until then.

JOHNNY: Isn't it a little early in the morning for you non-street people?

GEORGE: Right now I have enough adrenaline coursing through my body to do me for the day. A drink might help.

GEORGE pours himself a drink.

Are you thirsty? Can I offer you something?

JOHNNY: I smell coffee.

GEORGE: That I can provide. But we don't have any milk . . .

JOHNNY: Lots of sugar. My liver can still process all that stuff.

GEORGE sweetens the coffee and passes it to JOHNNY.

Mmm, good. It's not Tim Hortons, but it will do.

GEORGE: Look, Johnny, how long are we going to sit here staring at each other, making accusations and small talk? I was only planning to be here for an hour or so. Pretty soon, people will begin to miss me.

JOHNNY: Let's cross that bridge when we get to it, okay?

GEORGE: No. I've let you dictate this whole situation, say the most obscene things, but it's obvious you would be content to stay here all day waiting for me to confess—and it won't happen. The only possible outcome of this involves the police, who have a lot of their own weapons. They do not take kindly to people waving handguns around. I don't want you to be shot, Johnny. There are options.

JOHNNY: What options?

GEORGE: Give it up. The gun. This whole fiasco. Everything. Or kill me.

JOHNNY: Or kill you. Those are pretty limited options.

GEORGE: Those seem to be your only ones.

JOHNNY: Hey, I could shoot you in the crotch. The middle ground. You'd still be alive, but you'd be kinda unable to pitch. How do you feel about that?

GEORGE: Unenthusiastic.

JOHNNY: I could shoot myself. I could still do that.

GEORGE: No, Johnny. That, too, would be an unforgivable sin. Killing yourself is a grave offence, and an irreversible one.

JOHNNY: So, if you don't want me to shoot myself, I take it you'd rather have me shoot you? You religious people are weird.

GEORGE: We try to look at the big picture. With a little help, all things are possible. I know other people who have gone through what you have and who are managing to lead productive, happy lives. They are dealing with it.

JOHNNY: A thousand leaves can fall from the tree and they'll all land on the ground differently. I landed kind of hard.

GEORGE: All right then. Would you really shoot me, Johnny? If push came to shove, would you put a bullet through my head? Would that make the nightmares go away? Would it avenge Sammy and Angela? Would that make Johnny Indian sleep better? Would it?

JOHNNY: It's better than doing nothing. Something is always better than nothing.

GEORGE: I don't think you could do it. Pull the trigger.

JOHNNY: Oh, you do not want to play that game.

GEORGE: I think it is a game. I don't think you're serious. How do I know if you even have a bullet in that thing?

JOHNNY: It's not much use without one. I know that much. But if it is empty, I could always throw it at you. It is kind of heavy.

GEORGE: That's almost funny.

GEORGE drains his drink.

JOHNNY: Finished. Feel better?

GEORGE: A little. How are *you* feeling?

JOHNNY: Pretty good, all things considered. I see that light at the end of the tunnel.

GEORGE: Could be a train coming directly at you.

JOHNNY: Either way, it will be over.

GEORGE: Will it? How?

JOHNNY fires a bullet at the family photograph, nearly missing GEORGE, who reacts by falling over onto his back. He crawls away like a crab.

My God, Johnny! Why did you do that?!

JOHNNY: I don't think you believed me. That I would use this. I think you believe me now.

GEORGE: You're crazy!

JOHNNY: No . . . I think "dissociative" is the term they used to describe me once. Not quite sure what it means.

GEORGE: You . . . you . . . said you had only one bullet. You just used your one bullet. Ha!

JOHNNY: I lied. I have two. I think. No, it's three. See, can't remember shit these days, especially numbers. Never was good at math. Care to see if I got any bullets left?

GEORGE: No, no, I don't. But, Johnny, look at you. You're shaking. Sweating. I really wish you'd stop waving that gun around.

JOHNNY: All those years ago . . . you'd pretend to be nice to me, like you were my friend, then you'd hurt me. All these years you hoped I'd forgotten, but I didn't. It's been so long, you probably almost forgot.

GEORGE: I never hurt you, Johnny.

JOHNNY: Liar.

GEORGE: In my life I have committed many sins, but that is not one of them.

JOHNNY: Yes, you have! Yes, you have! Why won't you admit it? You're just afraid your wife and family will find out. That's it, eh? You don't want them to know. Or your bosses! You're just afraid, aren't you? Aren't you!

GEORGE: I'm not afraid.

JOHNNY: I can wait all day. All day.

GEORGE: You will have to wait a lot longer.

JOHNNY gets noticeably weaker. The last outburst seems to have sapped all her energy.

Though I don't think you can.

JOHNNY: I've waited over forty years. I can wait longer.

GEORGE: Johnny, unless you get some help, I doubt you'll see the end of the day—

JOHNNY: Stay away. I said that back then and I'm saying that now.

GEORGE: This can't be doing your condition any good.

Pause.

You know, there is a third way out of this.

JOHNNY: A third way? What third way?

GEORGE: I will be honest with you, Johnny. Yours is not the first allegation about St. David's.

JOHNNY: I knew it.

GEORGE: Reverend Anderson and Reverend LeBrett were under suspicion. Some allegations came forward in the late eighties. But Reverend Anderson died in '76 and Reverend LeBrett in '91. With them gone, there was little we could do. But we did try.

JOHNNY: You've been jerking me around. You knew all the time.

GEORGE: This is the first allegation against me. Remember LeBrett? He was young like me, and had the same kind of hair. Maybe it was him, Johnny. Maybe it was him.

JOHNNY: I don't believe anything you say.

GEORGE: We could open an internal investigation. As I said, we believe in cleaning up our own messes. We could launch an inquiry. You could testify. What do you think of that?

JOHNNY: You'd just lie. How many of you guys have actually gone to jail for what you've done?

GEORGE: I don't know.

Pause.

So I take it you're not interested in my suggestion?

JOHNNY: The fox would be watching the henhouse.

GEORGE: So it's a stalemate again.

JOHNNY: Help yourself to another drink. Maybe it will loosen your tongue. I remember how loose your tongue used to be.

GEORGE studies JOHNNY for a second and takes a deep breath.

GEORGE: Okay, I've had enough.

He stands up and straightens his clothes.

I'm leaving.

JOHNNY: You move and I will shoot.

GEORGE: Then shoot. Go ahead. I already told you I don't think you have it in you. It's easy to shoot a chair, but not a real person.

GEORGE walks to the door. JOHNNY points the gun at him, desperately trying to intimidate the man.

JOHNNY: I will! I will!

GEORGE: THEN DO IT!

GEORGE puts his hand on the doorknob and JOHNNY changes tactics. On the verge of tears, she turns the gun to her own head.

JOHNNY: You bastard! You fucking bastard! I'm not joking this time!

GEORGE stops. It looks like JOHNNY could really do it this time.

GEORGE: Johnny, take it easy.

JOHNNY: I'll do it! I swear I'll do it!

GEORGE backs away from the door. JOHNNY doesn't move.

GEORGE: There's no need to do this, Johnny. Everything's okay. I'll stay.

JOHNNY: It looks like you were right. I couldn't do it. I wanted to pull the trigger. I tried. I tried really hard. But . . .

GEORGE: It's okay, Johnny. I'm still here.

JOHNNY: You deserve to die. You all do. But I can't. I'm weak. I'm the one who's dead.

GEORGE: That's not true. Let me help—

JOHNNY: KEEP AWAY!

GEORGE backs away, placating her.

GEORGE: Okay! Okay. I could spend hours standing here trying to explain what happened in those schools, but it wouldn't make a difference. There is no excusing it. We both know that. But if you break something, you have two choices: you can walk away, forget about it, and let other people deal with it; or you can try and fix it.

JOHNNY: How do you fix a people? How are you going to fix me?

GEORGE: A hospital. Some counselling maybe, for a start. Just don't give up, Johnny.

JOHNNY: I won't. At least not yet. Not while we still have some unfinished business.

GEORGE: That business is finished.

JOHNNY: I will say this for you, Assistant Bishop King, you don't rattle easy.

GEORGE and JOHNNY both sit and wait. They are silent, motionless. The tension between them becomes uncomfortable.

GEORGE: This is ridiculous. You have no idea what to do now, do you?

JOHNNY: Oh, I know what to do. If you try to leave again, I will shoot. If not you, then me. Either way, you'll have to have your carpet cleaned.

Another long silence.

GEORGE: So what now, then?

JOHNNY: I'm thinking.

GEORGE: You're some hostage taker. The state you're in, I could just wait here until you pass out.

JOHNNY: I won't pass out. At least not until I get what I came for.

GEORGE: When you came in here, what exactly did you expect of me?

JOHNNY: I expected the truth.

GEORGE: You've got it. We're done.

JOHNNY: I expected that if you were truly as religious as you claim, you couldn't lie. Especially with him looking down on you.

JOHNNY stares intently at the painting of Christ.

He looks so kind. If he only knew . . .

GEORGE: He does know.

JOHNNY: When you see him, what are you going to tell him? To his face.

GEORGE: Everything I've said to you.

JOHNNY: You'd lie to the boss? Why stop now, eh?

GEORGE: Johnny . . .

JOHNNY: Assistant Bishop King . . .

GEORGE: What if I did confess?

JOHNNY: Yeah . . .

GEORGE: Would that stop the nightmares? If I admitted to everything you claimed I did, would it make you sleep at night? Would it make you put down the gun? Would that light at the end of the tunnel show you the way? Tell me, Johnny, if I said I abused you all those years ago, what would happen? What would change?

JOHNNY: What . . . ?

GEORGE: Okay. I did it. I was a terrible man. I did terrible things. I lied. I committed unspeakable sins. I tried not to hurt you, Johnny, I really did. I remember stroking your hair afterwards. Indian children always had such beautiful, shiny black hair. I'm sorry.

JOHNNY is shocked. She doesn't know how to respond.

JOHNNY: You don't believe that. You're just saying it.

GEORGE: Does it matter?

JOHNNY: Yes, it matters. Of course it matters. I don't want you to say it just to say it. I want to see the same pain in you that I see every day in myself. Don't lie to me, you bastard!

GEORGE: So, let me get this straight. You won't accept a denial and you won't accept a confession? I seem to be damned if I do and damned if I don't. What to do?

JOHNNY: I'll tell you what to do! Make me believe. Make Sammy believe you. Make Angela believe you.

GEORGE: I've tried. You won't believe anything I say or do. Kind of puts me in a difficult position.

JOHNNY: This is important to me. This is all I have. Don't play games!

GEORGE: That's what we've been doing all morning. I'm just calling it what it is. Here, let's play another game.

GEORGE uncorks one of the bottles.

JOHNNY: What are you doing?

GEORGE: Starting a new game. You seem to want to play. I want you to smell this.

He hands JOHNNY the bottle. She is confused.

What does it smell like?

JOHNNY: *(inhales)* It's . . . oranges!

GEORGE: Grand Marnier. It's a liqueur made from oranges. Quite tasty. Now, if I remember correctly, you mentioned something earlier about oranges, didn't you?

JOHNNY: You used them to bribe us.

GEORGE: I used oranges to bribe you.

JOHNNY won't let go of the bottle.

JOHNNY: I'd never had oranges before. They were so sweet and juicy. I remember them. That was so long ago. I haven't had an orange since. Bad memories, the things you made us do. Can't stand them now.

GEORGE: Johnny, you don't seem to be enjoying this game. Would you like to play something else?

JOHNNY: I once kissed Dick after he'd just eaten an orange. I almost threw up.

GEORGE: They can make liqueur out of just about everything. I once was given a bottle of something made from maple syrup, of all things. Very Canadian, I thought. Didn't taste like maple syrup at all. More like bad Scotch. This, however, still retains the flavour of oranges, don't you think?

JOHNNY: *(in tears)* I hate you.

GEORGE: Are you ready to put down the gun now?

JOHNNY weakens. Her resolve evaporates. She looks at the gun in her hand and sets it down on the desk.

That's a good girl. So, Johnny, it's been quite the exciting morning, eh? I guess that is something I should also apologize for. I believe what you say, Johnny, I really do. But it wasn't me. So now what should we do?

JOHNNY is silent.

So now you're quiet after chewing my ear off all morning.

GEORGE picks up the gun and examines it before tucking it in a drawer.

My goodness, this thing does have another bullet in it. I guess I owe you another apology for doubting you.

JOHNNY: It's over.

GEORGE: Yes, it is.

JOHNNY: You do owe me an apology. A real one. For Sammy. For Dick. For Angela. For me. It's got to end.

GEORGE: Oh for . . . let's not start that again, Johnny. Let's see what we can do about you now.

JOHNNY: You win. I can't make you confess. It's that free-will thing of yours.

GEORGE: It's not exactly mine. I will—

JOHNNY: I was no different with the gun. I forced you to confess.

GEORGE: But I have the gun now, so everything is all right. You're going to be okay. Now, to—

JOHNNY: I'm tired. I'm sick. I'm through with you. I don't need your confession anymore. I have all I need up here.

She points to her head.

It's all here. If you want to hide behind what you think you believe, then go ahead. I know the truth . . .

GEORGE: No, you don't. You just think you do.

JOHNNY: I'm going to leave now.

GEORGE: I don't think that's in your best interests, Johnny. You need help. Everything that's just happened proves it.

JOHNNY: Would you shoot me if I tried to leave?

GEORGE: Of course not.

JOHNNY: That's good to know.

GEORGE: Where will you go?

JOHNNY: Somewhere. There's nothing for me here.

GEORGE: I don't believe there's anything for you out there.

JOHNNY: Nothing out there ever hurt me as much as what's in here. I'll survive.

She puts on her jacket.

GEORGE: You're just going to wander the streets?

JOHNNY: For a while. And what will you do, Assistant Bishop King, once I walk out this door?

GEORGE: Maybe I'll follow you until you can't walk anymore. Then I'll get you to a hospital.

JOHNNY: I don't think you should. You might not like what you see.

GEORGE: I just can't let you walk out of here . . . the way you are. It wouldn't be right.

JOHNNY: It's a little late to be talkin' about what's right and wrong, isn't it?

JOHNNY sees the Bible on his desk.

You know, one thing I could never figure out. I don't remember anywhere in this thing it saying that Jesus ever laughed. Why is that?

GEORGE: It does say he wept. Wept for the children.

JOHNNY: I guess we know why, eh? I was taught that when God discovered he was alone, he created laughter. When man discovered he was alone, he created tears. My granny told me that once, a long time ago. Maybe. Who remembers . . .

GEORGE: That . . . Johnny, I remember somebody telling me that, too. A long time ago. I thought it was so beautiful. A young girl . . . her name was . . . what was it . . . Lucy?

Laughing painfully, JOHNNY *opens the door.*

JOHNNY: Very good. It's always nice to be remembered. I was named after my grandmother . . . an old woman in big, baggy skirts. That's what I remember. She smiled a lot. But she had more to smile about. And you, King David, I will leave you with whatever you hold important. But I know that you've lied. To me. To your family. To God. To yourself. That's gotta suck.

GEORGE: No, it doesn't. An impaired memory is not something I will feel guilty about.

JOHNNY: I could have killed you, you know, like I thought I was going to. *Bang*, and you would have been gone. But I didn't. That surprised even me. I guess in the end it wouldn't have really solved anything. Wanting and doing are two different things. Goodbye, Assistant Bishop King, I've got places to do, things to go . . .

GEORGE: Ka . . . Ka . . . Ka-wapamitin . . . Lucy.

JOHNNY *laughs.*

JOHNNY: No. No goodbyes. No Lucy. Johnny. Lucy's dead. She's been dead for a very long time. I'm a ghost, remember?

Pause.

Boo.

She exits through the door. GEORGE *begins to follow her, then changes his mind. Sitting down at his desk, he attempts to drink from his empty Scotch glass. Taking a deep breath, he opens the drawer to retrieve the gun, but mysteriously it's not there. He checks another drawer. The gun is gone. Puzzled, he turns toward the picture of Jesus and the children as the sound of children's voices and the hymn echo in his memory.*

Lights go down.

End.

A VERY POLITE GENOCIDE
OR THE GIRL WHO FELL TO EARTH

Melanie J. Murray

For Zelda Bea.
Despite everything, our past is a lesson in perseverance and hope.
I love you no matter what.

Acknowledgements

The playwright wishes to note that prior to the creation and development of this play she worked as a journalist interviewing elders and veterans, and the stories and cultural knowledge they shared deeply informed the creation of this script. She wishes especially to acknowledge the following people and organizations for their contributions and support: Nina Lee Aquino, Keith Barker, Tara Beagan, Per Brask, Christine Brouzes, Diane Cornet, Eugene Desjarlais, Diaspora Dialogues, Isidra Cruz, Spy Dénommé-Welch, Waawaate Fobister, Cara Gee, Grassroots News, Lawrence Guiboche, Catherine Hernandez, Sandra Laronde, Hope McIntyre, the Manitoba Metis Federation, the Manitoba Theatre for Young People, Jennilee Martineau, Josh Murray, Nine Circles Community Health Centre, Cheryl Lynn Plett, Yvette Nolan, Donna-Michelle St. Bernard, Rose Stella, and Helen Thundercloud.

This play was made possible in part by the support of the Manitoba Arts Council.

Monologues from *A Very Polite Genocide or The Girl Who Fell to Earth* were produced by Sarasvàti Productions, Winnipeg, Canada, at the International Women's Week Cabaret of Monologues on March 10, 2006. Creative credits were as follows:

Josie Pichette: Livia Dymond

Director: Hope McIntyre

A Very Polite Genocide or The Girl Who Fell to Earth was publicly workshopped at Factory Theatre, Toronto, Canada, as part of the 2006 CrossCurrents Festival on April 7, 2006. The cast was as follows:

Josie Pichette: Falen Johnson
Elder Martin Drunken Chief: Gary Farmer
Robbie Drunken Chief: Darrell Dennis
Young Martin Drunken Chief: Byron Abalos
Mary Barnabé (later Drunken Chief): Michaela Washburn
Rougarou/Alley: Waawaate Fobister
Dr. Baker: Valerie Buhagiar

Director and Dramaturg: Yvette Nolan
Set Design: Camellia Koo
Lighting Design: Aaron Kelly

A Very Polite Genocide or The Girl Who Fell to Earth was workshopped with Native Earth Performing Arts, Toronto, Canada, in August 2008. The cast was as follows:

Josie Pichette: Falen Johnson
Elder Martin Drunken Chief: Mike Bernier
Robbie Drunken Chief: Tyler Pennock
Young Martin Drunken Chief: Cliff Cardinal
Mary Barnabé (later Drunken Chief): Karyn Recollet
Rougarou/Alley: Jeremy Proulx
Dr. Baker/Gertrude Lett: Catherine McNally

Director and Dramaturg: Yvette Nolan
Assistant Director: Tara Beagan
Artistic Associate: Keith Barker
Music Composition and Performer: Alyssa Delbaere-Sawchuk

A Very Polite Genocide or The Girl Who Fell to Earth was premiered by Native Earth Performing Arts, Toronto, Canada on December 6, 2008, at Buddies in Bad Times Theatre. The cast was as follows:

Josie Pichette: Falen Johnson
Elder Martin Drunken Chief: Paul Chaput
Robbie Drunken Chief: Gordon White
Young Martin Drunken Chief: Simon Moccasin
Mary Barnabé (later Drunken Chief): Paula-Jean Prudat
Rougarou/Alley: Waawaate Fobister
Dr. Baker/Gertrude Lett: Catherine McNally

Director and Dramaturg: Yvette Nolan
Assistant Director: Tara Beagan
Set Design: Laird McDonald
Costume Design: Anna Treusch
Lighting Design: Michelle Ramsay
Music Composition and Performer: Jennilee Martineau
Choreographer: Waawaate Fobister
Stage Management: Stephanie Nakamura
Production Management: Michael Cuttini

Monologues from the script were produced by Sarasvàti Productions, Winnipeg, Canada at Women Through the Ages: In Monologue on October 28, 2011. Creative credits were as follows:

Josie Pichette: Siigwan Ferland

Director: Hope McIntyre

Notes

The set: The stage picture is constantly transitory—set pieces on wheels that glide fluidly in and out of place.

Rougarou: The werewolf of Metis legend. A derivative of the French-Canadian "loup garou," and the Cree shape-shifter figures. As is the case in Metis mythology, this script intertwines Rougarou with another mythic character—a black dog that appears out of nowhere, holds unearthly powers, and often embodies the trapped spirit of one who has done wrong and is trapped between this world and the next. From Agnes Pelletier (as recounted in the introduction to *Metis Legacy II: Michif Culture, Heritage and Folkways*): "And what they said years ago was: 'You have to draw blood from this dog. If you drew blood from this dog then you saved a soul.' This is what they used to say, that's how you saved a person's soul, and then when you saved this person's soul, they'd tell you 'Thank you.' They'd really appreciate it."

Characters

Josie Pichette: 2000s character, granddaughter of Martin and Mary

Elder Martin Drunken Chief: 2000s character

Robbie Drunken Chief: 1980s character, son of Martin and Mary

Young Martin Drunken Chief: 1940s–50s character, husband of Mary

Mary Barnabé (later Drunken Chief): 1940s–50s character, wife of Martin

Rougarou: timeless character, shifts: human, black dog, werewolf

Alley: 1980s character, played by the actor who plays Rougarou

Dr. Baker: 1980s and 2000s character

Gertrude Lett: 1950s character, played by the actor who plays Dr. Baker

Voice of Rose

Guy's Voice

Lights up: ELDER MARTIN, *in the 2000s, at the youth centre, sitting in a sharing circle.*

ELDER MARTIN: I'm not too sure about this . . . I've never sat in circle before. But the guys at the centre keep ribbing me. How I keep sending kids to circle, but I don't ever come myself. So I guess it's my turn? And I'm supposed to tell all my bad feelings, right? We could be here all night! Look. I want to start by giving you all a song, okay?

ELDER MARTIN *begins to fiddle—plaintive, slightly off-beat.*

As he plays, JOSIE *becomes present in an overlapping moment: a university classroom, the 2000s.*

JOSIE: My project's title is "A Very Polite Genocide: The Devastation of the Metis" . . . in a report from . . .

She shuffles through her index cards.

Uh . . .

She shuffles more.

I'm sorry.

She starts to cry.

I . . . I'm not sure . . . if I can . . . I don't know what I'm doing . . . Oh God.

She fights to maintain composure.

I'm sorry. Okay. Okay. Okay . . .

She returns to her notes.

In the world's eyes, Canada is seen as a First World nation, while Aboriginal Canadians live in Third World conditions. According to Amnesty International, Canada has the third-best standard of living of all countries, while we drop to twenty-sixth place if the status of only our Aboriginal population is considered.

ELDER MARTIN: I know what you want. I know why Dave told me I had to come. He saw in the paper, that guy Robbie who used to come here, they found him. And I told Dave, way back a long time ago, Robbie was my blood. My son. I didn't want to tell him. But he kept questioning why I keep asking after this one guy. He was supposed to keep that . . . I know you all know. I know he was showing that paper all around. There aren't that many Drunken Chiefs. I know that's why you all paid for him to be cremated. "In a nice box," Dave says. "With an announcement, and viewing, in case anyone, *anyone*, wants to pay their respects." But I say it's over, so forget it. If I open up, I'll pour my guts out all over the floor. You don't want that mess. You don't. So, I told Dave I've got to quit working here, but he says the centre needs an elder too bad to just let me go. So, I'll tell you a story. It's a story told to me by no one, and it's one no one tells. It's something I don't understand, but maybe in the telling it'll make sense.

JOSIE: I'm sorry . . . I . . .

She rubs her hands, looks at them, and breathes deeply.

The United Nations definition of genocide: "the following acts committed with intent to destroy, in whole or part, a national, ethnic, racial or religious group, including:

killing members of the group;
causing serious bodily or mental harm to members of the group;
deliberately inflicting on the group conditions of life calculated to bring about its physical destruction in whole or part;
imposing measures intended to prevent births within the group; forcibly transferring children of the group to another group."

Canadians . . . We Canadians hear about genocide, and think it's something that happens somewhere else. What I intend to prove is genocide happens here. In a way so subtle it's easy to deny. Maybe . . . maybe it's planted inside us?

Shift to a small downtown apartment, the mid-1950s. YOUNG MARTIN *faces* MARY, *who is visibly pregnant and crying with her back turned to him.*

YOUNG MARTIN: Mary. Mary. I wish you wouldn't cry. All you do is cry. Look. I've got to go. I wish you'd look at me. I wish you'd . . . Mary! Mary. Look. *Look at me!* I'll try to write. I don't know how long it'll take for a letter to get to here from Korea. But when I can. Mary. Don't be like this. Can't you be strong for me? Can't you . . .

MARY: Me be strong. Why don't you be strong? Why don't you stay?

YOUNG MARTIN: I'm going.

MARY: They've been taking babies. They're going to take the baby, and maybe Robbie too, if you're not here.

YOUNG MARTIN: That's not true. It's just a story.

MARY: They've been taking them and you know it, Martin. What will I do with you not here? Will I say, "Oh yeah, I learnt real good in the residential how to be a mum? Oh yeah, the kids will be just fine without a dad?"

YOUNG MARTIN: Mary. You know I love you. Katha matoo . . .[1]

MARY: Don't you use those words. Those words aren't for you to use anymore.

YOUNG MARTIN: I'm going.

MARY: The priests taught you to bend over, but they didn't teach you to be a man.

A shift: the same small downtown apartment, the 2000s. JOSIE, cleaning with bleach, finds something written on the cupboard.

JOSIE: *(reading)* "They killed me." They killed me.

She takes the bleach, pours more onto her rag, and scrubs. It won't come off. She closes it, steps away, and then goes back.

"They killed me."

She takes the phone, dials.

Hi. It's me. I was just feeling . . . Give me a call, when you have the time.

JOSIE takes out a baggie of pot, rolls a joint. ROUGAROU appears, prowling on slowly, until JOSIE sees him, startles, and backs away. He snarls at her until she shifts out of the apartment into the classroom. ROUGAROU disappears. JOSIE continues her presentation.

Blood memory. The encoding of the past into our blood, our bones, our DNA. Handed over from one generation to another. We talk about this like it's history—something to be taken out, looked at, and put back on a shelf. Something not a part of us. But what if it's never over?

---

1 Cree: Don't cry.

The government began dismantling residential schools, and instead took children from their parents—often without consent or through deception—and placed them with adoptive non-Aboriginal families. My mother was . . . The children faced cultural and identity confusion and didn't fit anywhere. I. They . . .

A shift: a downtown street corner, the early 1980s. A car screeches away. ROBBIE *staggers on, bleeding and struggling to pull up his underwear and pants.*

ROBBIE: Motherfucking bullshit! Goddamn, fucking everything. Fuck!

He falls to the ground and stays there.

Fuck. Fuck.

A shift: the apartment. MARY *is scrubbing her floor.*

MARY: I said I want you to read it all to me.

GERTRUDE: "And it is my wish they remain in the care of the Children's Aid Society." It says, "I understand the . . . " Solemnity? No . . . "context and meaning," I'm sorry—the wording is "context and meaning . . . of the permanent commitment . . . to the . . . to the guardianship of the Children's Aid Society." Sign here.

MARY: My wish?

GERTRUDE: They'll be taken care of, which is every mother's want. You want the best for your children, so you're agreeing to their care. It's a gift. You're giving them a gift!

MARY: Do you have children, Mrs. Lett?

GERTRUDE: How is that relevant?

MARY: You come here like you're omnipotent—which the church teaches belongs only to God—and tell me what my wishes are. You say nothing of my rights should I not fit in the tidy package of what your form dictates "my" wishes to be. That's how it's relevant.

GERTRUDE: Whether it's relevant or not, it's none of your business. It's personal.

MARY: It's been personal for me from the start! You come into my home. I'm here, making lace I learned to make at the government school so I can decorate my baby's clothes the way *your* people's ancestors admired. In return, I'm asking you to spare me the courtesy. I want to know if you're a woman or a machine, so please be so kind as to tell me, personally, what you think of this situation? Then—*then*—we can talk.

GERTRUDE: I'm a mother, I am. All right? I walk in here, and think, "Is this what you would want?" I would never want my child to set foot in this. My children? All children! I want to keep all children a million miles away from this life.

MARY: This life?

GERTRUDE: This life. You have no family. I stepped over animal or human waste just down the hallway from your apartment. It's the circumstances, dear. No one would blame you for leaving this life behind. Sign here. Then I'll go. Here! Would you like help to write it? If you would prefer, you're free to mark an "x." Mark an "x," please. That's simple. Here—on this line. This line. Right here. Please. Or if you aren't able then let me. Let me do it for you. Let me help you. Help them. Here.

She marks an "x."

There. There!

A shift: the 2000s. ELDER MARTIN *is sitting in circle.*

ELDER MARTIN: I just worked in the kitchen, but then the younger guys tell me I should be the centre's elder. "I'm not an elder," I said. But Dave says I'm one of the Ahneegay-kaashigakick—"the ones who know." And I told him, "I don't know anything." And he said, no, the kids who come around need to know how I made it in the city. That whatever I did to make it in one piece—that's an important thing to share. He starts calling me Elder Martin, and next thing you know he sits this kid down across from me—tells me he's all mixed up. He's "at risk." The kid, Ryan, he's got tattoos all over him, so I show him the ones I got in the service. I try talking to him, only I can't think of any examples of how to be good. So I say, "I knew this guy once, and he was real messed up," only "this guy" was me and I'm still messed up. "I knew this guy, once who had it good . . . "

A shift: outside a church, MARY *comes tearing in, shrieking with joy—she is wearing a simple veil.*

MARY: *(shouting to offstage)* Come on!

She waits.

Come on!

She lifts up her dress and playfully displays a bit of leg. YOUNG MARTIN *runs on, wearing a suit, carrying a camera. They embrace and kiss.*

YOUNG MARTIN: I love you. I love you, I love you, I love you.

He fumbles with the camera.

MARY: The light *is* good.

YOUNG MARTIN: The light *is* good. *You* said it would rain. But I told you it would be good. Didn't I?

MARY: Neee.

YOUNG MARTIN: Didn't I?

MARY *laughs, throwing her arms around him.*

MARY: Ki-sa-gee-ee-tin oo-ma, my good man.[2] My good, good man.

YOUNG MARTIN: Maybe we should honeymoon at Duck Lake—I could finally meet your mama and she could teach you to render skunk fat!

MARY: Martin, don't talk of those things.

YOUNG MARTIN: I'm sorry I didn't take you home to get married. I know it's not the old way, but it's for love, and that's what matters.

MARY: Don't. Don't, okay? It's a happy day today.

YOUNG MARTIN: Okay. Okay.

Beat.

Hey, let's go take some pictures over in that park, eh? We can take our shoes off and dance in the grass. Come on, Mrs. Drunken Chief. Come on!

He bounds off and she follows, giving a quick pinch to his bum as they exit.

A shift: ELDER MARTIN *is sitting in circle.*

ELDER MARTIN: So I tell Ryan about the service. How when you sign up, there are guys, if they passed you or me on the street back home, they'd look right through you, but when their asses are on the line, how they treat us all like brothers. He's listening real good, and says, "I like you, and I want you to tell me what to do—how to get on the right track." Only I want to tell him I can't.

A shift: ROBBIE, *the early 1980s, cold, in the street, near a phone booth, and* JOSIE, *the 2000s, in the apartment, asleep and surrounded by bleach, rags, and a blinking answering machine. She wakes, looks at her hands, and washes them.*

JOSIE: One, two, three, four, five. One, two, three, four, five.

2 Cree: I love you, my good man.

Beat.

Okay. Okay.

She sees there's a message, hits play.

GUY'S VOICE: Hey, Jo, sorry I didn't call you back. We're all doing the usual Friday night thing. You can come if you want. Maybe I'll see you. Or whatever.

JOSIE starts to cry. She goes to the sink, washes her hands more aggressively.

JOSIE: One, two, three, four, five. Stop. Stop it. One, two, three, four, five. One, two, three, four . . .

She continues as the phone rings and the machine clicks on.

ROSE'S VOICE: Josie? It's your mother. I'm calling to tell you your mail's still coming here. We got a letter for you from the university. It says you're failing all your classes! All but one! It says you have a B in something called "Aboriginal Studies . . . " I don't know what . . .

JOSIE picks up the phone.

JOSIE: I'm here, Mom. Hi. You shouldn't be opening my mail. Because it's none of your business. Listen. I'm dropping out, okay? No. I said no. I'm going to keep taking the one course I'm not failing, and I'm dropping the rest. I . . . There's no point! You never want to hear it. You make me feel awful. These things hurt. Hello?!

She hangs up.

Damn it. Okay. Okay.

She washes her hands.

One, two, three, four, five. One, two, three, four, five.

She goes to the phone, dials.

Hi, Mom. It's me. Don't pick up. I just want to say, I wish I could talk to you. Do you ever wonder what that other life might have been? I lost those things too. Parts of who I am. I'm going to start looking. I look at my skin, and I know there's a story. Oh. Hello?

She hangs up.

ROBBIE: Hey, can I get the number for Rose Pichette? *(spelling)* P-I-C-H-E-T-T-E. Okay. Well her husband's name is Albert—Albert Pichette? Good. Thank you. Hi, is this Rose? Hi, Rose, this is Robbie. How are you? Yeah? Yeah, definitely. I'm sorry to call this late. Oh, that's good. Oh, okay I'll speak up. I'm calling from a pay phone actually. Happy holidays, right? I'll get right to the point, okay? I know we only met a little while ago, but I was glad to finally meet you. So, since you're my "long lost" sister and everything, I was wondering if you'd mind if I came for a visit? Yeah, that'd be nice too. I'd like that, but, actually, I meant tonight. I understand this is a little weird, but . . . But I promise I'd stay out of the way.

Beat.

Yeah, I understand. It's okay. Sure. So your kid's okay? Yeah, well that sounds really good to me. I guess you've always had that kind of life though, eh? Sure. Hey, listen, Rose, Merry Christmas, eh? If I don't see you? Okay.

He hangs up.

The phone rings in the apartment, JOSIE doesn't pick up and the answering machine clicks on.

ROSE'S VOICE: Josie, it's your mother. Listen. When you were little, I found my brother, Robbie Drunken Chief. I met him, and after, he kept calling and I was glad when he stopped. He's not worth knowing. He has problems. You know how Indians are, with their drinking and drugs.

ROBBIE exits.

We don't need that. We're good people. That's all I want. For you to be good. Don't tell other people about . . . If they know we're Indians, they'll . . .

As the machine cuts out, ROUGAROU *appears, rearranging the set to reveal a funeral home with a photo of* ROBBIE *and a small container of ashes. He approaches* JOSIE*, grabs her, and forces her into the funeral home. She takes to the floor, where she lies frozen. He sniffs at her then slips away.* JOSIE *takes in the Polaroid and the funeral home.*

JOSIE: Robbie Drunken Chief. I came to put the pieces together.

A shift: MARY *in the downtown apartment, writing.*

MARY: Auntie Agnes. Thank you for writing to me for Maman. It's been almost a month now since Martin left for the service. The people from the government came and took Robbie. When my daughter was born, they took her too. I never got to hold her or look into her eyes. They said I couldn't possibly know how to raise my babies. My breasts ache and leak. My body knows how to be a mother. This Christmas will not be . . . This Christmas . . .

MARY *goes to the cupboard, opens it, and* ROUGAROU *is there. She closes then reopens it. He's gone. She takes out a bottle and drinks a large slug straight from it, gasps, takes another slug, gasps, takes another, and gasps.* MARY *rips up the letter and closes her eyes.* ROUGAROU *enters through the cupboard, and approaches slowly. Her eyes stay closed as he slips his arms around her in a sexual way. His hand/paws slide along her body. He sniffs at her breasts as he slips down to the ground, pulling her down with him, and then exits, leaving her behind.* MARY *rises, takes up a new page.*

Dear Auntie Agnes: Thank you for writing to me for Maman. It sounds like her eyesight is fading much quicker now. Please tell her I miss her, and I've decided to come home for Christmas and will stay to care for her. There's nothing for me in Winnipeg anymore, and I'll be coming as soon as I can.

A shift: the 2000s, a clinic examination room. DR. BAKER *enters carrying a box of files. She pulls out her cellphone and dials.*

DR. BAKER: Hi, George? Hi. So, my answer is "yes." It'll be hard to say goodbye. You were here five, and *that* was a long time. I'm the only one left from the original staff! The only one! I wish I could say "mission accomplished," but really, I'm waving the white flag. But . . . do you think . . . George, listen: Am I selling out? You're right. You're right. I've done my time. I've done more than my time. Patients come, they're fucked up, I can't fix them—the best I can do is mild alleviation. I want to say, "Come on! Can't you just take care of yourself? Like, basic hygiene. Like, maybe *don't* share needles. Hey, maybe *don't* kill yourself." But you know what? I'm done! I'm done. It'll be like vacation. How many of your patients come in caked in their own excretions? Babies don't count! Because they don't smell like a forty-year-old who hasn't bathed in a month thawing out! I'm awful. I'm awful, right? I haven't had a life! A life! I held out longer than most! Longer than you! Okay. Okay. But I'm still a do-gooder. We're talking about fostering a kid. No really.

JOSIE enters, holding a clipboard.

Hey, I've got to go. I'll put in my notice and then we're set! Okay. Great. Bye.

(to JOSIE) Hi. I'm Dr. Baker. I'll take that—you sit there.

She does.

So . . .

Josie, what I can I do for you?

JOSIE: Well, I was headed back to my apartment from class, and then I was on the ground, in a flowerbed. I was lying in the dirt and snow, and I'd lost time. I fell out of time. I was walking and then I was down, looking up at the sky, and people were staring at me. One of them said there was a clinic here . . .

DR. BAKER: And how are you feeling now?

JOSIE: I'm okay.

DR. BAKER: Have you been drinking or taking drugs today?

JOSIE: What? No.

DR. BAKER: No?

JOSIE: No.

DR. BAKER: You can be straight with me. If you tell me you're using drugs, I don't go to the police or anything, yes?

JOSIE: No. No. Listen, I'm not . . . I'm not like that. The people in your lobby? I'm not like them. I would never come to this clinic. I don't live downtown. I go to university. I'm not Aboriginal. I'm not a drunk or a drug addict or anything like that. I'm in pre-med! I'm in pre-med, okay?

DR. BAKER: I didn't mean to offend you.

JOSIE: I just thought this was serious, so I came straight here, but if it's . . .

DR. BAKER: No, no, you're right. Losing consciousness is serious. What else?

JOSIE: Well, one of the people said I was twitching—like a seizure or something.

DR. BAKER: And you've never had a seizure or fainting spells before?

JOSIE: No. Never.

DR. BAKER: Family history of seizures or epilepsy?

JOSIE: I don't know. I mean . . . my mom was adopted, so I don't know about that side. There's this void, but . . . I . . . I'm all right now.

DR. BAKER: Are you?

JOSIE: I'll see my family doctor.

DR. BAKER: Fine.

JOSIE: No offence. Sorry.

DR. BAKER: Fine.

JOSIE: Okay. Thank you.

She goes to leave, hesitates.

I didn't mean to . . .

DR. BAKER: You know you could be Aboriginal.

JOSIE: What?

DR. BAKER: You said your mother was adopted. You said, "I'm not Aboriginal, I'm not a drunk or a drug addict." And I take offence to that.

JOSIE: I'm leaving.

DR. BAKER: Be my guest.

JOSIE exits.

Goddamn it.

She takes out her phone.

Hey, George, it's me again. When you get this, call me. Listen, I'm . . . I probably just need a pep talk, but . . . I don't know. Just . . . Call me, okay?

A shift: the street, ALLEY waits for a john. It's cold, and s/he smokes. ROBBIE appears.

ALLEY: Hey.

ROBBIE: Hey.

ALLEY: It's so fucking cold.

ROBBIE: Yeah.

ALLEY: Yeah.

ROBBIE: Hey, could I bum a smoke?

ALLEY: This is my last one.

ROBBIE: Oh.

ALLEY: I haven't seen you in a while.

ROBBIE: It's dead out tonight.

ALLEY: Sure.

ROBBIE: You know you still owe me that money, right?

ALLEY: Oh, for fuck's sake, Robbie!

ROBBIE: I'm just sayin'.

ALLEY: Okay.

ROBBIE: Okay.

Beat.

'Cause I know a guy. And we could get some stuff. And I'm meeting him later on.

ALLEY: Yeah?

ROBBIE: Yeah. In a couple hours, out back of the Paradise.

ALLEY: Well if I get any business, maybe.

Beat.

You hear how that girl went missing?

ROBBIE: What girl?

ALLEY: Some girl. It was in the news. She disappeared.

ROBBIE: Yeah?

ALLEY: And a couple of weeks ago, this other girl I sort of knew too.

ROBBIE: That's too bad.

ALLEY: Are you taking care of yourself?

ROBBIE: What's that got to do with anything?

ALLEY: People go missing. People with brown skin that no one cares to look for. Girls have been going missing. More than one. Not OD'ing, not straightening out. Just falling off the face of the Earth. Girls are falling off the face of the Earth.

ROBBIE: So?

ALLEY: So?

ROBBIE: Fuck the girls.

ALLEY: Oh? Fuck me? Fuck me?

ROBBIE: Not a chance.

ALLEY: Am I supposed to be hurt?

Beat.

Look, all I'm saying is we should look out for each other. Maybe we should check in every once in a while? You know. Keep track of each other. Keep track of each other's track marks?

ROBBIE: I don't need a fucking girlfriend!

ALLEY: Oh, fuck you!

ROBBIE: You're such a fucking scavenger. The last thing I want is a tranny-whore chaperone.

Exiting.

You better get me my fucking money!

ALLEY: Nice to see you too! Prince-fucking-charming.

A shift: outside a formal dance, the music gets momentarily louder as YOUNG MARTIN charges on, kicking or knocking over chairs and any furniture in his path.

YOUNG MARTIN: Motherfucking bullshit! Goddamn, fucking everything!

Continuing to knock the furniture about.

Fuck! Fuck! Fuck!

As he continues to kick or toss furniture around, MARY enters and watches him until he stops and stands, panting.

MARY: Umm . . . Hi?

YOUNG MARTIN freezes.

Umm . . . I'm uh . . . sorry. If you . . . if you want a ticket? I just left to go to the ladies' room, but I'm . . . I'm selling tickets . . . so . . . if you want one . . . you can have one? Or you can just go in . . . You can just go in? I won't tell anyone. Do you wanna just go in? 'Cause, I don't mind? Okay? You could just go in. Or . . . or . . . I could just go? Because . . . if you want . . .

YOUNG MARTIN: *(grunting)* Don't.

MARY: I'm sorry?

YOUNG MARTIN: Don't go.

MARY: Oh . . . I . . .

YOUNG MARTIN: You don't have to. Sorry.

He sees the mess he's made and begins to pick things up. MARY *also rights a chair, etc., until all is restored.*

Sorry.

Beat.

Sorry.

MARY: It's okay. Okay. Are you . . . okay?

YOUNG MARTIN: You ever notice how if you say a word enough it stops sounding like a word? Okay, okay, okay.

MARY: Okay, okay, okay. Yeah, that's true, I guess.

Beat.

It's been more than an hour since I sold a ticket. It's queer how they're having a dance for us even though they don't really want us to dance. Hey listen, you're from St. Michael's—you played fiddle at the Easter concert, right?

When I peeked inside your Father Lacombe was walking around on patrol like a soldier. I heard he told the band they can't play any slow songs.

YOUNG MARTIN: Father Lacombe's a faggot.

MARY: I beg your pardon?

YOUNG MARTIN: Sorry. I'm . . . sorry. I don't talk to girls much. Sorry.

MARY: Martin Drunken Chief, right?

YOUNG MARTIN: Right.

MARY: I'm Marié-Angelique Barnabé. From St. Mary's . . . Mary from St. Mary's. Pleased to make your acquaintance.

She extends her hand to him, but he doesn't take it.

YOUNG MARTIN: You know, you're pretty brave to just hold out your hand like that after you just saw me go crazy.

MARY: I've seen worse.

YOUNG MARTIN: Have you?

MARY: Sure.

YOUNG MARTIN: Where?

MARY: Well . . . most fights—there's two people, you know?

YOUNG MARTIN: Yeah.

MARY: But look at you now, right? You and the chair have made up and now you're good friends!

YOUNG MARTIN: Yeah.

He offers his hand, which she shakes.

Pleased to make your acquaintance, Mademoiselle Marié.

MARY: Likewise. Everyone calls me Mary, actually.

YOUNG MARTIN: Mary, eh? So why aren't you in there with the other girls?

MARY: 'Cause I don't like them and they don't like me.

YOUNG MARTIN: Really? Why wouldn't they like you?

MARY: 'Cause Sister Pierrette always favours me because I'm a halfbreed and my skin's not so dark, so somehow she thinks maybe then I'm just a little more likely to be "saved." She's always giving me stupid little duties like this one. The other girls, they see me, see her being "nice" to me, and it makes them suspicious or angry or both.

YOUNG MARTIN: There's lots of halfbreeds at my school. They treat you bad no matter who you are at St. Michael's.

MARY: Both my parents are Michifs from Duck Lake. When I was little, Maman, her sisters, and Kohkom only spoke Cree to me, and Dad and his brothers spoke Michif and French. So I thought there was one language for women and another for men. Maybe that's still true, right? When I first came, the nuns didn't like any of those languages and hit me pretty hard with a ruler. My maman says her father's the town priest, so I have one up on them! I think she's joking, but sometimes she says things like they're funny so they don't cut so deep, you know? My dad fishes along the lake, but I don't ever get to see him anymore 'cause he has to leave before school's out for summer . . . Jeeze, I'm going on and on, and you probably think I'm just a shitty halfbreed now, right?

YOUNG MARTIN: Why would I think that?

MARY: Lots of boys spit on halfbreed girls.

YOUNG MARTIN: Oh, yeah? Well lots of my friends are halfbreeds, only they're too stupid to admit it, and I don't even know my roots, so who knows, eh? I have cousins here at school, and they say my mom died and my dad and grandpa took all my brothers and sisters to hide when they came to force us into school. They say I was left with them 'cause I was too young to go into the bush, so when I was old enough, my uncle sent me to school along with all my cousins 'cause a priest convinced him it was for the best.

MARY: Listen, Sister's gonna be by to check on me soon, and if she catches me alone with a boy I'll be stuck saying the rosary so many times my mouth'll fall off.

YOUNG MARTIN: You're right, I'd better go. I got in trouble and Father Lacombe said I was supposed to wait in the bus. I can't believe he's not out here yet either.

YOUNG MARTIN goes to leave.

MARY: Hey, Martin?

YOUNG MARTIN: Yeah?

MARY: Do you want to run away with me?

YOUNG MARTIN: What?!

MARY: I was actually going to go run away. I have a bag hidden around back, then I felt bad about taking the cash box so I came to put it back. I'm thinking we'd get along better if there were two of us. Do you want to? We don't have much time.

YOUNG MARTIN: Okay!

MARY: Okay. Okay! Let's go!

They run off.

A shift: JOSIE *is in the classroom.*

JOSIE: Stats Canada figures indicate our country's Aboriginal population experiences life expectancies five years shorter than all other Canadians.

The United Nations definition of genocide:

killing members of the group;
causing serious bodily or mental harm to . . .

Did I already . . . ?

Beat.

Assimilate: "to absorb; to make part of oneself; to be absorbed." I'm not feeling well. This is not who I am. I get As. But am I . . . What if I'm the successful product of this?

ROUGAROU appears. JOSIE sees him. They dodge each other until she is again pushed to the funeral home. He slips off.

There's a photograph of a group of students at the school Mary went to. Mary . . . your mother . . . my grandmother. I don't really know what she looked like—but I imagine she's there. I look at the faces. All the girls sit in rows. They're all looking at the camera. Any one of them could be her. They each have the same bob haircut; they're all holding their readings, and they all have the same expression. They have contempt and loss in their faces. They're apprehensive, and it's easy to tell, just below the surface, they're at war, and they're looking the enemy right in the eye.

A shift: ROBBIE *in a prison cell. His cellmate lies with his back to the audience, curled and covered.*

ROBBIE: Hey, Joe?

Beat.

You all right?

Beat.

Come on, man, I know you're awake . . . You okay? You'll be okay. They got you good, eh?

Beat.

Bet you miss your mom even more now. Remember how you cried and cried like a little boy your first night? Tellin' me all about how disappointed you made her? You'll be glad when she shows up for her visit next week. You can hold on to that to make it through the hours. Maybe when you see her face it'll feel like home. Like a little piece of home? Some people are like that. Like you can make a home for yourself in their heart.

I got fostered with this really religious couple when I was sixteen. They weren't bad people, just cold. When I talked to them, I could see their eyes shut down. But their son, George—he was a bit older and didn't live with them—one day he came for dinner. He was really tall and his eyes kind of twinkled. He was like magic. He talked to me like I was a real person. And when I talked, I could tell he was listening. I wasn't just some fucked-up Indian kid to him. I could tell that right away. He was all asking me questions about what I thought about politics and what I thought about the foster system. After dinner he convinced his folks to let him take me to the movies. I remember being in his car and I was stealing glances at his face—his profile. The whole way to the movies, I just wanted to look at him. He had big lips like pillows—they looked so soft. You know, I don't even know what movie it was. I just remember sitting beside him in the theatre and feeling the heat of his body in the next seat. It was like electricity, and feeling like I was going crazy. And I just wanted to memorize what it felt like to be sitting next to this guy.

After, we get into his car and he says I look like I don't really want to go home. And I say he's right. And then I can't believe it, because he's leaning in, and he's kissing me, and he puts his arms around me. Those pillowy lips and the rub of his stubble. And he's touching me. And . . . And . . .

Beat.

And, oh god, you know? I hadn't ever been touched before. Not really. So, George, when he touched me, it felt like . . . like fire and magic—or, I don't know what. 'Cause there aren't any words for it. And he's touching me, and he's holding me, and it's so impossible, and it's too good, and I start to shake so hard, and he's just holding me, and holding me, and the snot starts getting all clogged up in my nose, but I just don't care, and he's not asking for anything in return, and I can hear his heart beating in my ear, and he's so warm, and . . . And then suddenly it feels like home. It just feels like home. And the world feels new and like maybe my life's not all going to shit.

Beat. ROBBIE *gets up.*

Joe? You sleeping now?

Touches him.

Joe?

ROBBIE*'s cellmate stirs and is revealed to be* ROUGAROU. *The pair "recognize" each other.* ROUGAROU *slowly moves to stand, revealing a knife. They slowly circle each other.* ROUGAROU *makes a cut along his hand/paw—blood flows. He holds the knife out and* ROBBIE *takes it, cutting himself in the same way.* ROUGAROU *offers his bloody hand to* ROBBIE, *who takes it with his own.* ROUGAROU *enfolds* ROBBIE *in his arms, embracing him.* ROBBIE *at first resists the embrace, then settles into it.* ROUGAROU *guides* ROBBIE *to the cot.* ROBBIE *sleeps.* ROUGAROU *exits.*

A shift: the downtown apartment. MARY *is unpacking.* YOUNG MARTIN *quietly enters, hiding something behind his back. He sneaks up slowly behind her, shadowing the previous entrance of the* ROUGAROU *in his previous scene with her.* MARY *doesn't see* YOUNG MARTIN *as he moves in closer, eventually tapping her shoulder.*

MARY: Zayzeu![3] What are you doing creeping around all quiet? What have you got back there?

---

3 Michif: Jesus!

He dodges so she can't see. She whips him with a towel.

YOUNG MARTIN: Hey!

MARY: Hey yourself! What are you hiding back there?

They dodge around each other—it becomes a game. Eventually YOUNG MARTIN *swings out the fiddle he's been hiding and starts to play.*

Hey!

YOUNG MARTIN: *(over his playing)* It was for sale at the pawn shop! I got it cheap! I thought it'd be a nice house-warming gift.

YOUNG MARTIN *starts to dance while playing and* MARY *joins him. They enjoy dancing. It becomes a full-out jig—*MARY *dances the steps of the Red River Jig. They cheer, scream, and continue dancing, stamping, and fiddling, increasing in volume until* ROBBIE *wakes and pounds on his bed.*

ROBBIE: Shut the fuck up!

YOUNG MARTIN *and* MARY *stop.*

MARY: *(panting)* Welcome to the neighbourhood, eh? Guess the walls are pretty thin. Guess we'll have to be quiet tonight too.

YOUNG MARTIN *begins playing a soft, slow song.* ROBBIE *sleeps.*

YOUNG MARTIN: Ah, don't let that jerk bother you, my sweet. Whoever he is, he's all alone tonight and I've got you. And you're the prettiest thing for miles around. *(of the fiddle)* It's pretty good—way better than the one I had at school.

MARY: You'd better put that thing down and kiss me, you big moose.

He does.

A shift. ELDER MARTIN *is sitting in circle in silence. He lifts his fiddle and plays a bit of the tune from Neil Young's "Helpless," then stops.*

ELDER MARTIN: The boy—Ryan's sitting there, all smiles, like he's ready to sign up for Bold Eagle the next day. And I can't stand it. If he knew any more about me, he'd hate me. I tell him I don't want to talk anymore. I tell him he should do whatever he wants, 'cause things don't get better. He looks at me, and I can see he really sees, and then he turns and goes.

A couple weeks after, we found that little kid in the basement with his pants down and head smashed in. The police are there and they're looking for Ryan. The next day I come into work and Dave's smudging the halls with sweetgrass. And I tell him it stinks like incense from when I was a kid. He asks me if I'm okay, and I say, "Yeah, why shouldn't I be?"

Dave says, "That boy, Ryan? He's dead too." The police, six of them, surrounded him and shot him, because he was "resisting arrest," paper says. He didn't have a weapon or nothing. Only he was a suspect, and now he's dead too. Dave tells me to go home, but I just say "no" and work like always.

I knew this guy once. This guy, he was a boy once too, when an older boy crept into his bed at night and tore a hole inside him. And this guy, he knew, when he was a kid, and now that he's grown up, that he needed to keep this secret or this hole might spill all his insides out right onto the floor. And this gaping hole, this sucking wound, it became a part of him. When he was a boy and the priests and brothers called him worthless, this boy's hole had a gravity that sucked the words in and made them a part of him. And this wound was always open and always ready, so when Father Lacombe took this boy into the cloakroom that first time, the boy knew exactly what to do. And when it became a weekly appointment, this boy's hole knew to suck it up. To suck it up.

ELDER MARTIN *takes up his fiddle again, plays more of the tune from "Helpless," singing the chorus aloud until he breaks up and stops. Beat.*

I can't be your elder. You looked at me, and you thrust this title on me, and like magic, somehow, I should know what to do, but I don't.

A shift to JOSIE *in the funeral home.*

JOSIE: The only Drunken Chief in the phone book was a very angry woman. She says, "I don't want to hear no more about no fuckin' Robbie, and I don't want to talk to any more *fuckin'* cops." I don't know her. I don't know that life, but I'm looking. Weeks later, I see a poster taped to a light post, flapping in the wind. "Missing: Robbie Drunken Chief." Then at a coffee shop, I pick up a paper and there's a short story buried in the City section. Known sex trade worker. Last seen outside a North End hotel. Previous arrests. History of drug abuse. "Soup kitchen workers noticed Drunken Chief's absence." It's the sort of thing I would usually not even bother to read. That most people will just skim over, "And isn't it terrible. Oh, yes, it's so sad. I wish I could do something about it. But what can you do? People make their own choices in life."

I'm looking at your photograph, small and slightly blurred on the page and the humanity of your face is undeniable. You're smiling, half laughing. You had this moment of goodness in your life. You were not alone. Someone took your picture to capture a moment of happiness. You were undeniably alive.

I feel it welling up in me. I get up. Something inside me is breaking. Out into the street, I don't know where I'm going, but I go. I'm puking in the snow, and steam is rising off, and I walk without knowing where I'm going: I'm sobbing, snot running down my face, blinded by tears, vomit on my clothes. People are swerving to avoid me, and oh no, oh no, oh god, I'm a crazy Indian, and "isn't it sad, and I wish I could do something, but what can you do? People make their own choices . . . " Oh, god . . . Oh, god . . . Oh, god . . . People make their own choices.

A shift—split scenes: YOUNG MARTIN *in Korea and* ROBBIE *in his prison cell. A buzzer sounds. The men rise in synchronicity, make their cots, face the audience, and stand at attention. Over the following* MARY *enters the apartment, pregnant, with a bucket, and starts scrubbing the floor. She feels her baby kick, and hums.*

ROBBIE: I don't really remember you.

YOUNG MARTIN: I wish that I could talk to you.

ROBBIE: I wish I could talk to you.

YOUNG MARTIN: This war is fought at night. When day ends, we're at 100 per cent stand-to, all the men, dead silent. My finger tense on the trigger.

ROBBIE: The first time I ever hurt a woman was when I was around six. This was my second foster family. She was a sweet lady, and she went to put her arms around me, so I bit her, hard, on her breast. I can still remember the taste of the blood was like metal. The piece of her I spat out. And there I was. I laughed and laughed and laughed.

YOUNG MARTIN: I try not to think of your body.

ROBBIE: I tried to straighten out a few years ago. I don't know what I was thinking, but I got married.

YOUNG MARTIN: There'd been days of rain. I was shoulder to shoulder with my men in the trench yesterday when we came under heavy shelling.

ROBBIE: She got angry that I wasn't coming home every night.

YOUNG MARTIN: The shells were exploding, and it had gotten so muddy so suddenly.

ROBBIE: "You fucking bitch."

YOUNG MARTIN: Explosions. And then I felt this weight, and it was one of my men falling against me. Falling and taking me down with him because I was sliding in the mud, clay in my mouth, I pushed him away.

ROBBIE: I hit her and hit her and hit her until her face was broken.

YOUNG MARTIN: And I said, "Jesus, what the fuck are you doing?" Only then I saw he was dead, that part of his face was gone. That his blood was on me.

ROBBIE: I looked at her face and I felt like an artist, and it was finally quiet.

YOUNG MARTIN: Everything got quiet again. And I walked away.

YOUNG MARTIN begins to exit.

And I just started laughing and laughing and laughing . . .

He laughs while exiting.

ROBBIE: *(to MARY)* You fucking bitch. You fucking bitch! You fucking bitch. All I ever wanted was you. All I ever wanted! You . . . fucking . . . bitch.

A shift: JOSIE in the university classroom.

JOSIE: If I'm one of *them*, not one of *us*, and *they* don't sit in these classrooms, do I belong here? When I'm lost in it? What if . . . What if all this is an equation, that's logically solved . . . that all adds up . . . to me?

She starts over.

My project's title is "The Devastation of the Metis: A Very Polite Genocide."

The United Nations definition of genocide: "the following acts committed with . . . with . . . with . . ."

She falls to the floor in a full-fledged seizure. ROUGAROU appears and drags/carries her to the funeral home.

A shift: a 1980s clinic examination room. DR. BAKER paces and prepares the room.

DR. BAKER: Okay. Okay.

She steadies herself. ROBBIE enters.

Hello, Robert, how are you doing today?

ROBBIE: Okay.

DR. BAKER: Okay? Good! You can have a seat there. Is it still snowing out there? Can, I just . . . Open up? How's it feel? Is it hard to swallow?

ROBBIE: No.

DR. BAKER: What about a burning sensation in your mouth or throat?

ROBBIE: No.

DR. BAKER: You don't need to be embarrassed.

ROBBIE: I'm not.

DR. BAKER: Well . . . I'm looking in your mouth. I'm not stupid, you're not stupid. If you can't be open with me, it's going to be hard for me to treat you.

ROBBIE: I am being open with you.

DR. BAKER: Robert, I'm looking in your mouth. I can see you have oral thrush. I can imagine the symptoms, and I know it can't be comfortable. Bullshitting me is not good for either of us. I can easily prescribe some anti-fungal medication if you feel it would be helpful to get rid of the yeast infection in your throat and mouth. Would you like me to prescribe something?

ROBBIE: Yes.

DR. BAKER: Good. When I saw you before you said the last time you'd seen a doctor was when you were incarcerated. I've requested the transfer of your medical records, but nothing's come. How long were you in for?

ROBBIE: This time?

DR. BAKER: How about overall?

ROBBIE: About three years.

DR. BAKER: Needle drugs?

ROBBIE: No.

DR. BAKER looks at him.

Yes.

DR. BAKER: Still using?

ROBBIE: No.

DR. BAKER: No?

ROBBIE: No.

DR. BAKER: Methadone?

ROBBIE: No.

DR. BAKER: We have programs that . . .

ROBBIE: No.

DR. BAKER: No?

Beat.

Okay. Listen, Robert, our clinic is the sort of place where you don't have to put your guard up. Yes? You can be straight with me. You tell me if you're thinking about using again, and I won't be calling your parole officer. That's not how I operate, okay?

ROBBIE: Yeah.

DR. BAKER: I'd like to have a long-term doctor-patient relationship. I'm looking at starting up a special program at the clinic for . . .

ROBBIE's expression stops her.

Your return appointment was two weeks ago. I'm glad you came, but I wish you had come in when you were scheduled to. God only knows what treatment you got inside, but it's time to start taking care of yourself, okay? I can connect you with resources . . .

ROBBIE laughs.

Is there a problem?

ROBBIE shrugs.

I know most people don't like seeing the doctor. Is there a problem? Do you have a problem with me?

ROBBIE: No. It's just. When I came in last time, I didn't expect you to be a woman.

DR. BAKER: Oh. Is that a problem?

ROBBIE: Yeah it is!

DR. BAKER: Oh, I can . . .

ROBBIE: I'm kidding. Only kidding, okay?

DR. BAKER: Okay.

ROBBIE: All right.

DR. BAKER: You have a right to care. It's your basic right as a human being. I don't care if your skin is brown, or if you love other men. These things don't matter to me. My interest is keeping you well. May I talk seriously to you, Robert?

ROBBIE: Yeah.

DR. BAKER: All right. The results of the biopsy we took of the lesions we were looking at have come back. I need to prepare you and I need you to listen carefully. The results aren't good. When it comes to the lesions, what we're looking at is Kaposi's sarcoma—which most people shorten to KS. KS is pretty rare. It usually appears on men much older than you, or those with weak immune systems. Which is why I turn to your blood work. Given your history and the symptoms you present, I want to test you for Acquired Immune Deficiency Syndrome, which is something we're just starting to see here. AIDS for short. Have you heard of AIDS?

ROBBIE: Yeah, but I heard it hadn't spread here yet.

DR. BAKER: Well apparently it has.

ROBBIE: Bullshit!

DR. BAKER: Robert . . .

ROBBIE rises to exit.

ROBBIE: Bullshit!

DR. BAKER: Okay. Okay. Robert—

DR. BAKER blocks his exit.

I need you to calm down. Take a minute. Breathe. Please. There are steps we can take . . .

ROBBIE: Get the fuck out of my way.

DR. BAKER: No. I. No. Listen. I'm not going to let you go. I want to help. Do you have someone I can call? Please.

He charges toward her, throwing her out of his path, and exits. She shouts after him.

Hey! Come back! Please! Come back—when you're ready! Don't . . . Damn it!

A shift: the apartment. MARY *is pregnant.* YOUNG MARTIN *enters carrying a metal case, sees* MARY, *and freezes.*

MARY: It's about time! The cab already left, so we'll have to call another one. The bus leaves in forty-five minutes, so we can still make it. I'll just run downstairs and call another cab, okay? Okay, Martin? Okay?

YOUNG MARTIN: Yeah.

MARY *exits.* YOUNG MARTIN *puts down his case and stares at it.* MARY *returns.*

MARY: All right I called, and they said they'd be here right away. Hey, you look like you just got caught with your hand in the cookie jar. Where were you anyway? Did you forget we had to leave at six?

YOUNG MARTIN: No.

MARY: No? So why were you . . . Ah, we don't have time for this! Can you help with the bags? Yours is really heavy.

He doesn't move.

Martin? What's wrong? Hey?

YOUNG MARTIN: I'm going to stay.

MARY: What? No.

YOUNG MARTIN: I'm going to stay.

MARY: Come on, I told you, it's not a big deal. It's just a visit for a week, and Maman's happy she's going to be a kohkom.

YOUNG MARTIN: You'll have a better time without me.

MARY: What? No, no, no! I told you. I want you to meet Maman. We'll have a really good time. She's sweet, and she's going to like you. She said she's going to have a goose for us! And she's probably been preparing for weeks!

YOUNG MARTIN: No, I'm going to stay here.

MARY: Why, what's here?

YOUNG MARTIN: I just want to stay here.

MARY: Where have you been going lately?

YOUNG MARTIN: What?

MARY: Are you seeing someone else?

YOUNG MARTIN doesn't react.

Are you?

YOUNG MARTIN: No.

MARY: No?

YOUNG MARTIN: Of course not.

MARY: I need you to come with me. It's beautiful at the lake. My family will love you. You can see what it's like in a normal family. It'll be good for you.

The cab honks.

YOUNG MARTIN: Good for me?

MARY: Don't be that way.

Honking.

We have to go!

YOUNG MARTIN: You go.

MARY: Martin.

YOUNG MARTIN: Go.

MARY: Martin.

YOUNG MARTIN: Go. Just leave me.

A long honk. MARY exits. YOUNG MARTIN opens his case and takes out a gun. ROUGAROU appears, watching confrontationally as YOUNG MARTIN raises the gun to his mouth, holds, and then lowers it. ROUGAROU holds out his hand/paw and YOUNG MARTIN gives him the gun. ROUGAROU takes it and YOUNG MARTIN is left alone, shaking, as ELDER MARTIN, in the 2000s, speaks.

ELDER MARTIN: You tell me to talk to these kids about how I made it through? The tiny part of me that's still alive—you want me to take it out and show everyone how it bleeds? Well it bleeds, okay. How much more do you want? Are these the tears you wanted? Are you happy now?

A shift: the apartment. JOSIE is smoking up and staring at her hands.

JOSIE: This is my skin. This is my skin.

She starts singing to the tune of "Scooping Up My Baby Bumble Bee" as she finds the phone book.

I'm looking for Robbie Drunken Chief.
Won't my mommy be so mad at me?
I'm looking for Robbie Drunken Chief.
Won't my mommy be so proud of . . .

She stops and stares at the phone book.

R. Drunken Chief. 589-4323.

JOSIE quickly puts the phone book away, goes to the sink, takes out bleach, and uses it to wash her hands.

One, Two, Three, Four, Five. One, Two, Three, Four, Five.

JOSIE continues to wash, counting under her breath. MARY enters, very pregnant, carrying groceries, and sees JOSIE.

MARY: Are you from the government?

JOSIE: What?

MARY: What do you want now?

JOSIE: I don't understand . . .

MARY: You see? You see how I keep my house clean? I work hard to keep things just right. The last government woman said after the assessment she might bring Robbie back, if I'm "deemed fit."

JOSIE: They took Robbie from you?

MARY: Don't talk to me like I'm stupid. Just tell me what you want and I'll do it. I keep a good house, and I can cook. And the people at the Eaton's warehouse said they'd hire me in a second if I wasn't expecting. I'll get a job as soon as the baby comes. I'll have my baby, and I'll have Robbie back. I'll pay for a sitter, and I'll work to feed us.

JOSIE: I'm looking for Robbie Drunken Chief.

MARY: I told you. The other government agent took him. She took him thirteen days ago. Are you here for my assessment?

JOSIE: No . . . I . . . I'm not with the government.

MARY: Oh.

JOSIE: Oh.

MARY: Why are you here?

JOSIE: I don't know.

MARY: You said you're looking for Robbie?

JOSIE nods.

We'll I wish I knew where he is, but I don't, and they won't let me visit him. So could you please leave?

JOSIE: They took Robbie from you?

MARY: I said I want you to leave.

JOSIE: All right.

JOSIE goes to leave.

MARY: If you find Robbie, tell him . . . his mommy . . . that I love him and I want to bring him home. That I'm going to bring him home. Okay?

JOSIE: Okay.

A shift: ROBBIE in a Narcotics Anonymous meeting, reciting the serenity prayer.

ROBBIE: " . . . the serenity to accept the things I cannot change, the courage to change the things I can, and the wisdom to know the difference."

Beat.

I started step four, and I was talking to my sponsor about making my list of resentments. I'm looking at this list, and it's so long. It took me days and days, and I kept adding things. I don't know how I'm going to let it go. I'm mad at my mom for letting me go, my dad for fucking off, the people who fostered me for fucking me up, and I'm pissed at the government, the city, the country—whatever—for fucking it up for me and all the rest of us. And you want me to let it go? I walk down the street and the Indians are drunk or high and dying. And the girls and the boys that walk the streets and the white guys who pay for it, and the people in their cars who drive by and look away and the ones who stare like it's the drive-through zoo. Why aren't we all rioting in the streets? Don't you tell me it's okay—that this is the way it is. "The things I can not change." Well fuck you—I'm not accepting it, I never agreed to this bullshit. Fuck that. No. It's so wrong. And it's not okay with me.

A shift back to JOSIE *at the funeral home.*

JOSIE: My friends and I used to drive downtown and look at the hookers. We'd look at them, and we'd laugh and laugh. Them not us. In the safety of the car, we're *us*, and they're *them*. And I liked it. It was gratifying. It made me feel so much better, so much smarter than those boys and girls who'd fallen deep into the cracks.

A shift: MARY *in the apartment. In the next room a violent, drunken party can be heard.* MARY *sits, listening, surrounded by a mess of empty alcohol bottles.*

MARY: Dear Auntie Agnes, I've been in the city for three weeks now looking for work, but not finding much. I'm broke and hungry. I promise to stay away from now on like you asked if you could please just send more money.

MARY *drinks. The noise escalates into audible violence. Someone shouts, "Give us a song!" and dizzying fiddle music is added to the noise.* MARY *self-protecively grabs a knife from the mess that surrounds her and waves it at the perceived threat. She goes to the cupboard and carves, the fiddle squealing everyone else into silence:*

"They killed me."

The noise rushes back in, with the addition of a hard pounding and knocking from off. She clutches the knife. The pounding escalates. She goes to the cupboard *for a fresh bottle—*ROUGAROU *is there. She turns away from him, closes her eyes and keeps them closed as he approaches, runs his paws and snout along her body, then kneels and leans against her. She accepts this contact and rests his head on her lap, wraps her arms around him, and strokes his fur, cradling him maternally.* ROUGAROU *leaps from her lap and* MARY *stands with him. They circle each other and dodge around. It becomes a game like the one she played with* YOUNG MARTIN *earlier.* MARY *laughs and eventually begins to lose her breath.*

Okay, okay. Maman's tired, okay?

They stop circling.

I want to tell you a story your kohkom told to me and her mother told to her and her mother before her, so one day, when you have kids of your own, you can tell this story too. Okay? Okay.

My maman's great-grandmother was neighbours with this family: the wife was Therese, and the husband Jacques. Therese came from the colony and grew up there, but Jacques came from the States, and no one knew much about him.

Jacques heard there were lots of Saskatoons growing in the south, so they packed up their kids, the pails, and supplies onto the cart and headed out. The whole way there Jacques was grouchy. They got to picking, but the sun was beating down, so the kids went off to swim and just Therese and Jacques kept picking, only Jacques was so grouchy he wasn't good company.

MARY *and* ROUGAROU *begin slowly circling again.*

Therese tried to talk to him, but he kept moving farther and farther away until he disappeared into the bush. Then she heard her children screaming. She ran to the creek, and there on the bank was a great big wolf with red eyes. Therese screamed for Jacques, but he didn't come. She started throwing rocks at the wolf and hit it pretty hard on the head, so it turned and disappeared into the bush. Therese and the children ran back to the cart, and Jacques was there. She told him what had happened, and asked why he didn't come when she called. He said he didn't hear her, but Therese saw Jacques had a bump on his head the same place she'd hit the wolf. She didn't say anything.

Later, in the fall, Therese was working alone in her garden—

The circling continues, growing more intense. MARY *casually picks up the knife.*

—using a knife to cut squash from the vine. The wolf with red eyes came bounding out of the bush straight for her. As he pounced, Therese took the knife and stabbed him in the gut.

MARY *stabs the air between the two of them, and her arm remains extended with the blade pointed at* ROUGAROU.

The wolf howled in pain and moved into the undergrowth. The howling started to sound like a man, not an animal, so she carefully went to see. She saw Jacques lying there—bleeding. He said, "I couldn't tell you I was a rougarou. You had to make me bleed to set me free. So thank you, now I'm free forever." And with that he died.

MARY *rotates the knife so the handle is pointed out.* ROUGAROU *takes the blade; the circling begins again.* MARY *stops and closes her eyes. He slides up behind her as before. Her eyes stay closed as he slips his arms around her; his hands/paws slide along her body while he holds the knife.*

Thank you.

ROUGAROU *drives the knife into* MARY*'s stomach and she clenches at it inside her as he moves away from her. The noises resurge and reach another crescendo. More pounding.* MARY *pulls the knife from herself, bleeding, and holds it toward the pounding. The noise fades away as the knocking becomes less violent.* YOUNG MARTIN*'s voice is heard:*

YOUNG MARTIN: *(from off)* Mary? Mary?

Enters, sees her.

Oh. Mary. Oh, god.

He takes a step closer; she holds the knife out farther.

I cracked up. They sent me home . . . I tried to write, but . . . Mary. I'm sorry. I'm so sorry. Oh god. Oh god. Oh god. Ooh.

MARY moves to him, gives him a quick, powerful stab in the belly, dropping the knife between them. YOUNG MARTIN clutches himself, bleeding, then reaches out to her, smearing their blood on her face like war paint.

Thank you.

MARY goes to the cupboard, opens it with the expectation of ROUGAROU being there, but he is not. She takes a bottle from the cupboard and drinks.

Mary?

She continues drinking.

Mary?

She opens another bottle and drinks from both. YOUNG MARTIN watches as she vacantly continues drinking, lowering himself to the floor in a stupor. ROUGAROU creeps on from behind and drags/carries him off.

A shift: ALLEY and ROBBIE on the street. ROBBIE half-heartedly holds an "LA or Bust" sign. ALLEY has a Polaroid camera.

ALLEY: Here comes a car, hold it up. Hold it up!

He does. The car passes.

ROBBIE: I keep telling you, we're in the middle of Manitoba—no one's going to take us straight to LA. We need to make a sign for somewhere closer.

ALLEY: Come on, cheer up, Sour Grapes! We're going to see the sun!

ROBBIE: Right.

ALLEY: Here, let me take your picture holding the sign. Come on, hold it up! Good.

S/he takes a picture.

How many months?

ROBBIE: Six months.

ALLEY: Six months! Six months clean! See! Aren't you proud of yourself?

ROBBIE: Sure.

ALLEY: You better be. Of course you were just copying me. You had to make it look easy, just to piss me off.

ROBBIE: It wasn't easy.

ALLEY: Damn straight it wasn't. Which is why we deserve a little sun.

ROBBIE: Come on.

ALLEY: What?

ROBBIE: Come on, can we please change the sign?

ALLEY: No. It's "LA or Bust."

ROBBIE: So maybe it's "bust?" We've been here for three hours.

ALLEY: It's not "bust."

ROBBIE: No?

ALLEY: No.

ROBBIE: Okay.

ALLEY: Did you tell your wife?

ROBBIE: She's not my wife!

ALLEY: Ah, but she *is* you're wife. Who'd have thought *you'd* have a wife? What were you thinking?

ROBBIE: I don't know. I was stoned. I was stoned and she had money. She has a restraining order anyway. I'm not supposed to call her.

ALLEY: Did you love me?

ROBBIE: What?

ALLEY: Did you, do you, love me?

ROBBIE: I don't know "love." I didn't love her. I thought, "If I have a wife, a house, and all this stuff, I can forget." When I'm inside, I tell myself, again, "When I get out, I'll start a new chapter. I won't fuck up this time." And then I find out I've got this disease, and . . . Nothing's past. I can't escape the past, because the past is part of now and part of the future. That's it. It's all tangled together. A big fucking mess.

ALLEY: Well, what about right now?

ROBBIE: Right now?

ALLEY: Yeah . . . Will you love me right now?

ROBBIE: I can't . . . you know that I can't . . .

ALLEY: I didn't say fuck me. God. I'm trying to be romantic, and all you can think of is your cock!

ROBBIE: Oh, come on.

ALLEY: Come on yourself. I'm asking if you'll love me. Right now. In this moment. Because if you can love me, right now, then I'll love you too, right now. And there's nothing but now anyway. So can you?

ROBBIE: I don't know what you're talking about.

ALLEY: Oh really.

ROBBIE: Really.

ALLEY: Well, I think you do. Someone loves you. Right now, at this moment, you have someone who loves you.

ROBBIE: Oh, come on.

ALLEY holds up the Polaroid.

ALLEY: Come on yourself. Smile for me. Oh, put the stupid sign down and smile for me! Come on! "Fargo or Bust!"

ROBBIE laughs as ALLEY takes a picture.

There. I think this one'll be a good one. We should throw it in an envelope and mail it to your wife. And you can write her a letter, letting her know you're sorry. Are you sorry?

ROBBIE: Of course I'm sorry.

ALLEY: You should write her a letter. All right? All right?!

ROBBIE: All right.

ALLEY sees a car approaching.

ALLEY: Hold up the sign, hold it up!

The car unexpectedly stops offstage for them and they run off to catch their ride. A shift: the same street. MARY, *wearing her clothes from the dance, runs on laughing and out of breath.*

MARY: Come on!

YOUNG MARTIN *runs to join her.*

YOUNG MARTIN: I'm coming, I'm coming!

MARY: We made it! We made it.

YOUNG MARTIN: He'll come looking for me.

MARY: Of course they will, but we'll be long gone!

YOUNG MARTIN: We will?

MARY: Sure. I saved up enough to buy a ticket back to Duck Lake, but since I'm with you, it should be enough to get both of us to the city instead.

YOUNG MARTIN: Don't you want to go home?

MARY: If I went home, that'd be the first place they'd look. If we go to the city, we can get jobs, we can get a place, and they probably won't find us.

YOUNG MARTIN: A place?

MARY: Sure. A little place with a good stove. I know my maman's recipe for bannock by heart. We can live off bannock and lard sandwiches for the first little while if we need to.

YOUNG MARTIN: I don't know. What if they find us?

MARY: If they find us they'll beat the shit out of us!

YOUNG MARTIN: So we can't let them find us.

MARY: Exactly.

YOUNG MARTIN: I'll protect you.

MARY: You will?

YOUNG MARTIN: Sure.

MARY kisses him.

MARY: Things will be okay now. Now that we've gotten away. We won't have to run anymore. I can build a home in your eyes. I'll watch out for you, and you'll watch out for me. Okay?

YOUNG MARTIN: Okay.

A shift: the 2000s, the centre.

ELDER MARTIN: Okay.

He stands.

I'm going. I'm gonna go. All right.

Taking everyone in.

You want me to keep coming here? Okay. I'll come back to circle. And I'll talk. And listen. Okay? Right now, though, I've got to face the music. I've got to go make it better. Be better.

ELDER MARTIN exits.

A shift: JOSIE is in the classroom.

JOSIE: In the back pages of the local paper: "Body parts found. Suspected to be the remains of missing Aboriginal male prostitute."

Beat.

I can't. I'm sorry. I need to go.

JOSIE steps back from the presentation as ROUGAROU joins her. She pulls back his head covering to see the face of the person underneath, takes him, and kisses him gently. She places the covering back and takes his hand; they walk together to the funeral home. ROUGAROU settles next to ROBBIE's urn.

Listen . . . she loved you. And I want to know you, only I don't know how.

ELDER MARTIN enters from behind JOSIE. She doesn't see him. He moves in closer, eventually tapping her on the shoulder.

Jesus! I didn't hear you.

ELDER MARTIN: Sorry.

JOSIE: That's okay.

ELDER MARTIN: Okay.

JOSIE: Okay.

ELDER MARTIN: Did you know Robbie well?

JOSIE: No. Did you?

ELDER MARTIN: No . . . no. I think, maybe . . . I would've liked to have known him.

JOSIE: Me too.

ELDER MARTIN: You too?

JOSIE: Sure . . . I mean, who isn't worth knowing, right?

ELDER MARTIN: Maybe some people aren't worth knowing.

JOSIE: To some people he wasn't.

ELDER MARTIN: But you wish you had?

JOSIE: I wish everyone had someone.

ELDER MARTIN: Do you?

JOSIE: What?

ELDER MARTIN: Do you have someone?

JOSIE: I . . . Uh . . .

ELDER MARTIN: Do you have someone? Someone who would care? Someone who would go out and look for you and keep you?

Beat.

I've been trying to figure out how this could have happened, but I can't get the story straight.

JOSIE: Me too. I came here . . . I didn't know I'd find you. Maybe somehow we . . . Where have you been all this time?

ELDER MARTIN: I don't know. I went away. I didn't have courage to stay, I didn't know if I'd be coming back, or hoped I wouldn't. And maybe, really, I didn't. Your grandmother, Mary, didn't have anyone. She was filled with emptiness—became a part of the emptiness: drank, got consumed by it, and died real young. Me, I shut down, ate in soup kitchens, and eventually started working in one. Then I saw him. A boy who looked a lot like me and a little like you. I knew it was him. Right away, I knew. Just like when I see you now. I figured it was too late. But I made sure he had something to eat, and a coat when it got cold. It was me who noticed when he stopped coming around. I almost didn't come here today, 'cause I was scared some ghost from my future past might show up. And here you are.

JOSIE: Here I am. Boo.

ELDER MARTIN: Ha! What about your mum?

JOSIE: She's alive, only we can't talk. We don't connect. There's something we lost.

ROUGAROU intentionally knocks the urn to the ground—the ashes spill out.

Shit!

They both look to ROUGAROU, who nods and exits. Beat. ELDER MARTIN carefully collects the ashes into his hand.

ELDER MARTIN: "Dust to dust, ashes to ashes." I always hated that in school. Even though I never knew my stories, I always felt those church stories left me out. Left a lot out.

Have you heard the story of the Sky Woman?

JOSIE: Sort of. I'm taking an Aboriginal Studies course at school. We talked about the Sky Man.

ELDER MARTIN: Ah, no! Mary always said it was Sky Woman. She used to tell stories to Robbie her family taught her, even though he was too young to get them. That's where I first heard it.

JOSIE: Do you think you could . . . Would you tell it to me like she told it to him?

As JOSIE and ELDER MARTIN share the following story, MARY and ROBBIE become present, positioned on an opposite diagonal to JOSIE and ELDER MARTIN. MARY's voice is heard, just under the surface of the present moment, telling the same story to ROBBIE. As the four of them share the story, YOUNG MARTIN takes ELDER

MARTIN's former seat in circle, followed by DR. BAKER and ALLEY reappearing on the periphery of the stage.

ELDER MARTIN: Okay. If you want, I'll try to tell it to you the way Mary did . . . the way it was passed down to her. She used to say each time you tell a story it gets better. Maybe it becomes new. I'll tell it so one day you can tell it to someone too. Okay?

JOSIE: Okay.

ELDER MARTIN: So your great-great-grandmother told it to your great-grandmother, who told it to your grandmother, who told it to me and Robbie, and now I'm going to tell it to you.

Okay?

JOSIE: Okay.

ELDER MARTIN: So, there was the first people, the Sky People, and they lived in the air. Underneath was only water. There was a girl, and she was sick—the Sky Woman. An elder told her family to dig up a tree and put her in the hole, because this would heal her. They started digging, right at the base of a big tree. But as they were digging, the tree fell through the hole and the girl's hair got caught in the branches. She fell with it, and dirt fell too, down to the water. Swans swam to catch her, and landed her on the back of the Great Turtle. The water animals like otter and beaver tried to dive to find the tree's earth-covered roots, but they died of exhaustion. Then elder toad dove. For a long time she stayed underwater. They thought maybe she died. But then she came up, and spat out a mouthful of dirt onto the Great Turtle.

ELDER MARTIN goes to transfer the ashes to JOSIE's hands. She at first jerks away, but he persists and she takes them.

The earth had the power of growth. It grew into an island, and from it, the world. Sky Woman lived there, made a home, and from her came all people. See, Mary said, "even from dirt and dust comes something." So maybe there can be a new start, even when it seems like everything's lost. Like there's hope, even in dust.

JOSIE: And no matter how far you fall.

ELDER MARTIN takes some ashes from JOSIE's hands and spreads them across her face like war paint, as he did to MARY with blood.

ELDER MARTIN: Thank you. Thank you.

Lights.

KIHĒW

Curtis Peeteetuce

Dedicated to the many family members who attended St. Michael's Residential School in Duck Lake, Saskatchewan. Also to my cousin for sharing his account of events the night the youth burnt the building down.

Acknowledgements

Thank you to Kennetch Charlette, mentor and dramaturg, to Gordon Tootoosis Nīkānīwin Theatre for the wonderful opportunity, and to the alumni of the 2007 Circle of Voices program: Deidre Badger, Jaired Henderson, Danny Knight, Demetrious Knight, Aaron Shingoose, and Cory Standing. Nanaskimonawaw.

kihēw was first produced by the Saskatchewan Native Theatre Company (now Gordon Tootoosis Nīkānīwin Theatre) for the 2007 Circle of Voices youth theatre program in Saskatoon, Saskatchewan. It featured the following cast and creative team:

Patricia Kihew: Deidre Badger
Terry Kihew: Jaired Henderson
Winter Kihew: Danny Knight (as Walter for the 2007 production)
Ghost: Demetrious Knight
Joel Kihew: Aaron Shingoose

Director: Kennetch Charlette
Stage Manager: Damien H. Bartlett
Set/Props Design: Mark Eriksson
Lighting Design: Tim Cardinal
Costume Design: Jeff Chief
Sound Design: Kennetch Charlette, Tim Cardinal, and Cory Standing
Musical Composer: Daniel Fortier

Characters

Patricia Kihew: Cree female, in her fifties or sixties.
Joel Kihew: Cree male, seventeen.
Terry Kihew: Cree male, eighteen.
Winter Kihew: Cree female, seventeen.
MaryAnne Kihew: Cree female, fifteen.

Setting

Stone Pipe First Nation, present day.

Scene 1 (Patricia's House)

Monday, August 20, 2007. The sound of bells and a drum crossover to that of a kettle boiling on a woodstove. PATRICIA *Kihew enters her kitchen and tends to it. There is white gauze around her elbow. As she prepares a cup of tea the music fades and a news* ANCHOR *takes to the airwaves.*

ANCHOR: Approved by the federal government and courts last year, the Indian Residential Schools Settlement Agreement will provide $1.9 billion to former students of residential schools run by the government and religious organizations until the mid '70s.

Before too long, PATRICIA *notices a collection of stapled sheets on her table. An open envelope sits right by it. She picks up the stapled sheets.*

It's expected that each person can receive amounts anywhere between $10,000 and $40,000. As the deal states, students who take the settlement won't be able to sue the government, churches, or any other defendant in the class action. Compensation applies to nearly 80,000 residential school survivors. A government update this month said settlement could be implemented by the 19th of September.

The silhouette of a girl comes up.

The payout could begin in November and fully distributed by April 2008. Former students have until the end of the day to decide whether to opt out of the largest class-action settlement in Canadian history. Latest stats indicate that opt-out numbers are low.

She is holding a feather in one hand and a rosary in the other.

In other school news, Friday's premiere of *High School Musical 2* drew an estimated audience of 17.2 million, making it the most-watched basic cable program ever. The Disney Channel can now brag about more than a one-hit TV wonder—

PATRICIA shuts the radio off. She sighs deeply and addresses a man standing by her door.

PATRICIA: So, Mr. Rich Lawyer Man, you gonna just stand there at my door or what? Fine. No skin off my arse. It's all about money for you, isn't it? Close the damn door! Mosquitoes will get in.

So I guess you're wondering if I'm gonna sign these papers or not. Should Patricia Kihew pick A or B? Take the settlement or opt out? Well I still got till the end of the day so just hold your damn horses!

PATRICIA grabs the tea and sits.

I was with my cousin Stella the other day and we were talking about this whole settlement thing. We're not sure what to make of it yet. I mean, for some it might be a good thing, but for others it's definitely a bad thing. Like for her grandson. Imagine him. A young man with so much potential . . .

Another light comes up on a young man at stage left.

He liked dancing. Like all young people nowadays, he had promise, but too much anger. Always in trouble that one. His mom didn't wanna handle him . . . so she signed him up for that boarding school out east in the valley. I'm sure if she knew better she would've done otherwise. Anyways, his settlement gave him $110,000. Can you imagine that? Who the hell in their right mind gives a troubled young man that much money?

The young man continues to play out PATRICIA*'s story.*

Well, you know what happened then. Uh-huh, that's right. Suddenly . . . he had it all. Brought himself some rich clothes, two new cars, cut his hair, and even changed his name. All of a sudden he had as many new friends as there are mosquitoes on the reserve. Bloodsuckers. But to him they were friends.

So him and his new friends lived it up. Travelled from city to city, club to club, party to party. Sure enough, in six months they went through all that money. One hundred and ten thousand dollars! And you know what happened? Like a can of repellent sprayed all over his world, the bloodsuckers were gone.

The young man sits on an empty chair.

All of them. He ended up selling his cars and eventually drank that money up, too. In the end, he sat in his lonely room in some dirty old hotel, and drank himself away.

You think he died? Namoya, but he might as well be dead. See, he suffered alcohol poisoning and now lies in a hospital room . . . unable to speak, listen, or even smile . . . this young man who had it all . . .

They gave him $110,000, this young man. But they might as well have given him a death sentence . . .

A light fades on the young man as a doctor takes him away. PATRICIA *recomposes in the chair.*

I suppose you think you're gonna hear another damn sob story. Or maybe you want to hear a sugar-coated story? Huh? Well shit no! I got another story to tell you. About that old building that used to sit just off the west end of the reserve . . . about my sister MaryAnne . . . and it starts with my nosimak . . . my grandchildren . . .

PATRICIA repositions to indicate a time transition.

Scene 2 (Patricia's House)

A cold, rainy evening a week earlier. PATRICIA's grandson enters stage right and sits at the table. His name is JOEL. PATRICIA watches him enter and takes a seat at the table beside him. She begins to question him about some incident.

PATRICIA: So? What happened?

JOEL: When?

PATRICIA: Don't get smart, Joel! You know when.

JOEL: We were only there for a little while, then all of a sudden it just burned down.

PATRICIA: Not that. I mean what you saw. Did you see anyone?

JOEL: Maybe . . .

PATRICIA: Tell me!

JOEL: I don't know.

PATRICIA: Cripes! Can't get a damn straight answer out of you.

JOEL: I'm going to bed.

PATRICIA: SIT DOWN! I didn't say you could leave!

JOEL: Well what then?

PATRICIA: You are going to sit your arse in that chair and tell me.

JOEL stops himself from swearing.

JOEL: Ff . . . Dammit anyway! I don't wanna! I wanna go to bed!

PATRICIA: Well, too bad. If your mom were still alive you could live with her and do whatever you want. Or maybe you could go back to living on people's couches in the city, or even worse . . . end up in jail. So tell me.

JOEL: I did. I told you, all of a sudden it was there, then it wasn't.

PATRICIA: What?

JOEL: I don't know! Sounded like someone else was—

PATRICIA: There. What did they look like?

JOEL: How should I know?

In frustration, PATRICIA retreats to a corner of the room.

PATRICIA: Ahh! Dammit Joel! You're just making this worse.

PATRICIA attempts another strategy.

I know you're only here on probation, but if they get the idea you might be getting into trouble, they're gonna send the RCMP. Then they're gonna take you away.

JOEL: Well, what's the use telling you then?

PATRICIA: 'Cause you can go to jail! That's why. Is that what you want? Well . . . is it?

JOEL: No.

PATRICIA: Well there's nothing I can do about it unless you tell me who you saw. So start talking.

JOEL: I told you. Me, Terry, and Winter came from Auntie Veronica's. She let us take some leftovers before we left.

PATRICIA: Yeow! She let you go to that old building?

JOEL: Yeah. Well, no. We told her we were gonna camp out at the lake.

PATRICIA: Dammit, you kids. Why do you have to go and lie all the time?

JOEL: See? I knew you were gonna get mad.

PATRICIA: What were you guys doing there in the first place?

JOEL: Terry wanted to make a video. Some kind of submission to get into film school or something.

PATRICIA: Cripes! What the hell were you kids thinking?

JOEL: I don't know. We were just bored. There's nothing to do on the reserve.

PATRICIA: Jesus Christ Almighty! What the hell am I supposed to do with you? Well, first you're gonna talk, then you're gonna bring your cousins here in the morning and they're gonna talk. So if you wanna stay here tonight, you're gonna tell me what you know.

JOEL: Nah. I'll just go to Auntie Veronica's.

PATRICIA: Go ahead. It's pouring rain out there. Walk out in the storm . . . see if I care . . . have a good walk . . .

The sounds of rain and thunder are heard in the distance. PATRICIA *prepares a kettle.* JOEL *stares at her.*

JOEL: Okay then!

PATRICIA: Right from the beginning . . .

JOEL: The beginning?

PATRICIA *does not respond.*

We got there after suppertime . . .

Music: the sound of the drum begins playing intermittently with the sounds of an acoustic guitar.

Scene 3 (The Building)

Early evening. The outside of an abandoned building. Three young people enter as the music fades: JOEL, TERRY, *and* WINTER. TERRY *leads the group with a flashlight.*

TERRY: Come on, you guys, hurry up.

WINTER: Hold on, you. I'm the one carrying everything.

JOEL: Cha, not even. Just carrying a backpack.

WINTER: Well, look at you. A pouch of tobacco and a stolen camera.

JOEL: I didn't steal it. I borrowed it.

WINTER: How come you just didn't ask me then?

JOEL: Because . . . you were talking to your mom about watching your baby and I didn't wanna disturb you.

WINTER: Yeah, whatever.

TERRY: Here's where we get in. Here, Joel, hold these.

TERRY hands him a flashlight and tripod.

JOEL: What the hell? Now I'm the one carrying everything.

WINTER: So? You carry that big zit you call a face all the time. I never hear you complain.

JOEL puts a hand to his face.

TERRY: You guys ever been here before?

WINTER: Are you kidding? It's been shut down for years now. We're not even supposed to be here. Remember that letter they sent to everyone on the reserve?

TERRY: What? You mean the one they sent about Treaty Day? Woo hoo, five whole bucks. As if, I'm not picking mine up. If I'm gonna shake some mountie's hand and say thanks, I'm doing it for, like, thirty bucks.

WINTER: Not that one. The one that says anyone caught here will be subject to criminal prosecution. That means get charged.

TERRY: On the reserve? I doubt it. No one cares what happens to Indians on the reserve.

JOEL: So who all went to school here?

WINTER: What? You mean out of our whole family? There's only like twelve Kihews on the planet.

TERRY: Yeah, we should be on the endangered species list.

WINTER: I don't think Mosom went to residential school. He just worked. Probably Kohkom, though. This place looks old and ancient . . . just like her.

TERRY: Hey, don't talk like that. Help me out here, Joel.

JOEL and TERRY attempt to open the door.

WINTER: Why is it always a guy who gets asked? How do you know I'm not stronger than him . . . or you, for that matter?

TERRY: 'Cause, Winter, men are warriors. We're warrior braves. Plus, I'm the oldest. Which means I'm the wisest. Oh . . . and the best! So there. Pull, Joel.

They get the door open.

Ha! See?

WINTER: I could've done that myself.

JOEL: Yeah . . . with one of your powerful farts.

TERRY: Come on then, let's go inside.

The three young people enter the building.

JOEL: What the hell's that stink?

TERRY: Smells like stale water that's been sitting too long . . . kinda mouldy.

JOEL: Just like your house, Winter.

WINTER: More like your shorts.

TERRY: Sshh . . . listen.

The group stops to listen.

JOEL: What? I don't hear anything.

TERRY: Exactly. It's quiet isn't it? Really quiet.

JOEL attempts to be dramatic.

JOEL: Too quiet.

The group hushes for a brief moment before WINTER shouts down the hallways.

WINTER: *Hello?*

JOEL and TERRY are startled. WINTER laughs.

JOEL: Shit.

WINTER: You should have seen yourselves. What was that? "Warrior braves"?

TERRY: Just nevermind. Joel, turn the camera on.

JOEL takes out the digital camera and tripod. WINTER puts the backpack on the floor and sits.

WINTER: So how long are we gonna be here anyway?

TERRY: I don't know. Maybe a couple of hours or so. Hopefully enough to go viral and submit something to that film school.

WINTER: A couple of hours? What the hell? Well, whatever, I just needed to get away from baby girl for a while.

JOEL: You want to get away from your baby Autumn?

WINTER: Yeah. Being a parent does get hard sometimes, dumbass. You wouldn't even understand. You're still just a kid.

JOEL: I'll be eighteen in two months. You're no better. Look at you.

JOEL points the camera at WINTER.

Nineteen-year-old single mom Winter Kihew lives with her mom on Stone Pipe Reserve. She made it to grade ten then got knocked up at seventeen, probably a one-night stand.

TERRY: Hey.

WINTER: Shut up. I love my baby girl. I just need my mom to take her once in a while so I can have "me" time.

TERRY: Joel, Autumn's your niece, too. So don't even talk like that.

JOEL: Sorry. Holy.

WINTER: Pass me the tobacco, Joel. I'm gonna roll a smoke.

JOEL passes her the pouch.

JOEL: Here, roll me one, too.

TERRY takes to the front of the camera.

TERRY: Okay, is it recording?

JOEL: One sec.

WINTER: Better not break my camera, you.

TERRY: Quiet, Winter.

WINTER: Dad should've got me a new iPhone. I mean, he didn't mail *you* anything for Christmas, so I guess I should be glad.

TERRY/JOEL: Quiet!

WINTER: 'Kay then. Holy.

In an instant, a faint sound is heard in another part of the building. The three young people freeze.

JOEL: What the hell is that?

TERRY: Nothing. There's probably a weasel in the building or something.

WINTER: No, it's not. Oh my goodness . . . it's the ghost. Aaaaa!

TERRY: Shut up, Winter. Okay, here we go.

JOEL: And four, three, two . . .

He motions for TERRY to start.

TERRY: Ahem . . . hey . . . no, hi . . . uh, tanisi. I'm Terry Kihew and we're in old St. Philip's Residential School. I'm here with my cousin Joel, who's on the camera.

JOEL waves his hand in front of the camera.

And my sister, Winter.

JOEL moves the camera to WINTER, then back to TERRY.

WINTER: What's up?

TERRY: We're here on Stone Pipe First Nation to investigate the mysterious ghost who is said to be roaming these halls.

WINTER lets out a haunting laugh.

WINTER: Mua ha ha ha . . .

TERRY and JOEL give her a reprimanding glance.

TERRY: Okay, cool. Um, move over there and change the angle.

JOEL: Ooh, good idea.

JOEL moves downstage.

WINTER: What's with the cloth?

JOEL: Quiet. Okay, and four, three, two . . .

TERRY: There are many stories about this place, but one we're interested in is about a student who passed away in this old building many years back. Some say it was sickness. Little else is known, for there are few on the reserve who know little else.

WINTER laughs.

What?

WINTER: Do you hear yourself? Little else is known, for there are few on the reserve who know little else.

WINTER finishes rolling a smoke and hands it to JOEL.

TERRY: So?

WINTER laughs.

Shut up, you're breaking my concentration here.

JOEL: Come on, hurry up. We should go walk around and check it out. Score me a light.

TERRY: Why the hell would I have a light? I don't even smoke. You probably dropped the lighter outside.

WINTER: You mean you don't have a light, Joel!? What the hell?

TERRY: Good. You guys stink when you smoke anyway. And save some tobacco for the seance.

JOEL: Dammit.

JOEL places his cigarette on the floor.

Okay then, Terry. Let's wrap up this intro part.

TERRY: So the question remains: Is there really a ghost in this old building? Tonight, we'll find out. What I have here with me is a seance kit, but not just any one . . . an Indian Seance kit. It comes with tobacco, cloth, and candles. Which I guess are useless now. But my expertise as . . . as . . . as a ghost contact . . . guy . . . will be good enough.

JOEL and WINTER try not to laugh.

That's right . . . tonight you will witness as we contact the ghost. And find out why it's here . . .

JOEL: And cut. Okay, so there's the intro.

TERRY: Right on. What did that run at?

JOEL: I don't know.

TERRY: Joel! You're the camera guy here. You're supposed to time everything.

JOEL: Well now you tell me.

TERRY: From now on, time everything.

JOEL: Okay.

TERRY: And write everything down. Like the scene number, the take, everything.

JOEL: *Okay everything holy!*

WINTER: I don't know why you're making such a big deal out of this, Terry. You think another stupid ghost-hunt video will go viral or get you into film school? Shit.

JOEL: You know in the movies it's always the doubter that dies first? And the ghost hunters always live.

WINTER: You couldn't hunt a rabbit if it died on Kohkom's front step.

JOEL: Yeah, well . . . you're dumb.

WINTER: Nice comeback. The only reason you're doing this is to impress your probation officer. You probably have the hots for her or something.

JOEL: Not even.

WINTER: And what the hell are you doing with cloth and tobacco, Terry? You know you're not supposed to piss around like that.

TERRY: Oh, give me a break, Winter. I'm an artist, and every great artist in this world takes chances . . . one who disturbs the norm. One who thinks outside the box and isn't afraid to try new things.

WINTER: You got that line from a movie.

TERRY: No . . . the internet.

WINTER: Gawd, you're an idiot. Even I know not to mess around with the culture.

TERRY: Yeah . . . and what the hell is culture anyway? And what kind of culture? There's prison culture, hip hop culture, pop culture. Don't go getting on some high chair, Miss Culture with a grade ten education.

WINTER: Don't you ever listen to elders speak?

TERRY: I don't go to Bingo.

JOEL: Should I be writing this down?

WINTER: I mean feasts and wakes and stuff. It's about knowing that our ancestors died so we could know and respect our ways. Even I know that. And here you are doing the exact opposite.

TERRY: Yeah, and most of that is gone, isn't it? That's what they did with all the residential schools and shit. Took our language, our history, our culture . . . and now it's all gone. So how can you say I'm disrespecting something that may not even be our true culture?

WINTER: Figure it out, dumbass.

JOEL: D-u-m-b-a-s-s.

TERRY: Be a hater if you want, but we'll be the first to prove that ghosts are either true or false. If you don't wanna cash in when I become a producer, that's your problem.

JOEL: Yeah. If you didn't want in on this, you should have said so in the first place. I gotta take a leak.

JOEL goes to a corner of the room.

WINTER: What the hell? Don't go there, go somewhere else!

JOEL: As if! You didn't care when we were kids. Ahhhhhhhhhhhhhhhhhh . . . oh yeah, that's what I'm talking about.

WINTER: Shit.

WINTER turns her head. She stands a bit offstage.

TERRY: Hurry up.

JOEL: Cha, is that it? That really was a leak.

JOEL returns to the camera and kneels beside it.

WINTER: Anyways ghost is a moniyaw thing. A white person's word. They just brought that idea here from England or something so we would stop believing our own ways. I think we're old enough to know by now that ghosts don't exist. It's spirits.

JOEL: So tell me why we should believe this.

WINTER: Duh. They tell us all the time when we go to wakes and memorials. Our loved ones are gone to a better place. They're gone home to be with the ancestors. Hello . . . tanisi?

JOEL: Well, maybe you're right. Maybe you're not.

WINTER: I am right. You know I'm right. Look at Terry, trying to do an Indian ceremony with a white man's seance. We're on the reserve, not England. You can't just mix two ceremonies together. If you wanna see this spirit you should learn about it in our own way.

TERRY holds up the pouch of tobacco and emulates a prayer ceremony, but in a monk-style voice.

TERRY: Oh Great Spirit . . . of the grandfathers and grandmothers . . . you who are so omniscient and . . . great . . . help us see the ghost—

WINTER: Spirit.

TERRY: Shut up. The ghost who is still here. Taaaaannnisiiiiii . . .

WINTER: You know how disrespectful that is? Next time I'm not going along on one of your stupid adventures.

TERRY: Good.

WINTER: In fact, when we're done here I'm gonna tell all the girls you believe in moniyaw ghosts. Then you'll never score with an Indian woman.

TERRY: Go ahead. I'll just move to Germany. They love us Indian men over there anyway.

WINTER: Yeah, good luck with that. Just give up this idea of ghost hunting. It's stupid and you're a pretty smart guy, Terry. Why not just be like Dad and go work on the rigs or something?

JOEL examines the door.

TERRY: 'Cause guys who work on the rigs end up being rich alcoholics and never come home to their families, that's why. You think I wanna end up like Dad?

WINTER: At least it'll be a real job.

TERRY: Whatever. I'll find a real job. But I'm not leaving until I find out for sure if this ghost exists or not.

JOEL: Looks like no one's leaving anytime soon.

TERRY: What?

JOEL: This door's jammed. We're locked in.

WINTER: What? What the hell did you do, Joel?

JOEL: I didn't do anything.

WINTER: Dumbass!

TERRY: Settle down. We can just smash a window later or something.

WINTER: How do we do that, genius? The windows are barred.

TERRY: Oh . . .

WINTER: Shit! I don't wanna be stuck here!

JOEL: Relax. There's gotta be a back door or emergency exit.

TERRY: Right. That's exactly right. So just simmer down, Winter.

In an instant, the faint sound from earlier is heard, but louder. It is almost the sound of a voice.

JOEL: Shit. Did you guys hear that?

TERRY: Yeah, ssh. Listen.

The sound almost fades out.

JOEL: What the hell is that?

WINTER: It's your talking weasel. *Shut the hell up! Go to bed!!!*

The sound repeats in a distant hallway.

JOEL: Whoa!

TERRY: Joel, turn the camera on.

WINTER: Gawd, this is so damn stupid.

TERRY: Winter, shut up. Boy, you just kill it.

JOEL: Should we go check it out?

TERRY: I don't know. You wanna?

JOEL: Yeah. Let's go.

TERRY: Okay, come on, Winter.

WINTER: Cha . . . you guys go. I'm staying here.

TERRY: Fine. Stay here. We'll be right back. Come on.

TERRY and JOEL leave. WINTER sits alone with the backpack.

WINTER: So stupid . . . *Can I eat something?*

TERRY/JOEL: *No!*

WINTER: *Well, I'm gonna roll a couple of smokes for after. And hurry up. I'm getting hungry.*

WINTER sits alone and begins to roll a smoke.

Damn tobacco's getting all dry and shit. As if they forgot to bring a light.

Suddenly, the sounds of whispers are heard, and a faint noise in a nearby corridor.

Back already? Good, let's find a way to get out of here.

The sounds of whispers are heard again.

Yeah, yeah, psst, psst, blah, blah. Let's get going.

The whispers are around a corner. WINTER freezes and looks in that direction.

You guys?

Pause.

Guys?

WINTER stares and, for a brief second, observes a young girl. Lights snap out.

Scene 4 (Patricia's House)

The lightning continues outside, but the rain is not as heavy. A short time has passed. JOEL *returns to where he was sitting at the table.*

PATRICIA: So, Winter saw someone?

JOEL: I don't know. I'm just guessing.

PATRICIA: Then what?

JOEL: Well . . . Terry and I checked out the building.

PATRICIA: Yeah . . .

JOEL: And when we got back, Winter was kind of quiet all of a sudden.

PATRICIA: What do you mean quiet?

JOEL: When we first got in the building, she couldn't stop complaining. Then when we saw her again, she was just quiet.

PATRICIA: Did she say what that person looked like?

JOEL: No. Terry and I didn't see anyone . . . I gotta use the washroom.

JOEL *doesn't move from his chair.*

PATRICIA: Cha . . . well go ahead. You don't need my permission to piss.

JOEL: Kohkom, I'm tired. Can I just go to bed?

PATRICIA: Might as well. I'm still gonna talk to Terry tomorrow.

JOEL: What about Winter?

PATRICIA: Nevermind, she's got her hands full with Autumn.

JOEL stands still.

Well, go to bed then!

JOEL exits. Lighting state returns to the present.

PATRICIA watches JOEL leave, then addresses the lawyer who is still by her kitchen door. She sips a cup of tea while holding the rosary.

So, that's what my nosim Joel told me about a week ago. Holy, you just gonna stand there all day? Your skinny white legs are gonna get tired and burnt. But it's your choice.

PATRICIA sips on a cup of tea while staring at the stapled papers.

So A or B . . . money or no money?

She puts them back on the table again.

You know, I was thirteen when they took us away . . . I can still remember her. She looked just like my kohkom. Strong features and very beautiful. She was always making me laugh, even when times were tough.

Two young people enter as PATRICIA's story is narrated.

It was the summer she was supposed to get married. She was only fifteen, but back then it was still common to get married at an early age. MaryAnne was so happy. Plans of a future husband and family. That's all she talked about.

The two sit together.

Wasn't long before those bastards showed up . . . and took us to that place.

Suddenly the two are apprehended.

You know the worst thing about being in a residential school? It's not about getting strapped . . . it's not even about getting abused . . . it's the fear of never getting out and seeing your family again. Mom died of sickness that year and Dad moved away . . . it was the last time we saw our parents. Somehow those damn people found a way to take us from our homes, our families, and our way of life.

But that doesn't even compare to what they did to us . . . what they did to her . . . and them taking away baby . . . nevermind. Not long after, they transferred me to another school. Far away.

I never saw them again . . . like that, just gone . . . Bastards! So I guess in many ways, this is misery money. You expect me to accept that?! Hey! The day's not over yet, Rich Lawyer Man. Don't you try and leave yet. There's still some more to tell. That next morning I sat with my son's boy, Terry.

PATRICIA sips on a cup of tea as lights fade out.

End scene.

Scene 5 (Patricia's House)

Musical interlude. TERRY enters and sits alone at the table, looking somewhat nervous. He walks in with a slight limp.

TERRY: Where's Joel?

PATRICIA: Getting wood.

TERRY: Oh . . . cool.

TERRY rolls up his pant leg and reveals a wound on his shin.

PATRICIA: What the hell's wrong with your leg?

TERRY: Nothing. I just fell when we were trying to get out.

PATRICIA: Cha. Well that's what you get for not listening to me.

TERRY: Huh?

PATRICIA: I was trying to tell you the other day to stay away from that building.

TERRY: No you didn't. That was Joel.

PATRICIA: Oh be quiet, you! That damn kid pays more attention to his music than his own family. That guitar doesn't even rightfully belong to him.

TERRY: I thought his foster parents bought it for him.

PATRICIA: Yeah right. He probably just grabbed it without anyone knowing.

TERRY: Umm . . . well, why not just pawn it then?

PATRICIA: Awas, the cops will find out and take your cousin away.

TERRY: Why do you always assume Joel steals everything?

PATRICIA: Stealing is wrong! Taking things that don't belong to you is wrong! And it'll come back to him someday. Here, put some of this on, it'll help.

TERRY: What is it? Vaseline?

PATRICIA: Cha, no . . . bear grease.

TERRY: Kohkom, do I have to put bear grease on? It smells.

PATRICIA: Oh quit being like that!

TERRY: Is this what you put on your arm?

PATRICIA: Yeah.

TERRY: What happened to your arm?

PATRICIA: Nevermind about my arm. Just put it on.

PATRICIA applies some of the bear grease on TERRY's leg.

TERRY: Ow!

PATRICIA: Sit still!

TERRY: It hurts.

PATRICIA: Didn't your mom ever teach you to about bear grease? Cripes! Fine, here then. Do it yourself. Don't say I never tried to help you.

TERRY dresses the wound on his leg, somewhat carefully.

Look at the sight of your face.

PATRICIA grabs a cloth from the counter.

TERRY: What?

PATRICIA: Let's see.

PATRICIA takes a look at TERRY's face, grabbing him by the chin, and starts to clean it.

TERRY: Um, no it's okay, Kohkom.

PATRICIA: I'm not going to have my grandson looking like he just came from the damn bush.

TERRY: Please, can you not do that?

PATRICIA: What the hell is wrong with you? Why don't you kids listen?

PATRICIA pushes TERRY's face away. TERRY looks at her with shock. She stops and looks at TERRY, realizing what has taken place. PATRICIA tosses the rag back onto the counter.

I didn't mean to do that. I just wanted to . . . nevermind.

There is an awkward silence between the two.

Why the hell did you even go there in the first place? Huh?

TERRY: Kohkom, how come you're always getting mad?

PATRICIA takes a good look at TERRY.

PATRICIA: I . . . don't know . . .

PATRICIA retreats to a corner of the room.

You know your family went to school there?

TERRY: Yeah, Dad told Mom a little before he left.

PATRICIA: Huh?

TERRY: Yeah, that you went school there. That's why you never want us to go there. We know.

PATRICIA: Yeah, but you don't even know what happened there.

TERRY: Yeah I do, but we're not supposed to talk about it.

PATRICIA: Yeah . . .

TERRY sits staring down at the floor.

I don't even know why I asked about those settlement papers.

TERRY: Settlement papers?

PATRICIA pauses, realizing TERRY heard her.

So that's why Mom talks the way she does.

PATRICIA: Huh? What does she say?

TERRY: Oh shit, um . . . nothing.

PATRICIA: Tell me. Now!

TERRY speaks with fear, and rather fast.

TERRY: She talks about how she needs to be nice to you and everything in case Dad never comes home.

PATRICIA: She what? When the hell did she say this?

TERRY: All the time. She always talks about it. Please don't get mad . . .

PATRICIA: How the hell did she find out?

TERRY: Band office probably. They talk about everything. Are you gonna take settlement money, Kohkom?

PATRICIA: No! Are you crazy?!

TERRY: How long did you go to that school, Kohkom?

PATRICIA: Too long. Anyways, it's none of your business!

TERRY: When did you go there?

PATRICIA: That's enough! I mean it!

TERRY: Sorry . . .

PATRICIA: Cripes!

PATRICIA takes a seat at the table.

I didn't want anyone to know.

TERRY: To know what? That you went there?

PATRICIA: Not that. I didn't want anyone to know about your other kohkom . . .

TERRY: Kohkom who?

PATRICIA: Nevermind! Stop asking questions! I told you it's none of your damn business!

TERRY: You mean Kohkom MaryAnne?

PATRICIA: *Shut up! Just shut the hell up about that!*

It is as if PATRICIA is ready to hit TERRY.

TERRY: Okay! Sorry, Kohkom!

PATRICIA: *Don't you ever say her name! You hear me?!*

TERRY: Okay . . .

PATRICIA: Better not! So you said you saw someone in that old building. Who was it?

TERRY: I don't know for sure. I remember Winter was just quiet all of a sudden . . .

Lights fade.

Scene 6 (The Building)

WINTER enters nervously and paces around the room. She looks around dark corners to see if anyone is near. TERRY and JOEL enter and startle her.

WINTER: Aggh! Shit, you!

TERRY: Holy, what's wrong with you? Did you have a paranormal experience sitting here by yourself?

WINTER: No.

TERRY and JOEL take a seat on the floor.

JOEL: She probably just got scared. Girls always get scared when they're alone.

WINTER: Shut up, you.

TERRY: You are scared, aren't you?

WINTER doesn't respond.

What's wrong?

WINTER: Nothing . . . I just wanna get outta here.

TERRY: Why? Scared you'll never see Autumn again? I thought you wanted to get away from her.

WINTER: Shut the hell up, you.

TERRY: Not until we see something. Activity should be picking up soon.

JOEL: Cha, I thought you were gonna roll some smokes.

TERRY: Settle down, we don't have a light, remember?

JOEL: I'll roll a couple then.

TERRY: You shouldn't have come in the first place if all you're gonna do is complain. Just don't tell Mom when we get back. Here, eat something.

WINTER shakes her head in refusal.

JOEL: Hey, I will. Score me some, bro.

TERRY passes the backpack to JOEL instead.

You gonna eat, too, or what?

TERRY: Nah. I'll have something after. Boy, this place sure does get dark quick, eh?

JOEL: And kinda chilly, too. Look at all the cobwebs. Must be some big-ass spiders here.

TERRY: Hey, you know what this place was before, Joel?

JOEL: Yeah . . . the old residential school.

TERRY: And do you know what happened in residential schools?

JOEL: Of course, kids got strapped for speaking their language, got their hair cut off, then like got put in foster homes in the '60s or something.

TERRY: There's more than just that.

JOEL: What do you mean? How much more?

TERRY: I heard my mom and dad talk about this place once. You know what else happened?

JOEL: What?

TERRY: Do you really, like really wanna know?

JOEL: Spill it then. Holy shit.

TERRY: Students and babies were murdered here . . .

JOEL pauses while eating and stands.

JOEL: *What?!* What the hell? How come you didn't tell us that in the first place, dumbass?

TERRY: 'Cuz I knew you wouldn't come if you knew.

JOEL: You asshole! That's why you wanna make this fuckin' video! Did you know, Winter?

WINTER doesn't respond.

Fuckin' asshole!

TERRY: What's wrong? You scared?

JOEL: No. What the hell are we doing here? We shouldn't be here!

TERRY: Why not?

JOEL attempts to exit.

JOEL: I'm outta here!

TERRY: What are you doing? The door's jammed, remember?

JOEL: *Dammit!* You ass! You brought us here and didn't even tell us! And you, too, Winter. You probably knew and didn't even say anything.

TERRY: She didn't know. I never told her.

JOEL: What the hell are we going to do now? No one even knows we're here.

TERRY stands.

TERRY: Good. Then we won't get in shit! So quit being like that and relax. Holy, you think we we're gonna be murdered or something.

JOEL: We shouldn't be here, you guys. It's not right. There may be more spirits in this place than you think!

WINTER: Terry, we should just take off.

TERRY: Holy, you two. Settle down! No one's going anywhere yet.

JOEL: You can't make us stay here. We can take him, Winter. There's two of us and one of him.

TERRY: Oh, please. I'll kick your ass and wipe these walls with your shorts. That's if they're not stained already. We won't be here much longer. Okay? So just sit your ass down, eat, and roll yourself a goddam smoke!

JOEL gives TERRY a disappointing glance and sits.

JOEL: *Fuck!*

TERRY: Let me remind you: We didn't see anything when we walked around, did we? Did we?

JOEL: No . . .

TERRY: Well there ya go. People come here all the time. Probably smoke up, drink, who knows what else.

WINTER: I don't wanna know.

TERRY: Plus, this door was closed when we got here, right? That means there's gotta be another way out. That should ease your minds a little.

JOEL goes back to rolling a smoke.

JOEL: How come no one ever talks about what really happened here?

TERRY: They do. Just not around city Indians like you. Who cares? There's probably nothing to talk about. Everyone that went here is older now. Those are the ones that are getting all this money.

JOEL: And here I thought it was just about getting the strap. That's why Kohkom's so angry.

TERRY: Yeah. And now you know why Indians are so screwed up.

JOEL: Not everyone's messed up.

TERRY: Yeah, maybe not the apples. You know where "apple" really comes from? It means all the ones who were forced into foster care and forgot who they were. Red on the outside and white on the inside.

JOEL: You trying to say I'm an apple?

WINTER: Can we please not talk about this?

TERRY: No, I mean all the ones who got abused and are now messed in the head! Now when everyone gets their money, drinks it up, and goes broke again . . . we'll be the lost ones who once had it all?

JOEL looks over at WINTER.

JOEL: Why aren't you saying anything? You think the same thing, too?

WINTER stands and reaches for the flashlight.

WINTER: I just wanna get the hell outta here.

JOEL: No one in our family died here. Right, Terry?

TERRY doesn't respond.

Terry!!

TERRY: I guess you guys don't know about our other kohkom . . .

In an instant, the whispers that WINTER heard earlier are heard again, faint, in the hallways. Everyone freezes.

JOEL: Whoa, what the hell is that?

TERRY: Joel, grab the camera.

WINTER: You guys, I wanna go now. Please.

TERRY: Joel, I said grab the camera!

TERRY grabs the digital.

JOEL: Screw you! I'm not doing this.

TERRY: Fine, I'll check it out. How do you work this thing?

JOEL: Put it down, Terry!

WINTER: Hey that's mine. Don't break it, you guys!

The sounds in the hallways grow louder.

TERRY: Well turn it on then.

JOEL: Leave it alone!

WINTER: I think someone else is here, Terry. Can we please just go?

TERRY: Well if someone is here, they're not getting any footage before I do.

JOEL: Let go!

TERRY: Fuck off!

TERRY punches JOEL and knocks him to the ground. WINTER intervenes.

JOEL: What the hell was that for?

TERRY: Come on then, you little shit. I got something for you!

WINTER: Quit it, you guys!

JOEL: Piss off!

TERRY: Yeah . . . gonna go home and cry to Kohkom now?

WINTER: Smarten up!

JOEL: What's wrong with you, man?

TERRY retreats to a corner of the room.

WINTER: Enough!

JOEL retreats to another side of the room.

You guys, I think this place has like a bad vibe or something.

TERRY: What do you mean?

WINTER: Well, look at us. Getting pissed off. Fighting, swearing. What do you think? We can't even get out of here.

TERRY: Listen.

The sound of a back door opening is heard in the distance. Everyone freezes.

JOEL: Someone's here!

WINTER: Shit. See?

TERRY: Sshh. Quiet.

They hear the sound of a struggle, and of someone pushing against the door.

WINTER: They're trying to get in. Listen.

They hear someone in pain. The voice is faint, almost cursory. Then a bottle smashes on the floor somewhere, followed by the sound of the door closing.

JOEL: They're closing the door!

WINTER: Go find out where it is!

JOEL attempts to leave. Suddenly, the image of a young girl appears and then fades again without them noticing.

They hear the sound of a baby crying and freeze. Lights fade out.

Scene 7 (Patricia's House)

PATRICIA sits on the chair with a cup of tea.

PATRICIA: So, Mr. Rich Lawyer Man . . . am I just shocking you with my story or what? You feel like crying home to your wife yet? Good . . .

You know, no one talks about getting themselves better. All they talk about is money. Holy boy, I'm gonna buy a new car! A new TV! Then after that, I'm gonna go somewhere far away, like Hawaii. How the hell is a fifty-two-inch

TV gonna help you get better? We're all better off just wiping our arses with these settlement papers.

PATRICIA throws the papers on the table. She unwraps the dressing on her arm and puts bear grease on it.

I only told my late husband and son about it. But I didn't think my grandson knew about MaryAnne.

She was pregnant when they put us in that school. Pregnant from the man she was supposed to marry.

The priests and nuns knew, too, but didn't do anything till it was time for the baby to come. She fought long and hard, boy. One priest and two nuns couldn't hold her back. She just kept kicking and screaming, "She's my baby!" Real strong, just like our mom and all the women in our family. She almost bit one of those nun's fingers off when they covered her mouth. I was there. I remember . . . They took her . . . took her from us. They smothered MaryAnne . . . they smothered her with a pillow . . . till she just stopped moving.

PATRICIA struggles with her emotion.

Misery money. That's all this is about. Well, everyone can have it . . . everyone's chasing it, you greedy lawyers . . . *you can all have it . . . shove it up your fucking arses for all I care.*

Lights fade.

Scene 8 (Patricia's House)

JOEL enters the kitchen with a small pile of wood. PATRICIA watches him. He pulls out the pouch of tobacco and proceeds to roll a cigarette.

JOEL: Where's Terry?

PATRICIA: In the bathroom.

JOEL: So can I go to Auntie Veronica's?

PATRICIA: Cha. No. We're not done yet.

JOEL: I already told you everything. Why are we even doing this? It's pointless.

PATRICIA: Joel, I really need you to tell me now.

JOEL: What?! Tell you what?! What do you want to know?!

PATRICIA: I need to know who you saw in that building.

JOEL: I don't know. The room was smoky, then it just burned down.

PATRICIA: Dammit! You want to be taken away or what?

JOEL: Well at least if I go to jail, I'll have three meals a day.

PATRICIA: Don't get smart, you!

JOEL: And you know what else? I won't have to worry about drinking bad water all the time!

PATRICIA: That's enough.

JOEL: Or have to walk everywhere just to visit people!

PATRICIA: Joel!

JOEL: I hate it here.

PATRICIA: Shut up!

JOEL: Why the hell did I agree to stay here? I might as well go to jail. And you . . . you try to be a guardian. All you do is get pissed off! You don't even know how to be a kohkom!

PATRICIA grabs JOEL by the shoulders and shakes him.

PATRICIA: *What do you want? What the hell do you want from me? Huh? I don't know how to care. I forgot how, okay? So what the hell do you want you little—*

There is an immediate silence as PATRICIA slaps JOEL across the head. She and JOEL freeze. JOEL gets up and leaves. TERRY enters.

No, wait. Don't go. Wait, please . . . don't go.

PATRICIA takes a moment to compose herself, losing orientation and holding the wrapping around her arm.

TERRY: Kohkom?

TERRY helps PATRICIA to grab a seat.

Kohkom, are you okay? Here, just sit down . . .

PATRICIA: Just get me some tea.

TERRY: Okay.

TERRY grabs her cup of tea.

Anything else? Maybe you should go lie down or something.

PATRICIA: No. No, nosim. Please, just let me sit here.

TERRY: Okay.

PATRICIA: Terry . . . please, nosim, please . . .

TERRY: What, Kohkom?

PATRICIA: Did you see who started the fire?

TERRY: I don't know . . . the room was too smoky.

Lights fade.

Scene 9

WINTER enters and sits quietly, close to TERRY, who prepares the equipment for recording. WINTER grabs his sleeve and moves in closer to him as she looks around the room.

WINTER: Terry.

TERRY: Quit. Just relax. I wanna get something on video.

WINTER: This isn't *X-Files*.

TERRY: No, Winter, this isn't *X-Files*. I'm calling this . . . Rez-Files.

TERRY hums the X-Files *theme music.*

WINTER: There is someone else in this building. I heard a door open. You think spirits open doors? I don't know who the hell she is or how she got in? But someone else is here! You know what that means?

TERRY does not pay attention to her.

It means someone knows we're here. You think people aren't going to get pissed off knowing we're here? And what do you think will happen then?

TERRY continues to put the camera into position.

Well, I'll tell you. Elders will meet; the council will meet. Then they'll call a stupid band meeting where everyone will know. They'll point us out, give us shit, and Mom will end up being embarrassed.

TERRY: Yeah, so? Shit happens.

WINTER: So? So Mom's not even from here. It's hard enough she has to take care of us on Dad's reserve. She'll probably want us to leave. I'm not moving up north. I'd rather go to the city. Then I'll have to be a single mom living by myself while you go out spirit hunting.

TERRY: Ghost hunting.

WINTER: *Shut up!* I can't relax. How the hell can I relax? I can't take care of Autumn myself. I can't even properly take care of her living with Mom. If I have to live on my own they might as well take Autumn away. And it'll be all your fault.

TERRY: What? All my fault? Hey, no one made you come here, Winter. So don't even try and blame this shit on me.

WINTER: I shouldn't have come here in the first place.

JOEL enters.

JOEL: I can't find that door, but whoever that was locked it, I just know it.

WINTER: Great . . . so the door's are locked, the window's are barred, and there's no way out.

JOEL: *Hey, who the fuck's in here?*

TERRY: Shut up! You'll scare it away.

JOEL: What the hell are you doing?

TERRY: I have my first case. I just know that sound was a ghost.

WINTER: Oh, shut your hole already! That thing was a person. Someone else was here and we gotta take off.

JOEL: What if they're still here?

TERRY: You gotta take off. I gotta record . . .

JOEL: Hey, dumbass. I'm not gonna get caught in here. I'm on probation!

TERRY arranges the cloth, tobacco, and camera.

TERRY: What the hell are you getting bent out of shape for? No one's gonna rat you out! You wanna ditch out? Go ahead, wussy!

JOEL: Let's go, Winter.

WINTER: I'm leaving. If she rats us out, you better not tell Mom I was here.

TERRY: It's not a person, you guys. It's a ghost. This shit is real and I'm gonna be the one who catches it on tape.

JOEL: I don't wanna go to jail, man!

TERRY: You're not going to jail, all right?

JOEL: I'm serious, Terry. I'll take off before they take me away.

TERRY: Yeah? And where are you gonna go?

JOEL: I don't know. I'll shack up on some reserve far away. Change my name, the way I look—

TERRY: And you think that's gonna make everything cool? Running away? You ran away from foster care like how many times? And they found you just like that.

WINTER stands and begins shouting.

WINTER: *Okay, listen here! You wanna piece of me?*

TERRY: Winter!

WINTER: *Come on then. You scared or what?*

JOEL: *Yeah!*

TERRY: You guys, what the—

WINTER: *You wanna rat us out. We'll rat you out, too!*

JOEL: *Yeah!*

WINTER: *My brother will kick your ass! So come on . . . bitch!*

TERRY stands.

JOEL: *Yeah . . . bitch!*

TERRY: *Enough!* Both of you. I said I'm gonna get this on tape and that's what I'm gonna do. Film school is my ticket off the reserve and I didn't walk all this way to have both of you fuck it up for me. You got that? Oh Great Spirit . . .

WINTER: Shit!

JOEL: You smell smoke?

JOEL exits.

TERRY: No, that's just you and your nicotine fits. Oh Great Spirit . . . of the grandfathers and grandmothers . . . you who is so omniscient and great . . . help us see the spirit of the young woman who is still here.

They sit in silence and listen. They hear nothing. WINTER attempts to open the door. TERRY chants the words of the seance in repetition, while holding the cloth and tobacco.

Oh Great Spirit . . . of the grandfathers and grandmothers . . . you who is so omniscient and great . . . help us see the spirit.

After a three-peat of the ceremony . . . silence.

Should I do it again?

WINTER stands by TERRY, holding his shirt.

WINTER: Come on, Terry. I wanna go. I don't wanna get busted here.

TERRY: Just a few more minutes.

Suddenly, the sounds of faint voices are heard.

It's coming from over there. I'm gonna get it.

WINTER: *No!* Fuck that, you're not leaving me here alone.

TERRY: Come along then.

WINTER: No! Terry wait. Wait. I did see something earlier.

TERRY: What?

WINTER: I saw something earlier.

TERRY: The ghost girl?

WINTER: I think so . . . or maybe . . . I don't know.

TERRY: Shit! Why didn't you say so? Where?

WINTER: Just right around the corner there. I wasn't sure. I thought it was just someone else in the building. But maybe . . .

The voices disappear.

TERRY: Sshh, listen.

WINTER: What?

TERRY: It's gone.

TERRY *positions the camera.*

All right then. It's still early. I guess we just wait for it.

WINTER: Don't leave me alone!

TERRY: I won't. I'll be right here.

They sit in a brief silence.

I told you ghosts are real.

WINTER: I didn't say I saw a ghost. I said I wasn't sure.

TERRY: Yeah, well, at this point if someone was just pissing around, we would've known by now.

WINTER: You think so?

TERRY: Come on, you think anyone would sit in this place all day and hope someone would show up?

WINTER: Probably not.

TERRY: There you go.

WINTER: I didn't say I believe . . . yet.

TERRY: You sure sounded like a believer a minute ago.

WINTER: We shouldn't have come here. I'm scared, Terry.

TERRY: Are you for real?

WINTER: Yeah . . .

TERRY: Well, just sit close. It'll be all right. Besides, its only moniyaw ghosts that are harmful, right?

WINTER: I guess so.

TERRY: You really think an Indian spirit would be harmful? I don't think so.

WINTER: Maybe you're right.

The two siblings sit in silence for a brief moment.

Terry?

TERRY: Yeah?

WINTER: If this girl's spirit is really here, why do you think they tell us at funerals that they go to a better place?

TERRY: I don't know. Maybe that's if it's done right. Maybe the ones who didn't have a proper goodbye get stuck or something.

WINTER: Like they don't go to the ancestors?

TERRY: Yeah, like they don't go home.

WINTER: So what do you think takes them home?

TERRY: I'm not sure. Probably more than an Indian-slash-whiteman seance.

WINTER: Do you think there is more than just one spirit here?

TERRY: Probably. What about you?

WINTER: Well, they say so many things about how we go home. Like one time an elder came to the school when I was in grade nine.

TERRY: Yeah?

WINTER: And said we are called by our Indian name to come home. That's why we need to know that kind of stuff.

TERRY: Oh yeah . . .

WINTER: Another said we are called to one more ceremony before we finish that journey home. Nothing wrong with thinking that, is there?

TERRY: As long as you believe, I suppose. I never thought of it that way. Maybe you're right, Winter. There are some things I need to learn before being some kind of a ghost hunter.

WINTER: Terry?

TERRY: What?

WINTER: Do you remember what you said about our other kohkom?

TERRY: Yeah . . .

WINTER: You meant Kohkom Patricia's sister, right?

TERRY: Yeah . . .

WINTER: She died here, didn't she?

TERRY: Yeah . . . that's what I heard Dad say.

Instantly the sounds of faint voices, cacophony, and crying are heard.

JOEL: Shit! Hey, you guys!

TERRY and WINTER are startled. The noises are louder now. TERRY and WINTER freeze.

TERRY: WHAT?

JOEL: Someone's outside! Field! They're leaving in the field!

TERRY: Shit. Get over here.

JOEL enters running.

WINTER: Are you okay?

JOEL: Holyshit holyshit holyshit—

TERRY: What, man!?

JOEL: There's a fuckin' fire in the other room!

WINTER: What?!

TERRY: *What?!* What the hell did you do?

JOEL: Nothing! I don't have a light, remember?

TERRY: Pack everything up.

Smoke enters the room.

WINTER: Nevermind that! How the hell do we get out of here?

TERRY: Shit! I don't know . . .

JOEL: Holyshit holyshit holyshit!

WINTER: Shit! We gotta get out!

JOEL: Terry! What do we do?

TERRY: I don't know. *Hey!*

JOEL: WE GOTTA OPEN THE DOOR!

WINTER: TERRY I GOTTA GET THE HELL OUTTA HERE! BACK TO BABY AUTUMN!

They hear a window smash followed by an eruption of flames. TERRY *falls to the ground, hurting his leg.*

TERRY: Shit! My leg, you guys!

JOEL: Get off your ass! Come on!

The sudden voices are loudest at this moment. All three are coughing continuously.

WINTER: Help! We wanna get outta here!

TERRY: Somebody! Let us out!

JOEL: Open the door! Please!

The noise is heard again. Voices are intermixed, like the language of broken Cree. The young girl appears again. Suddenly she stops and slowly turns to see the three cousins. She turns around once again and leaves.

WINTER: *Who the hell is that?*

TERRY: *Nevermind! Just follow her!*

JOEL: *Come on!*

They all run out except TERRY, *who returns to sit at the table with* PATRICIA *as she enters.*

TERRY: And that's what happened, Kohkom. I don't know who it was.

PATRICIA *sits in shocked silence.*

PATRICIA: Oh my god . . .

TERRY: What?

PATRICIA: Huh? Oh, not now. I'll tell you about it another time.

TERRY: I think I already know.

Silent pause.

Kohkom, if they think it was us, are they gonna take us away?

PATRICIA: No. No one's taking anyone away. Not anymore. Don't say anything to anyone, you hear me? Not a thing.

JOEL *and* WINTER *enter.*

TERRY: Okay . . .

JOEL does not say a word. He simply goes to the tap and gets a drink of water. TERRY, JOEL, and PATRICIA all stand silent in the kitchen, unsure of the right words.

TERRY and JOEL take notice of WINTER, who does not say a word to anyone. She immediately takes to the table and pulls out a chair for herself.

WINTER: Hi, Kohkom.

PATRICIA: Yeow! Aren't you supposed to be taking care of your baby?

WINTER: Mom's watching her for a while.

PATRICIA: Oh . . .

The room is uncomfortable, the silence almost deafening. No one is sure what to say. There is an occasional cough, a shuffle of feet, a glance . . . until it becomes too unbearable. Then all try to speak at once.

JOEL: Well, I think—

TERRY: Maybe we—

WINTER: Kohkom, I—

PATRICIA: There's so much—

Silence again.

There's so much I want to talk about. Not just with you, but with the whole family. But I just haven't been ready all these years. I've been so afraid to talk for so long. But I'll be ready soon . . .

Next week, there's a lawyer's coming to see me. About something important. And I'd like you, Joel, and Terry to be here when he does. Can you do that?

TERRY: For sure.

JOEL: I guess so.

WINTER: Why?

JOEL: But we didn't do it. Why do we need a lawyer?

PATRICIA: It's not for you; it's for me. You should go home now. Go be with your baby. I need to get some rest. I'm gonna need it. All right?

ALL: Okay. For sure.

PATRICIA: Okay, nosim. Now get the hell outta my house. Kohkom's tired.

WINTER gets up to leave. As she nears the door, she turns around, returns quickly to the table, and puts her arms around Kohkom.

WINTER: Kohkom, I saw her, too. We all did. She helped us get out. I don't know if the boys are ready to believe it. But we all know, and we love you very much . . .

WINTER kisses Kohkom on the cheek and makes for the door. PATRICIA sits in silence for a brief moment. As the lights crossfade to the present, she grabs the papers on the table next to the envelope.

Lights fade.

Scene 10 (Patricia's House)

PATRICIA sits in the chair as the day with the lawyer is coming to an end.

PATRICIA: I've lost a lot family. My husband, my daughter, my son, my sister, and her baby. And because of my anger and my actions, I almost lost my grandchildren.

That old building burnt down and my nosimak got out safely. No one said anything. No one cared. No fire trucks came. Not even the law. And people are liking it that way. Many say it's a good thing that old building is gone.

And you know what? My sister MaryAnne is finally going home. We're doing a special ceremony for her and all our loved ones who never made it out of that place. To honour them.

There's a dark history hidden, Mr. Rich Lawyer Man. I don't expect you to have pity on me or us as Indian people. That's not why I asked you here today.

I'm taking the settlement. Now just because I am doesn't make everything all right. This is not forgive and forget. See, I'm not doing it to forget, I'm doing it to remember . . . what they did to me. For what they did to MaryAnne . . . and for taking her baby away. That's right. They took her baby away and shoved her into some foster home, and I want to use this money to find her. So I'm asking you, sir . . . please help me find her. Help me find MaryAnne's baby and bring her home . . .

JOEL, TERRY, and WINTER enter. TERRY is leading with the camera in hand.

TERRY: And this is where the song was written, at the home of our grandmother, Patricia Kihew, on Stone Pipe First Nation.

PATRICIA: What are you guys doing?

TERRY: Oh, hi, Kohkom. We're just putting the finishing touches on my new video. It's called "Hey Ya Hey Country."

JOEL: Yeah, it's about this song I wrote.

TERRY: But actually, it's about mixing pow-wow singing with country music. I figure since my seance video didn't come through, I'll submit this to get into film school.

WINTER: Idiots.

JOEL: Wanna hear it, Kohkom?

WINTER: Kohkom . . . what happened to your arm?

PATRICIA: I hurt myself.

WINTER: How?

PATRICIA: On a door.

JOEL: On a door?! You mean . . . you?

PATRICIA: Well? Sing, dammit!

The song is performed—the music of a local musician.

I know there are a lot things you people must think about us. About how we're all helpless now. Well take it from me, we're not. We're survivors. We're still here and we'll always be here. I've been so afraid for so long to talk about this . . . about my experience . . . but it's time for healing.

I don't know what happens from this point on. I can only pray that the road ahead is one filled with healing. I believe my prayers will be heard . . . and because of that, I have hope. Nanaskimon.

My arm? That's a story for another time . . . another time . . .

The music grows louder as the family stands in a semicircle at centre stage.

Lights fade out.

End play.

DEAR MR. BUCHWALD

Yvette Nolan

For Helen Thundercloud, who goes on in me.

Dear Mr. Buchwald was commissioned from Native Earth Performing Arts by the Osgoode Hall Graduate Law Students Association and premiered on May 1, 2010, at the Osgoode Professional Development Centre in Toronto with the following cast:

Falen Johnson
Craig Lauzon
Michaela Washburn

It has since been adapted into the short film *A Common Experience* by Shane Belcourt and Yvette Nolan.

Projection:

The Letter

Projections throughout: Helen's wedding, Helen's status card, Helen and Yvette, Helen, St. Mary's photos.

MICHAELA: Pitblado LLP
Commodity Exchange Tower
2500-360 Main Street
Winnipeg, MB R3C 4H6
January 19, 2010

FALEN: Dear Richard Buchwald,

Enclosed you will find a cheque for the balance due for services you and Pitblado rendered in the matter of my mother's estate in regards to the Indian

Residential School Settlement. I received the settlement yesterday, in the amount of $19,000. My brothers have already paid $2,100 in fees, so here is the final $2,203.46.

My mother—

MICHAELA: Helen Chabot born in Maniwaki, Quebec, January 5,1943, to Suzanne and Frank Chabot, sister to Peter, Joe, Max, Viviane, and Stella. There was another brother, a twin, who drowned as a teenager.

FALEN: —was taken from her community when she was seven years old—

MICHAELA: —to the sanitorium, with tuberculosis. She was there for years, because the medication for TB didn't work on Indians. From there she went to residential school, first at Spanish—

CRAIG: 1954, 1955.

MICHAELA: —then at Kenora.

CRAIG: 1957, 1958, 1959, 1960, 1961.

FALEN: She married out of residential school at seventeen.

MICHAELA: The nuns gave her a wedding—

CRAIG: October 1, 1960.

MICHAELA: —though it was not the wedding the nuns gave Maria in *The Sound of Music.*

CRAIG: St. Mary's Residential School.

MICHAELA: When the marriage ended, she applied for her status back.

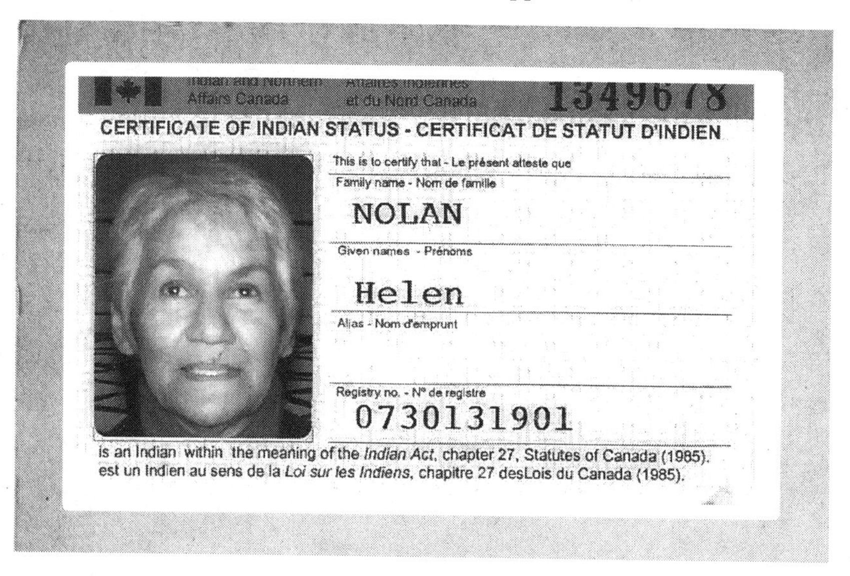

Indian and Northern Affairs Canada
Affaires indiennes et du Nord Canada
1349678

CERTIFICATE OF INDIAN STATUS - CERTIFICAT DE STATUT D'INDIEN

This is to certify that - Le présent atteste que

Family name - Nom de famille

NOLAN

Given names - Prénoms

Helen

Alias - Nom d'emprunt

Registry no. - N° de registre

0730131901

is an Indian within the meaning of the *Indian Act*, chapter 27, Statutes of Canada (1985).
est un Indien au sens de la *Loi sur les Indiens*, chapitre 27 desLois du Canada (1985).

CRAIG: "Dear Mrs. Nolan, thank you for applying to become an Indian—"

FALEN: She died two years ago—

CRAIG: May 14, 2007.

FALEN: —at the age of sixty-four.

MICHAELA: Heart.

CRAIG: Bad smog days.

MICHAELA: Hard life.

CRAIG: TB.

MICHAELA: Twice.

CRAIG: Fire in '81.

MICHAELA: Yeah, damage inside and out.

CRAIG: Always getting pneumonia.

MICHAELA: Hard on the heart.

CRAIG: Then those three bad smog days . . .

MICHAELA/CRAIG: Hard on the heart.

FALEN: We found the IRS claim in her papers. My brothers were insistent that we apply for the settlement, although they were estranged from my mother at the time of her death, had not seen her for five and twenty years, respectively.

CRAIG: Patrick James, born in 1969, and Michael Charles, born in 1964.

FALEN: It has taken the three of us, and you, two years to secure this settlement, of which Pitblado's cut represents 22.6 percent. I am sure that is fair payment for the work the firm has done, and I don't care at all about the money—I am in fact giving my share to charity—but I do want you to think about the system, and consider how difficult it must be for Aboriginal people who do not have access to lawyers, education, English as a first language, and who may not live in an urban centre to negotiate the system and actually apply for and receive a little bit of money.

Are you thinking about it now? Are you thinking that you're sorry but you've worked hard to get where you are, and you have expenses, and overhead, and you can't just do *pro bono* work? I am thinking, too, Mr. Buchwald, day and night, about how everything in this country is built on the premise of this being a land of plenty, resource-rich, tolerant, and rife with opportunity.

I am not angry with you, Mr. Buchwald, or with Pitblado, or with the government that is trying to undo decades of harm with a little bit of money. But I do wonder at how many people must be making a living off the First Peoples of this land, still, after all this time, all the while complaining that we should just get over it, pull ourselves up by our bootstraps, and stop being a drain on the resources.

The money has made me mad, Mr. Buchwald. I hope that giving it away will afford me some peace. I hope it inspires you to consider your position and the good you do in the world.

In spirit,

MICHAELA/CRAIG: In spirit,

FALEN: Yvette Nolan.

Projection:

The Road Forward

The Royal Commission on Aboriginal Peoples

People to People, Nation to Nation

CRAIG: A word from the Commissioners:

MICHAELA: "Canada is a test case for a grand notion—the notion that dissimilar peoples can share lands, resources, power, and dreams while respecting and sustaining their differences. The story of Canada is the story of many such peoples, trying and failing and trying again, to live together in peace and harmony."

FALEN: "But there cannot be peace or harmony unless there is justice. It was to help restore justice to the relationship between Aboriginal and non-Aboriginal people in Canada, and to propose practical solutions to stubborn problems, that the Royal Commission on Aboriginal Peoples was established. In 1991, four Aboriginal and three non-Aboriginal commissioners were appointed to investigate the issues and advise the government on their findings."

The sound of Jennifer Kreisberg's song "The Road Forward" comes up and plays as the projections roll. The actors stand and look at the audience. The final series of projections are photos of contemporary Indigenous people: actors, writers, judges, lawyers, leaders, activists, role models. There are so many of them. The music plays on.

Projection:

178 days of public hearings

96 communities

Dozens of experts

Reviewed past inquiries and reports

Our central conclusion can be summarized simply: The main policy direction, pursued for more than 150 years, first by colonial then by Canadian governments, has been wrong.

To bring about this fundamental change, Canadians need to understand that Aboriginal Peoples are nations.

Canada as a Fair and Enlightened Society

The Ghosts of History

We propose four principles as the basis for a renewed relationship: recognition, respect, sharing and responsibility.

The Apology in the House

REFERENCES

In essence, the entirety of the residential school program was to inject foreign languages and stories into our people to erase the Indigenous stories from our identity.

—Kevin Loring, Artistic Director, Indigenous Theatre of the National Arts Centre, May 2018

These reference materials, excerpts from the Canadian Indian Act and the UN's Declaration on the Rights of Indigenous Peoples, are intended to offer context for the persistent government policies at the root of the stories in this collection. While the language of Canadian policy has been revised and redacted, the culture it represents is implicit and pervasive within contemporary policy and is in sharp contrast to the UN's statement.

Indian Act: An Act Respecting Indians

R.S.C., 1985, c. I-5

114 (1) The Governor in Council may authorize the Minister, in accordance with this Act, to enter into agreements on behalf of Her Majesty for the education in accordance with this Act of Indian children, with

(a) the government of a province;

(b) the Commissioner of the Yukon Territory;

(c) the Commissioner of the Northwest Territories;

(c.1) the Commissioner of Nunavut;

(d) a public or separate school board; and

(e) a religious or charitable organization. [repealed 2014]

(2) The Minister may, in accordance with this Act, establish, operate and maintain schools for Indian children.

115 The Minister may

(a) provide for and make regulations with respect to standards for buildings, equipment, teaching, education, inspection and discipline in connection with schools;

(b) provide for the transportation of children to and from school;

(c) enter into agreements with religious organizations for the support and maintenance of children who are being educated in schools operated by those organizations; and [repealed 2014]

(d) apply the whole or any part of moneys that would otherwise be payable to or on behalf of a child who is attending a residential school to the maintenance of that child at that school. [repealed 2014]

* * *

118 Every Indian child who is required to attend school shall attend such school as the Minister may designate . . .

119 (1) The Minister may appoint persons, to be called truant officers, to enforce the attendance of Indian children at school, and for that purpose a truant officer has the powers of a peace officer.

(2) Without restricting the generality of subsection (1), a truant officer may, subject to subsection (2.1),

(a) enter any place where he believes, on reasonable grounds, that there are Indian children who are between the ages of seven and sixteen years, or who are required by the Minister to attend school;

(6) A truant officer may take into custody a child whom he believes on reasonable grounds to be absent from school contrary to this Act and may convey the child to school, using as much force as the circumstances require. [repealed 2014]

Excerpted from the government of Canada, Department of Justice, source document http://laws-lois.justice.gc.ca/eng/acts/i-5/

Article 11 of the UN Declaration on the Rights of Indigenous Peoples states [in part] that:

Indigenous peoples have the right to practice and revitalize their cultural traditions and customs. This includes the right to maintain, protect and develop the past, present and future manifestations of their cultures, such as archaeological and historical sites, artifacts, designs, ceremonies, technologies and visual and performing arts and literature.

OTHER WORKS TO CONSIDER

There have been and will continue to be numerous artistic works that touch on the experience and impact of residential schools on Turtle Island. Following is an abridged list of other works worth consideration:

A Common Experience, Shane Belcourt and Yvette Nolan

Almighty Voice and His Wife, Daniel David Moses

Assimilation, Jack Dalton

Bearing, Signal Theatre (Michael Greyeyes, Yvette Nolan, Tara Beagan, Spy Dénommé-Welch, Catherine Magowan)

Children of God, Corey Payette

Fragments, Lara Kramer Danse

I Remember, Brad Bellegarde, a.k.a. InfoRed

In Care, Kenneth T. Williams

Kiss of the Fur Queen, Tomson Highway

The Mush Hole Project, Woodland Cultural Centre

Ora Pro Nobis (Pray For Us), Oskiniko (Larry Loyie)

Path With No Moccasins, Shirley Cheechoo

Reckoning, Article 11

River by the Residential Schoolhouse, Justine Chen and Spy Dénommé-Welsh

Seven Fallen Feathers, Tanya Talaga

Strength of Indian Women, Vera Manuel

Where the Blood Mixes, Kevin Loring

ABOUT THE CONTRIBUTORS

Tara Beagan is a proud Ntlaka'pamux and Irish "Canadian" halfbreed from Mohkintsis (Calgary, Alberta). She is co-founder/director of ARTICLE 11 with her most cherished collaborator, Andy Moro. She served as the artistic director of Native Earth Performing Arts from February 2011 to December 2013. A Dora Mavor Moore Award–winning playwright, she has been in residence at Cahoots Theatre, NEPA, the National Arts Centre, and Berton House. Five of her twenty plus plays have been published, and her first film script, *133 Skyway*, co-written with Randy Redroad, won the imagineNATIVE award for best Canadian drama. Beagan is also a Dora and Betty Mitchell Award–nominated actor.

Michael Greyeyes (Plains Cree) is an actor, choreographer, director, and educator. Selected directing credits include *A Soldier's Tale* and *from thine eyes* (Signal Theatre), *Pimooteewin* (Soundstreams), *Almighty Voice and His Wife* (Native Earth Performing Arts), and *Seven Seconds* (2010 imagineNATIVE Film + Media Arts Festival). Most recently Greyeyes co-directed *Bearing*, a dance opera exploring the legacy of Canada's Indian residential school system at Toronto's Luminato Festival in 2017. In addition to this work on stage and screen, he is an associate professor in the Department of Theatre at York University. Greyeyes's career is diverse with a stage and screen resumé spanning over twenty-five years. From his beginnings with the National Ballet of Canada and Eliot Feld's company in New York City to Nanabush in Tomson Highway's seminal work *The Rez Sisters* to his role as legendary Hunkpapa Chief Sitting Bull in the feature film *Woman Walks Ahead*, directed by Susanna White and co-starring Jessica Chastain, Greyeyes has built an extensive body of work, including writing in addition to the scholarship he is pursuing as an academic.

Larry Edward Guno was a lawyer, playwright, and political figure in British Columbia. He was first elected to the BC legislature in 1986 as an NDP member. Born in Aiyansh in 1940, he was a member of the Nisga'a nation, Frog Clan. He attended the Edmonton Indian Residential School from 1958 to 1962. He went on to be educated at Simon Fraser University and the University of British Columbia. He wrote the play *Bunk #7* but died in 2005 before it was finished.

Falen Johnson is Mohawk and Tuscarora from Six Nations Grand River Territory. She is Bear Clan. Falen is a writer, producer, director, and actor. Her plays *Salt Baby*, *Two Indians*, and *Ipperwash* have played in theatres across the country. Her writing has appeared in publications such as *Granta Magazine* and *Brick Literary Journal*. She has also been featured in *Canadian Theatre Review* as well as on *The Moth*, a storytelling podcast. Falen has earned TV writing credits for *Urban Native Girl* (APTN) and was a researcher on *Colonization Road* (Frog Girl Films). She co-hosts the podcast *The Secret Life of Canada* with co-creator Leah Simone Bowen.

Daniel David Moses is a Delaware playwright, poet, essayist, and teacher from the Grand River Six Nations lands in southern Ontario. His plays include *Coyote City*, a nominee for the Governor General's Literary Award for Drama, *The Indian Medicine Shows*, a winner of the James Buller Memorial Award for Excellence in Aboriginal Theatre, and *Almighty Voice and His Wife*, the Canadian play included in *The Norton Anthology of Drama*. He's also authored poetry collections, including *'A Small Essay on the Largeness of Light' and Other Poems*, and co-edited four editions of Oxford University Press's *An Anthology of Canadian Native Literature in English*. His most recent publication, with Exile Editions Classics, is *Coyote City/Big Buck City: Two Plays*. His honours include the Harbourfront Festival Prize, the Ontario Arts Council's Indigenous Arts Award, and election to the Royal Society of Canada. He teaches in the Dan School of Drama and Music at Queen's University, Kingston, Ontario.

Melanie J. Murray is a Metis feminist who lives, works, and creates in Winnipeg, Manitoba. She has written, directed, and performed in numerous theatrical productions and has published several biographical articles about Metis veterans and elders whom she had the honour to interview. Researching and writing *A Very Polite Genocide or The Girl Who Fell to Earth* compelled her to pursue work in community support and public health. Her work outside the arts has included coordinating programs for people living with HIV, youth living in care, and those seeking midwifery care. A passion for dismantling barriers and advocating for marginalized people encapsulates her life's work. Against her better judgment, she is working on a new fiction project in her non-existent free time. She loves her kid and husband even more than she loves sushi.

Yvette Nolan is a playwright, dramaturg, and director. She has been the writer-in-residence at Brandon University, Mount Royal College, and the Saskatoon Public Library, as well as playwright-in-residence at the National Arts Centre. Yvette was born in Prince Albert, Saskatchewan, to an Algonquin mother and an Irish immigrant father. She is based in Saskatchewan.

Curtis Peeteetuce is from the Beardy's & Okemasis Cree Nation in central Saskatchewan. Since 2001 he has had the honour of working with many wonderful and talented artists across Canada as an actor, director, musician, and playwright. He currently has two published plays: *Nicimos: The Last Rez Christmas Story*, and his latest, *Popcorn Elder.* With over twenty-five works produced, Curtis has dedicated all his accomplishments to his son Mahihkan. ekosi.

Donna-Michelle St. Bernard is an emcee, playwright, and agitator. Works for the stage include *Gas Girls*, *Salome's Clothes*, *The House You Build*, *Cake*, *Sound of the Beast*, and *They Say He Fell.* She is co-editor with Yvette Nolan of the anthologies *Refractions: Solo* and *Refractions: Scenes.* She is the former general manager of Native Earth Performing Arts and the current artistic director of New Harlem Productions.

Ojibway writer Drew Hayden Taylor is from the Curve Lake Reserve in Ontario. Hailed by the *Montreal Gazette* as one of Canada's leading Native dramatists, he writes for the screen as well as the stage and contributes regularly to North American Native periodicals and national newspapers. His plays have garnered many prestigious awards, and his beguiling and perceptive storytelling style has enthralled audiences in Canada, the United States, and Germany. His 1998 play *Only Drunks and Children Tell the Truth* (winner of the Dora Mavor Moore Award for Outstanding Drama) has been anthologized in *Seventh Generation: An Anthology of Native American Plays*, published by Theatre Communications Group. Taylor has travelled extensively throughout North America, honouring requests to read from his work and to attend arts festivals, workshops, and productions of his plays. He was also invited to Robert Redford's Sundance Institute in California, where he participated in a week-long Indigenous script-writing workshop. One of his most established bodies of work includes what he calls the Blues Quartet, an ongoing, outrageous, and often farcical examination of Native and non-Native stereotypes as explored through humour.

First edition: June 2018
Printed and bound in Canada by Rapido Books, Montreal

Jacket art, *Mending Ancestral Lands*, by Erika Iserhoff

202-269 Richmond St. W.
Toronto, ON
M5V 1X1

416.703.0013
info@playwrightscanada.com
www.playwrightscanada.com
@playcanpress